AMAZON BESTSELLING AUTHOR

BRETT KING

With contributions from

Alex Lightman, JP Rangaswami & Andy Lark

AUGMENTED
LIFE IN THE **SMART** LANE

augmentedbook.com

mc **Marshall Cavendish**
Editions

Cover design by Kylie Maxwell
Book design by Benson Tan
All content information is correct at press time. Care has been taken to trace the
ownership of any copyright material contained in the book. Photographs are used
with permission and credit given to the photographer or copyright holder.

Published by Marshall Cavendish Editions
An imprint of Marshall Cavendish International
1 New Industrial Road, Singapore 536196

Other Marshall Cavendish Offices:
Marshall Cavendish Corporation. 99 White Plains Road, Tarrytown NY 10591-9001,
USA • Marshall Cavendish International (Thailand) Co Ltd. 253 Asoke, 12th Flr,
Sukhumvit 21 Road, Klongtoey Nua, Wattana, Bangkok 10110, Thailand • Marshall
Cavendish (Malaysia) Sdn Bhd, Times Subang, Lot 46, Subang Hi-Tech Industrial
Park, Batu Tiga, 40000 Shah Alam, Selangor Darul Ehsan, Malaysia.

Marshall Cavendish is a trademark of Times Publishing Limited

National Library Board, Singapore Cataloguing-in-Publication Data
Name(s): King, Brett, 1968- | Lightman, Alex, 1961- contributor. | Rangaswami, J. P.,
contributor. | Lark, Andy, contributor.
Title: Augmented : life in the smart lane / Brett King, with contributions from
Alex Lightman, JP Rangaswami & Andy Lark.
Description: Singapore : Marshall Cavendish Editions, [2016]
Identifier(s): OCN 906658326 | ISBN 978-981-4634-03-8 (hardcover)
Subject(s): LCSH: Technology--Social aspects. | Technological innovations--Social
aspects. | Technological forecasting.
Classification: LCC T173.8 | DDC 303.483--dc23

Printed and bound in the USA
by Lake Book Manufacturing, Inc.

Change is the law of life. And those who look
only to the past or present are certain to miss
the future.

John F. Kennedy

To my daughter Hannah who has learned strength is
best measured from the inside. And to Michael Armstrong
and Peter Brooks whom I can never thank enough for
starting me on this journey.

Contents

Acknowledgements

My thanks to the team at Moven for giving me the flexibility to pursue this endeavour, especially Alex Sion and Mircea Mihaescu. My thanks to the coffee shops that allowed me to write while consuming their java, namely Las Vetas in Fairfield, Koffee in New Haven, the lobby lounge of The Algonquin Hotel in NYC, Coupa Café in Palo Alto, Les Deux Magots in Paris, Drip Café and Artista Perfetto in Taiwan, Truth Coffee in Cape Town, Scopa Caffe in Wellington and numerous Starbucks around the world. My thanks to the FinTechMafia for allowing me to bounce ideas off them constantly. The team at Voice America for keeping me on the air. Thanks to Rudi at Performance Flight for teaching an old dog new tricks. To Jay Kemp, Tanja Markovic, Leanne, Parker Blue and, most of all, Rachel Morrissey for keeping me sane and looking after me on the road and at home day after day. Thanks to Rose Marie Terenzio for helping get the word out and to Katharine Carpenter, Rachel Heng, Janine Gamilla and

Part 3: The Augmented Age

"As a long-time R&D project manager in military technology innovations and national security policy, I am deeply impressed by the potential value of *Augmented*. It has great potential to inform evolving security policy and creative new options, and to prepare government and industry leaders for the emerging future. King, Lightman and their contributors are to be congratulated for their thought-provoking work. The book should be required reading for professionals in the US and international defense and security organisations."

Dr. Christopher Harz, **RAND**, **DARPA**, **DHS** and **NATO**
research analyst and project manager, author of *Electric Blue*,
and co-author of *Food Security via Clean Energy*.

"If you wonder about what your life will look like in 20 years, read this book. Things are about to get real, and Brett and Alex lay it out beautifully in a way that is accurate, easy to understand and only a little bit scary."

Dave Asprey, New York Times Bestselling Author of *The Bulletproof Diet*

"You may think you've heard all there is to know about the dramatic changes to come in our digital future. Well, prepare to have your mind blown... again. In a crowded field of prognosticators, Brett King stands out for his clearly articulated vision of how technology is changing who we are."

Michael J. Casey, author of *The Age of Cryptocurrency:
How Bitcoin and Digital Money are Challenging the Global Economic Order*

"As one of the world's most followed and provocative voices in digital finance, Brett King has once again thrown down the gauntlet. Brett's vision of the future should be required reading for governments, think-tanks, investors, or basically anyone wondering how transformational technologies like artificial intelligence, robotics, Bitcoin and gene-editing may impact our society."

Seth Wheeler, former White House advisor on financial services
and Brookings Institution guest scholar

"Whole industries have been vaporised by technological progress but as Brett King show us, this trend is just getting started. *Augmented* is your guide to a world in chaos, where each wave of technological innovation collides with several others. Get ready, get smart; read this book."

Robert Tercek, author of *Vaporized*

"We live in a world where software is getting smart enough to automate tasks that only people could do just a few years ago. This is going to radically change the way we educate our children and the way people work in the future. *Augmented* is a wake-up call for a whole swathe of industries including the accounting profession. If your job can be automated, it probably will be.

Artificial intelligence, embedded experience design and real-time advice will undermine many of the professional services industries that grew rapidly last century. The future is one that is very different and King, Lark, Lightman and Rangaswami are the best guys on the planet to explain how we might get there.

In the next 20 years we'll see professions like accountants, financial advisors, bank tellers and others dramatically effected by automation, experience design and artificial intelligence. *Augmented* shows us that these changes are typical of historical disruptions, but this time the changes are happening much faster. This book really blew my mind. All I can say is: I'm glad I run a technology company."

Rod Drury, CEO of XERO

"When someone as obsessed and thoughtful about the future as Brett King gets ahold of a keyboard and sufficient time to think and write—watch out, world. Here comes a book that will broaden your mind and make you re-examine what you think you know about tomorrow."

David Wolman, author of *The End of Money*
and contributing editor at *Wired*

"What happens when you take accelerating exponential change for granted? The augmented world of the future described by Brett King and Alex Lightman is shaped by the profound consequences of this understanding. The social transformation, the radical impact on the very definition of being human and the huge economic upside of the global opportunities are all deeply analysed and richly illustrated in this inspiring book."

David Orban, Managing Partner of Network Society Ventures

"If you want real financial security and the ability to fund your dreams in the future, then you need to see what is coming next. Brett King's *Augmented* is a roadmap of the biggest changes and the most disruptive technologies we'll need to navigate to get there."

David Bach, New York Times Bestselling Author of
The Automatic Millionaire

Introduction

My six-year-old son Thomas won't need a driver's licence to own a car and it's highly likely he won't even own a car; he'll simply rent car "time" instead. Throughout his entire life, he will never be without a smart device which will soon tell him when to go to the doctor for advice (and his insurer will require him to wear it), he'll live in a smart house where robots clean and fridges or a household AI order groceries (delivered by a robot), he'll never use a plastic card or chequebook to pay for anything (and likely no cash either) and he'll interact with hundreds of computers every day that won't have a mouse or keyboard. Thomas is part of the so-called Generation Z which is growing up in a world so dramatically different from the world that their grandparents were born into that if you had predicted these changes 100 years ago, it would have simply been called science fiction.

You might be tempted to pass these changes off as the simple forward march of technology, but there is something more the team at Marshall Cavendish for making this happen. And, of course, to my co-authors in this endeavour, especially Alex Lightman who went above and beyond.

But most of all, thanks to Rebekah, Hannah, Matt and Thomas who put up with me when I went off to write for hours at a time, and then came back home bursting with crazy ideas on nanotech, robotics, AI, health tech and other such things.

From Andy Lark: For Sophia and Zach, I can barely imagine the worlds you will create and interact with.

From Alex Lightman: My sincere thanks to Brett King for inviting me to join him in writing *Augmented*, to my mother Elizabeth for instilling my love of reading and writing, to Eric Schuss for assistance with robots, to Eddy Waty for helping me to reach many of my goals in recent years, to Dr Mohammed Abdel-Haq for showing me how money and power move the world and to Paul Shepherd and Dr Chris Harz for three decades of best friendships.

This book is about the world that is coming, the changes society will need to make to adapt to that world but, more importantly, *it is about the journey that each of us individually will take to arrive in that future.* We will explore where we've come from and how we've found ourselves in potentially the most disruptive and innovative age of mankind's history. What will your life look like in 2025, 2030 and beyond? How will we get there? That's the essence of what we're trying to answer in the pages that follow.

This glimpse into that future is ultimately optimistic but, along the way, I wanted to see if there are any specific lessons we could learn as to how we might react to the seismic shifts coming. I interviewed and sought the contributions of some of the world's most pre-eminent experts in the areas of network effect, health care, artificial intelligence, robotics, consumer behaviour and sociological impact to ensure that you don't just get a single commentator's view.

In the last decade, I've spent my life talking to business leaders, entrepreneurs and media about the future. How banking, money and commerce are being fundamentally changed by smartphones, how identity and privacy are evolving, how consumer buying habits have shifted around buying books, music and TV and will never return to what they were in the past. What continues to astound me, the optimist that I am, is how many so often push back against technology changes and trends as they emerge.

I think it is fair to say that most people have a nostalgic view of the past; it is why we call them the "good ole days"! The world, however, never stays stuck in the past. So why is it the instinct of some to resist change, often passionately? What I do know is that despite any fears that we might have and challenges we fundamental taking place at a personal level and even in the way society itself functions. How many times a day do you check your smartphone for messages or check your Facebook newsfeed? How often do you log in to a website or use an app? Do you listen to music, read a book or play games on a device? How often do you walk into a new restaurant, hotel or office and immediately ask for the WiFi password? Have you ever taken a selfie?

While it is true that humans have been adapting to technology continuously, in the next two to three decades more changes will be thrust upon humanity than in the last 1,000 years. We'll have the technology to cure diseases and perhaps even extend life itself, we'll have machines that mimic or surpass humans in intelligence, we'll have self-driving cars, we'll land the first humans on Mars and we'll finally have the technology to live sustainably on the planet with abundant energy and creativity.

Shifts of these magnitudes often bring incredible opportunities, jarring sociological adjustment and, on many occasions, even violence.

The Internet, social media and smartphones brought us email, selfies, hashtags and YouTube, but they also brought us the Arab Spring, ISIS propaganda, Wikileaks, NSA's PRISM programme and the global Occupy movement. Social media gave us Facebook and Twitter and arguably propelled Barak Obama to the presidency in 2008, but it has also allowed some of the most hateful and racist vilification in recent history to find a home. It has created cyberbullying that has left numerous victims in its wake and has exposed intimate details of both famous personalities and secret government agencies.

Is all this technological advancement inherently good or bad for us? Are the emerging changes going to result in a new golden age, or an age of even greater disruption?

might face, the future is incredibly bright, incredibly interesting and coming at us fast.

Augmented is about how your life will change on a day-to-day basis as data, sensors, machine intelligence and automation enhance our world, and our place in it. It's about *how you will adapt to live in a smart world*.

I hope it will inspire you and supercharge your imagination.

Before we get started in earnest on this journey, I'll leave you with a quote from one of the greatest science fiction authors of our time, William Gibson.

> The future is already here—it's just not evenly distributed.
>
> William Gibson, *Economist*, 4th December 2003

Thanks for taking this journey, but then again... do you really have a choice?

BK

Part 1

250 Years of Disruption

Chapter 1

The History of Technology Disruption

"Every generation likes to think it is improving on the last, that progress is inevitable... But the truth is,... History has a way of repeating itself. It's just most people don't live long enough to see it happen."

Forever, Season 1, Episode 5, 2014

I wasn't there to see it but I imagine that the invention of the wheel was a pretty big deal at the time. As with every major invention since though, I'm also fairly sure that there was a priest, shaman, village elder, local trader or town official who cautioned why the wheel was bad for the town, how it was going to destroy jobs and lead to disasters of possibly apocalyptic proportions. History teaches us that technology is incredibly disruptive. Despite repeated attempts throughout history to resist changes to the way we live and work, we can't stop that forward march. Today, technology appears to be disrupting our lives faster than ever.

In the last 200 years, there has not only been a continuous cycle of disruption[1] through the introduction of newer and better technologies, there has also been a dramatic speeding up of those cycles of innovation. Researchers refer to this concept as technology adoption or innovation "diffusion". As technology becomes increasingly diffuse (or common) in society, new technologies face less resistance to adoption. As the world has become more interconnected, new technologies are distributed across a wide range of markets, at a much faster rate than was possible in the past. Take the iPhone as an example. Soon, technology like 3D printing will result in instant delivery of new products into your home, even faster than an Amazon Prime drone.

Technology Mass Adoption (in Years)

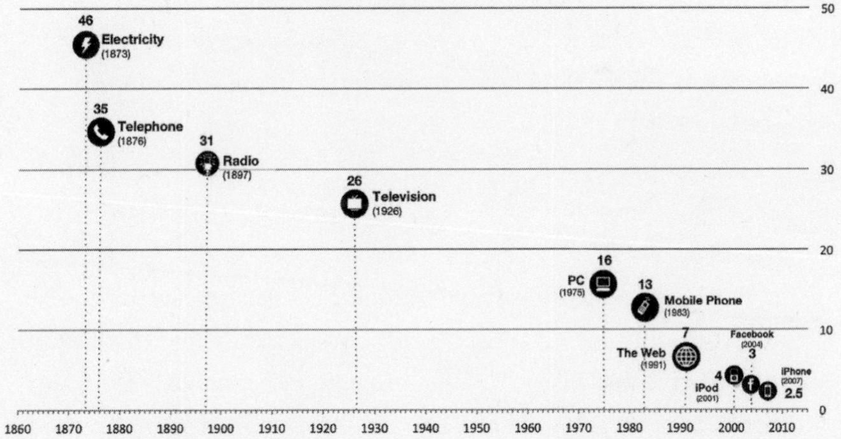

Figure 1.1: Years till mass adoption of specific technologies[2] (Source: Various)

We often talk about adoption of new technology in terms of "early" versus "late" adopters, but it is getting harder to tell the difference between these two groups as adoption

---

1 The term "disruption" is often overused today. When we refer to "disruption", we generally refer to disruptive innovations that fill unmet or future needs or created entirely new markets, and in doing so displace incumbents who fail to adapt (see Clayton Christensen's *The Innovator's Dilemma*).

2 In this case, until 25 per cent adoption in the US economy

cycles compress. In recent years as new technologies like the smartphone, Facebook, Angry Birds, Snapchat and WeChat emerged, they became mass-market propositions 30 to 50 times faster than technologies such as the aeroplane or telephone. We live in extraordinary, accelerated times.

Technology adoption and innovation has a compounding effect on the way we live when viewed over the long term. As we invent new technologies, they accelerate our ability to invent or create yet newer technologies. The invention of the printing press allowed more people to become educated and allowed knowledge to be distributed as never before. The invention of the integrated circuit (IC) not only allowed us to mass-produce consumer electronics and microchips, but also allowed us to rapidly improve design and fabrication methods for subsequent generations of computers and devices. Consequently, the time between major new technological advancements has been reducing over time. It's why, as consumers, we have come to expect major new features to be incorporated into every new iPhone.[3]

The graph on the following page shows what accelerated technology growth has looked like over the last 600 years. Statisticians call this sort of graph a "hockey stick curve" as it indicates evidence of an exponential growth scenario. In the 20th century, graphs like this appeared with increasing regularity, especially where technology was involved. This led to the hypothesis of what mathematician John von Neumann and futurist Ray Kurzweil dubbed the **singularity** (sometimes called the technological singularity)—a time when technological advancement reaches escape velocity. In theory, the singularity means that we could solve any problem mankind faces through the application of increasingly powerful computing.

---

3 "This is the best iPhone yet!" All Apple® and iPhone® trademarks are the property of Apple Inc.

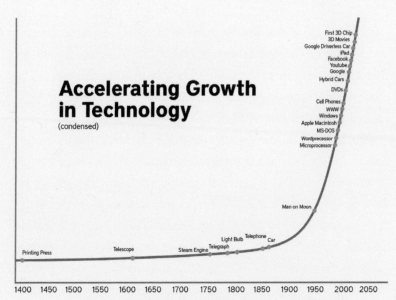

Figure 1.2: Major technology improvements are accelerating.
(Image credit: Asgard Venture Capital)

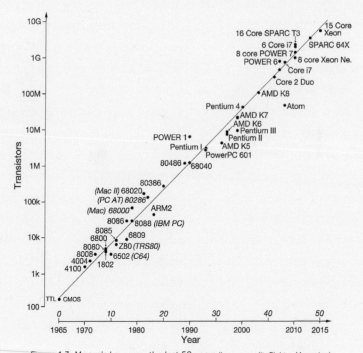

Figure 1.3: Moore's Law over the last 50 years (Image credit: Elektor Magazine)

The single most fundamental metric of these accelerated advancements in technology is embodied in a law known as "Moore's Law". Moore's Law is the observation that, over the history of computing hardware, the number of transistors in a dense integrated circuit doubles approximately every two years. While Moore's Law is now slowing down due to the limitations of physics, it has proven uncannily accurate the last 50 years. The law is named after Gordon E. Moore, co-founder of Intel Corporation, who described the trend in his 1965 technical paper.[4]

Today, technology is changing us faster than any other time in human history. The rate of change that society has to cope with is increasing from one generation to the next. The so-called Millennials (the generation reaching young adulthood around 2000) are a generation that appears mostly comfortable with these rapid innovations. Historically, however, the disruption wrought by new technologies has come with frequent social impact. Should we be wary of the disruptions new technologies bring or is it just history taking its course?

One of my favourite disruption stories is that of the Pony Express in the days of the so-called "Wild West". The Pony Express closed on 26th October 1861, just *two days* after the first transcontinental telegraph line connecting the eastern and western parts of the United States went into operation—now that wasn't a coincidence.

The telegraph was, in turn, rapidly disrupted by the invention of the telephone. Today, we know Western Union as a money transmitter but, back in 1856, Western Union was the largest provider of telegraph services across the United States, and by 1890 its reach extended even across the Atlantic. Inflation adjusted, Western Union was capitalised at around US$850 million dollars (US$41 million actual) in 1876. Western

---

4 "Cramming more components onto integrated circuits" by Gordon E. Moore was published in *Electronics* on 19 April 1965.

Union was operating more than a million miles of telegraph lines and two international undersea cables at the time.

When Alexander Graham Bell and his partners[5] patented the telephone in 1876, initially referring to it as a "talking telegraph", they offered Western Union the patent for the sum of US$100,000.[6] The established communications monopoly declined their offer, deciding that higher dividends were more important than investment in new technology.

Between 1881 and 1909, the Bell Telephone Company (known as AT&T from 1899 to date) subsequently battled Western Union until they had acquired a controlling stake in their business.[7] AT&T, now operating as a national telecoms monopoly, was forced to nationalise under the so-called "Kingsbury Commitment", one of the first major antitrust lawsuits brought by the US government against a monopoly. Despite the phenomenal success of the telephone, in 1913 there were still senior public figures trying to protect the incumbent telegraph industry, or they simply didn't appreciate that the telephone was a fundamental technological leap.

> "Lee DeForest has said in many newspapers and over his signature that it would be possible to transmit the human voice across the Atlantic before many years. Based on these absurd and deliberately misleading statements, the misguided public ... has been persuaded to purchase stock in his company..."
>
> The US District Attorney, prosecuting DeForest for selling stock "fraudulently" for his Radio Telephone Company in 1913

In 1913, the US District Attorney prosecuted Lee DeForest, one of the major telephone industry players of the time, for

---

5 Gardiner Hubbard and Thomas Sanders
6 The equivalent of US$2.5 million in 2010
7 Gerald Sussman. *Communication, Technology, and Politics in the Information Age* (Thousand Oaks: Sage Publications, 1997), 76.

fraudulently suggesting that voice could be transmitted across the Atlantic. Something millions of people do every day today. Was the District Attorney's objection to this technology scientific, based on a perceived risk to the stock market, or in an attempt to protect the existing telegraph industry? It hardly seems to matter now—it certainly didn't stop the telephone from changing the world.

As consumers, we seem to be constantly rushing to buy the latest shiny gadget, but perhaps we sometimes forget that all this technological progress comes at a price. It is doubtful that many of us mourned the fading of Motorola, Blackberry and Nokia from the commercial landscape as Apple and Samsung came to dominate smartphone sales, but I'm also sure that most of us were appalled at learning that Foxconn workers in China making iPhones were committing suicide[8] as a result of poor working conditions there.

At each stage of history, technology disruptions have been significant enough to create ripples that we still talk about today. When we call someone a "Luddite" nowadays, we are suggesting that person has an adverse reaction to new technologies. Other verbs in the common vernacular such as "Kodak Moments", "xeroxing" and "he sounds like a broken record" have been replaced by the more modern equivalents of "googling", "ubering", "tweeting" or "taking a selfie". Our language changes, our behaviours change, but society adapts.

Before we can predict what will happen over the next three to four decades as a result of emerging technology, it would be helpful to look back at technology disruption over the last 200 years to see if there are any long-term patterns or trends. If these patterns repeat, it is logical that we should be able to predict what disruptions the **Augmented Age** will bring.

---

8   Joel Johnson, "1 Million Workers. 90 Million iPhones. 17 Suicides. Who's to Blame?" *Wired*, 28 February 2011.

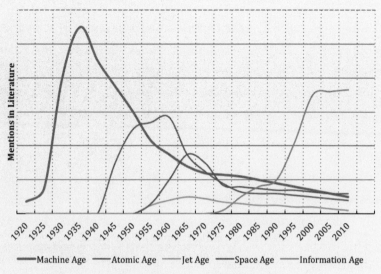

Figure 1.4: Mentions of "ages" in popular literature (Source: Google)

For the purpose of definitions, we'll use the accepted language and timeline for these "ages" as have been defined in modern literature and academia over the last 100 years.

The Industrial or Machine Age (1800–1945)

The industrial age or revolution was largely a transition to large-scale manufacturing processes focused around production methods, chemical and metals production (particularly iron), transitioning through the improved use of water (sewerage, plumbing, irrigation, etc.), to steam power and ultimately automated machine tools. The impact of the so-called Industrial Revolution was such that it touched the lives of people in many ways. In fact, it could be argued that almost every aspect of daily life was altered in some way over the space of 50 years by the machine age.

History shows us that once a new technology starts to take hold in an industry or in consumer markets, there is no successful defence for a traditional business model against that new technology beyond a few years, ever...

The Industrial Revolution was centred in Great Britain (the dominant world power of the day) and started about 1760, focusing initially on advances in the two largest industries of the time—the textile and agricultural industries. The changes in the textile industry really started to take hold in the early 1800s with the use of labour-saving machinery such as the stocking frame, spinning frames and power looms. Power looms were initially powered by water (mills) but, by 1803, Thomas Johnson and others were building looms based on steam engine technology. The steam engine typically drove a leather belt which, in turn, powered a "warp" and a "shuttle" that mimicked the way a textile operator worked a manual loom.

These labour-saving devices resulted in employers hiring unskilled, low-wage workers to replace the skilled "artisans" who dominated the textile industry at the time. Between 1811 and 1817, mass protests erupted across Britain, but centred mainly around textile mills in Nottinghamshire, Yorkshire and Lancashire. The textile workers who initiated these protests, which included smashing these steam machines,[9] were called "Luddites" by the press.

This is the first trend that we often see repeated historically. As a new technology emerges, which threatens to either revolutionise or disrupt an industry, protests arise and incumbent players may enlist the government's support to clamp down on the disruption. Within a decade, the new technology has become ubiquitous and employment patterns have altered irrevocably. History shows us that once a new technology starts to take hold in an industry or in the consumer marketplace, there is no successful defence for a traditional business model against that technology beyond a few years, ever.

The Internet turned 25 in 2014, and for most of the world it

---

9   *See* "Heathcoat of Tiverton, Lace Manufacturers," UK National Archives, Devon Heritage Centre (1791–1957)—1816 attack by Luddites on the Heathcoat lace-making machine. http://apps. nationalarchives.gov.uk/a2a/records.aspx?cat=027-4302b&cid=0#0.

is now an element of daily life. However, Pew Internet Research shows that as of 2014, 13 per cent (more than one in ten for those of you who prefer fractions) of Americans still didn't use the Internet,[10] and around 19 per cent didn't even use a computer. Maybe that doesn't sound like a lot, but it represents more than 30 million people in the United States alone. Having said that, the United States is the biggest incarcerator of prisoners in the world (around 22 million people, or 25 per cent of the world's prisoners), and most of these prisoners don't get access to the web, so this definitely skews the data.

The growth of the Internet has dramatically slowed in the United States since 2010, with just 2 per cent annual growth. However, the intriguing elements of Pew's research are the reasons *why* people don't use the web.

More than one third of those who don't use the Internet in the United States reject it as irrelevant, another third say it's too difficult or they worry about viruses and getting "hacked" while the final third say they can't afford web access. While the final third of users may be won over by cheaper smartphones or tablets, it is unlikely that the remaining technology laggards will have a change of heart. We can predict that Internet penetration in the United States will max out at around 90 to 91 per cent and smartphone penetration will reach saturation at around 80 per cent.[11]

Those figures are not representative of the world. At the time of printing, there are already more than ten countries in the world where smartphone adoption *exceeds* 100 per cent, meaning that in these countries most adults own a smartphone, but many own multiple phones. Countries like Singapore, Hong Kong, the United Arab Emirates, Sweden, South Korea and even Saudi Arabia all put the United States to shame when it comes to technology adoption.

10 "The Web at 25," Pew Research Center, February 2014, http://www.pewinternet.org/files/2014/02/PIP_25th-anniversary-of-the-Web_0227141.pdf.
11 Kamelia Angelova, "Here's When Smartphones Will Saturate the US Market," *Business Insider*, 5 January 2013, http://www.businessinsider.com.au/chart-of-the-day-smartphones-us-saturation-2013-1.

Today, we might classify people like those in the United States who obstinately refuse to adopt the Internet or smartphones as Luddites or even "Neo-Luddites"[12]. We can almost always find people in society who aren't simply sceptics in respect to technology but actively promote an anti-technology philosophy. The 2014 movie *Transcendence*, staring Johnny Depp, dramatises the supposed coming clash between the movement for machine or artificial intelligence (AI), broadly classified as the singularity, and an extremist group called R.I.F.T. (short for Revolutionary Independence From Technology) whose goal is to stop the development of AI. When a new technology like the ATM, mobile phone, the Internet or Facebook comes along, there are always those who are firm in their belief that "they'll never use [insert new technology trend here]". The oft-heard excuse is "it is a fad", that they'd never have a use for it or just don't think it is safe, useful, etc.

Who were the original Luddites? Did they simply just hate technology or is that too simple a classification?

The Luddites in early 19th-century England were named after the fictitious leader of the anti-industrialisation movement who was known as General or King Ludd. King Ludd was widely used as a pseudonym in written death threats to magistrates, food merchants and manufacturers at the time. The Luddites actually became a major militia force numbering in the hundreds. In fact, at one time there were more British troops fending off the Luddite protests and action at home than there were fighting Napoleon on the Iberian Peninsula.

By 1812, it had become a capital crime under British law[13] to break a steam machine or maliciously damage a factory or mill. In a mass trial at York in January 1813, over 60 men

---

12 Kirkpatrick Sale, "America's new Luddites," *Le Monde diplomatique*, February 1997, http://mondediplo. com/1997/02/20luddites.
13 Destruction of Stocking Frames, etc. Act of 1812

were charged as Luddites after an attack on a mill at Rawfolds, Cleckheaton. So why did the Luddites take such direct action against the machinery of the time? Were they anti-technology, as the name today implies?

Most of the Luddites were skilled artisans or workers who had made their living in the weaving and textile manufacturing industries. Prior to industrialisation, those sectors required a high level of technical skill, with many years of training, to operate the looms and weaving frames. The automation of factories took away the need for those specialised skills, and in doing so dramatically changed the nature and make-up of employment in the largest industry of the time. *The Luddites weren't against technology; they were simply against losing their jobs, their livelihood.* Unfortunately, they were fighting the inevitable.

The era of mass production accelerated globally in 1913, with the opening of Henry Ford's Model T Assembly Line in Highland Park, Michigan. In the early days, Ford built cars the same way as everyone else—one vehicle at a time, by hand, assembling the car from the chassis up. Ford's innovation was the development of an assembly line where a car was moved from station to station on a track, and at each station a new component of the car was fitted. The process involved a long list of sub-assembly tasks and specialised production of components so that the car could be produced in mass quantities cheaply and quickly. This reduced the price of the Model T to a point where the average family could afford to buy a car for the first time. By 1925, the Model T sold for just US$260 per unit, leading to 16.5 million units being sold. This record wasn't surpassed until the 1970s by the Volkswagen Beetle.

Ford's website says of the finished assembly line:

> "The ultimate step was the creation of the
> moving final assembly line. Starting with a bare
> chassis, it moved along the line and through
> each workstation until a complete car was driven
> off under its own power. An essential part of this
> process was that all feeder lines along the route
> were synchronised to supply the right parts, at
> the right time."
>
> The Evolution of Mass Production—Ford.co.uk

Mass production pioneered by Ford became a benchmark for manufacturing around the world. Ford established a minimum wage of US$5 per day for factory workers, and economists frequently cite this as a primary mechanism for the establishment of the US middle class. This is the second trend—new technologies generally create new jobs at a faster rate than those lost by these innovations, given enough time.

Social Effects of the Machine Age

The Industrial Revolution is widely credited with raising the quality of life. Before 1750, the average life expectancy was around 35, even in France and England where the quality of life was generally better. A core element of well-being was better farming and agricultural techniques and more widely available fresh produce, reducing the spoiling of food stuffs. The use of the steam engine and creation of factories enabled mass production of pipes, for example, which were used in agriculture and sanitation.

By the mid-1700s, the largest industry in Europe was farming and agriculture, with over 50 per cent of the population employed in this sector at the time. The Industrial Revolution resulted in growing unemployment as less manual labour was needed, but soon textiles grew to replace farming as the dominant employer. Between 1800 and 1950, agriculture went from employing more than half of the British and American workforces to less than 10 per cent. Early in the 20th century, the mining and steel industries had become the big employers, only to be replaced by the automobile, oil and gas industries. Later these were impacted by investments in the electronics, telecommunications, computer and information technology (IT) sectors.

At each stage of disruption, workers revolted and unions protested, trying to stave off the inevitable, while politicians and employers tried their best to navigate this shift and stay competitive and relevant. Repeatedly we've seen cities dependent on a single industry or dominated by a single affected corporation negatively impacted by these shifts.

A good illustration of how the introduction of tractors into the US farming community correlated with the reduction of workers employed (as a percentage of total workers in the economy) in the farming sector across the United States from 1900 through to the 1960s can be seen by simply examining the numbers. Farming jobs accounted for 42 per cent of the economy in the year 1900 but had dropped to under 5 per cent by 1970. The mechanisation of farming had a direct impact on employment patterns as we can see from the graph overleaf.

Ironically, preceding the industrial age, there was a massive boom in agriculture in the economies of countries like the United States and the United Kingdom. In fact, technology was at play here too. The agricultural revolution led to improvements such as crop rotation, improvements in plowing implements, more intensive farming techniques with higher labour inputs,

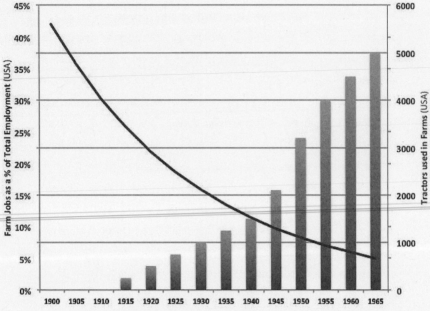

Figure 1.5: The correlation between tractors and reduced employment in farming

better breeding and animal husbandry, along with increases in farm size.

The disruptions in the next age were perhaps a little subtler, although the news of such changes tended to be more dramatic.

The Atomic, Jet or Space Age (1945–1975)

My childhood heroes had the *right stuff*. Neil Armstrong, Chuck Yeager, Yuri Gagarin, Alexey Leonov,[14] Buzz Aldrin, David Scott, Jim Lovell, Gordon Cooper and the other Apollo astronauts (just to name a few) captured our imagination, and pushed us beyond barriers that we could never have imagined. However, none of these amazing feats would have been possible without a supporting cast of thousands, and without leaps and bounds in technological capability. During this period, research and development around particle science was surging ahead, as

14 Or Alexei Arkhipovich Leonov

was the promise of cheap, near unlimited power from atomic energy. Each of these developments led to some of mankind's greatest achievements, and the most devastating weapons of all time.

Early in the 20th century, a German-born theoretical physicist and scientific philosopher postulated that it might be possible to harness the power of the atom for massive amounts of energy. His paper "Zur Elektrodynamik bewegter Körper" ("On the Electrodynamics of Moving Bodies"), which was published on 26th September 1905, led to both the theory of special relativity, as well as specifically an equation to quantify mass-energy equivalence, known simply as $E=MC^2$. The physicist, of course, was none other than the Nobel laureate Albert Einstein.

Prior to Einstein's revelations, worldwide excitement over Marie and Pierre Curie's discovery of radium in 1898 launched an era of optimism over the potential benefits of nuclear science. However, H. G. Wells' imagining of atomic war in *The World Set Free* in 1914, the Radium Dial Trials of the 1930s and the top-secret Manhattan Project to develop an atomic weapon in 1942 soon revealed a darker side to nuclear science.

At the outset of World War II, Einstein dispatched a letter to President Roosevelt (FDR) about the work of scientists Fermi and Szilard, who had expanded on Einstein's mass-energy equation. Their manuscript—combined with the work of physicist Frédéric Joliot in France—led Einstein to believe that in a nuclear reaction "vast amounts of power and large quantities of new radium-like elements would be generated." The more interesting leap that Einstein made was the understanding that "this new phenomenon would also lead to the construction of ... extremely powerful bombs of a new type."

His letter to FDR can be seen below:

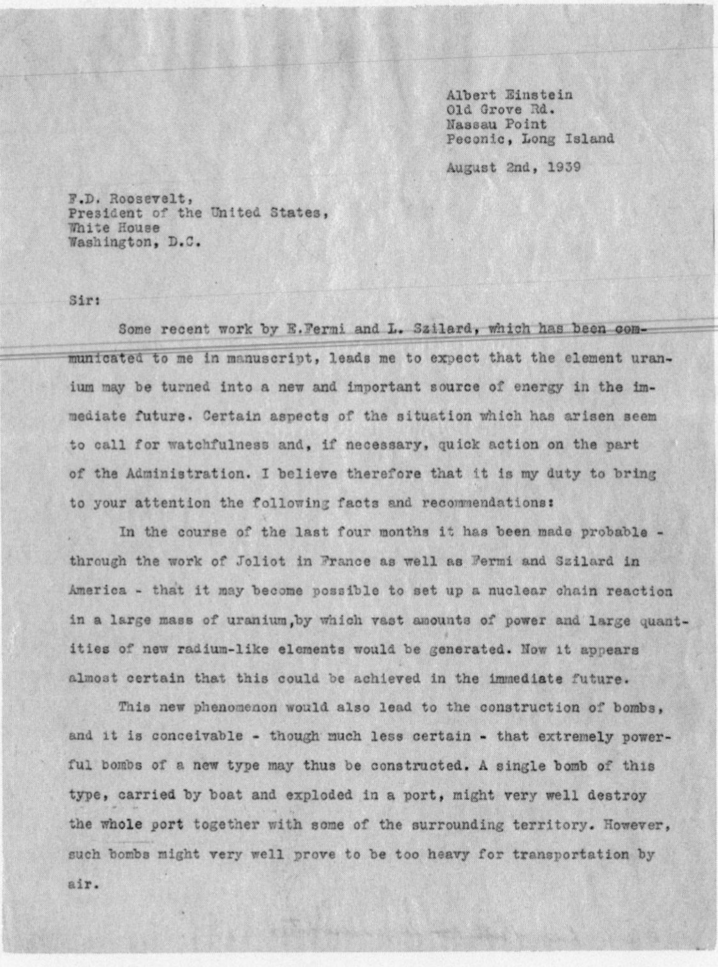

Albert Einstein
Old Grove Rd.
Nassau Point
Peconic, Long Island

August 2nd, 1939

F.D. Roosevelt,
President of the United States,
White House
Washington, D.C.

Sir:

Some recent work by E.Fermi and L. Szilard, which has been communicated to me in manuscript, leads me to expect that the element uranium may be turned into a new and important source of energy in the immediate future. Certain aspects of the situation which has arisen seem to call for watchfulness and, if necessary, quick action on the part of the Administration. I believe therefore that it is my duty to bring to your attention the following facts and recommendations:

In the course of the last four months it has been made probable - through the work of Joliot in France as well as Fermi and Szilard in America - that it may become possible to set up a nuclear chain reaction in a large mass of uranium,by which vast amounts of power and large quantities of new radium-like elements would be generated. Now it appears almost certain that this could be achieved in the immediate future.

This new phenomenon would also lead to the construction of bombs, and it is conceivable - though much less certain - that extremely powerful bombs of a new type may thus be constructed. A single bomb of this type, carried by boat and exploded in a port, might very well destroy the whole port together with some of the surrounding territory. However, such bombs might very well prove to be too heavy for transportation by air.

Figure 1.6: Einstein's letter to FDR on nuclear weapons (Source: National Archives)

While this line of research led to the birth of nuclear energy, it also—as Einstein postulated—led to the instigation of the Manhattan Project in 1942. The deployment of nuclear weapons became inextricably linked to advancements in rocket technology.

The V2 rocket (the *Vergeltungswaffe 2* in German, or "Retribution Weapon 2") was one of the most devastating long-range weapons of World War II. Hitler's forces successfully fired 3,000 of these weapons at London and its surrounds, Antwerp and Liège. The V2 was not the only advanced weaponry that the Nazis developed, but it was probably the most successful. The Germans also flew the first operational jet fighter and jet-powered bomber aircraft, the Messerschmitt Me 262 in 1941.[15] The Me 262, while a formidable fighter, entered operations too late in the war to have any meaningful impact.

At the end of the war, both the Union of Soviet Socialist Republics (USSR)[16] and the United States rushed to gather as much intelligence on German weaponry research as possible. In the final days leading to the collapse of the German army, there was an all-out effort by both Soviet and US forces to capture any of the rocket scientists who had worked on the V2 rocket and other such efforts. Ultimately, captured scientists were given the option to emigrate and work on US and Soviet rocket programmes or face life imprisonment. One of the leading rocket scientists working on the V2 programme was a German aerospace engineer named Wernher Magnus Maximilian Freiherr von Braun, or simply Wernher von Braun. Von Braun went on to lead the team that built the massive Saturn V rockets that took the Apollo astronauts to the moon.

In March 1946, about six months after the end of World War II, Prime Minister Winston Churchill gave an address at Westminster College during which he used the term "Iron Curtain" in the context of Soviet-dominated Eastern Europe.[17] This political antagonism played out over four decades in a so-called "cold war", but the most dynamic technological outcome of the period was the **space race**.

15 The He-178, a turbojet aircraft, flew a couple of years earlier in 1939, but was not a pure jet turbine aircraft.
16 Also known as the Soviet Union
17 Winston Churchill, "Sinews of Peace" address, 5th March 1946.

Figure 1.7: The launch of Sputnik started a "race" for space.

On 4th October 1957, the USSR launched a sphere with a diameter of 58 centimetres into an elliptical low earth orbit. It was called Sputnik (official designation "Sputnik-1"). *Sputnik* is a Russian word used to describe "satellites" (спутниковое or Sputnikovoye) but it can also be literally translated as "fellow traveller". In 1955, US president Dwight D. Eisenhower had announced the intention of the United States to launch an artificial satellite, but the Soviet Union caught the West completely off guard when Sputnik launched in 1957, sparking a rush of analysis and concerns.

Following the launch of Sputnik, the race for low earth orbit and the moon was on. The first man in space—Yuri Gagarin—almost didn't make it back to earth. As he fired his retro rockets, problems with an equipment module that hadn't detached meant that Gagarin experienced an uncomfortable ten minutes of wild gyration before the modules broke free of each other and Gagarin's re-entry capsule settled into a proper orientation.

It was less than five years after Sputnik that US president John F. Kennedy gave his famous "we choose to go to the moon" speech,[18] promising to put a man on the moon by the

18 12th September 1962

end of the decade. This speech launched the Apollo programme, and arguably the greatest single technological achievement of mankind to date. While there are conspiracy theorists who claim that the moon landings were some elaborate hoax, we know now that the technology to "fake" the moon landings simply didn't exist in the late 1960s. We also know that Chinese, Indian, European and US satellites have since taken photographs of the Apollo landing sites on the moon, showing ample proof that Armstrong and co. did irrefutably walk on the moon. Eight missions in all made it to the moon—Apollo 10 and 13 orbited the moon but did not land—but of the six missions that made it to the moon (i.e., landed), more than 840 pounds of moon rock, soil and core samples (just 48.5 pounds of that material came from the Apollo 11 mission) were collected.

For those who ask why we haven't returned to the moon, the answer is simple. The Apollo programme was an undertaking of massive proportions involving at its peak 4.4 per cent of the US federal budget, the equivalent of around US$200 billion in 2015. Less than a decade after the final Apollo mission, the US space agency's budget had shrunk to less than 1 per cent, and today less than US$7 billion a year is spent on flight programmes by the National Aeronautics and Space Administration (NASA). Still sounds like a lot of money, right? Not when your gross domestic product (GDP) is US$17.3 trillion (estimate from the second quarter of 2014).

"Asking if space exploration—with humans or robots or both—is worth the effort is like questioning the value of Columbus's voyages to the New World in the late 1490s."

Keith Cowing, founder and editor of
NASAWatch.com and former NASA space biologist

After Sputnik launched, nationalistic pride pushed both the Soviets and the Americans to a focus not seen since, competing against each other for the "firsts" of orbit, space walk, docking, etc. Previously such huge national efforts had been limited to wartime endeavours, but during the cold war, while the arms race was in full swing, the ability to claim the region of space local to earth orbit was just as critical a foothold in the minds of these two competing nations.

The atomic age was an age of massive economic growth. GDP growth hovered between 6 and 10 per cent for most of the 1950s and 1960s, and the demand for electricity growth was running at 7 per cent per year. While coal-fired plants were growing rapidly, projections showed that these facilities would not be able to cater for the growth expected through to the end of the century. Thus, nuclear was considered the more viable long-term option. In 1967, it was estimated that 56 per cent of the US generation capacity would be borne by nuclear power plants by the year 2000. Inflation in the 1970s, followed by the oil crisis, however, played havoc with the economy and the demand for growth of the grid shrunk.

Today, it is solar cell technology that is most likely to take the crown in the energy stakes. Solar was essentially a parallel invention of the space age. Bell Labs produced the first viable solar cell in 1954, and it was just four years later in 1958 that NASA's Vanguard 1, the first solar-powered satellite, launched.

Although solar was invented during the atomic age, it's only now that it has reached a price point where it can compete with the incumbent energy industry. The disruption of technologies borne in the post-war technology boom is set to continue, and by the sounds of it, that's great for all of us.

Social Impact of Rockets, Tronics and Nukes?

At its peak, NASA employed some 400,000 people, and it is said that this extended to another 20,000 universities, contractors and industrial firms around the world. It is said that 4.5 per cent of the US workforce was involved in the space race in some way or another in the mid-1960s. This was an unprecedented outlier in the typical ebbs and flows of various industry sectors and their contribution to economic growth.

To this day, Houston, Texas, and the "Space Coast" of Florida still bear the long-term economic benefits of the investments made in the space programme during the 1960s. A few of the benefits from NASA's investment in technologies over the last five decades include:

- **Teflon-coated fibreglass** today used as a roofing material
- **Liquid-cooled spacesuits and undergarments** which have been adapted into portable cooling systems for treatment of medical ailments such as burning limb syndrome, multiple sclerosis, spinal injuries and sports injuries
- **Lightweight breathing system for NASA firefighters** now used in fire-fighting apparatuses around the world
- **Robotic spacecraft servicing arms** and **artificial muscle systems developed by NASA** now used in artificial limbs designed for amputees
- **The design of NASA's space shuttle main engine fuel pumps** used as the basis to develop an artificial heart pump by Dr Michael DeBakey of the Baylor College of Medicine together with Johnson Space Center engineer David Saucier

Amongst the other cool NASA inventions or contributions we use every day are invisible braces, scratch resistant lenses, memory foam, infrared thermometers, smoke detectors, cordless tools, water filters, high-performance radial tyres, light-emitting diodes (LEDs), chemical detectors and even video-enhancing and analysis software.

The atomic or space age, while disruptive from a technology perspective, created many more jobs and much more wealth than it displaced.

The Information or Digital Age (1975–2015)

At the centre of technology innovation today lie three core *laws* or principles. Moore's Law, which we covered earlier in the chapter, and two other laws known as Metcalfe's Law (and the closely associated Gilder's Law) and Kryder's Law, a principle related to storage mediums. Collectively, they cover the core precepts of the digital age—computing power, networking and storage (or data). Computing and telecommunications have had a profound effect on the world and our behaviour over the last few decades.

Another way of thinking about it is that if you took every book ever printed throughout history (estimated at about 130 million individual titles), today we produce that same amount of content almost 1,000 times every second, or 80 million times per day!

To illustrate some of the mind-blowing statistics of the digital age, let's look at data storage and data transmission over networks. Between 1990 and 2005, the capacity of hard disks increased a thousandfold, and it continues to this today.

In 2015, it was estimated that Internet Protocol (IP) networks circling the planet would transmit 10 zettabytes of data. In 2008, we estimated that we would do 1 zettabyte in 2015, so we've already exceeded that tenfold, and we're expected to see another tenfold increase between 2014 and 2019.

To put that into perspective, if you were to size the "data", or content, stored in the entire Library of Congress, the largest

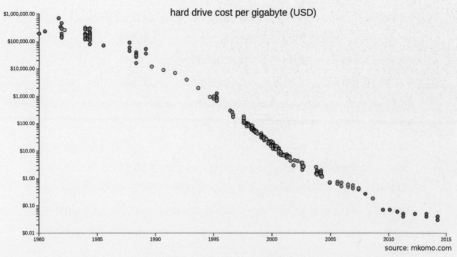

Figure 1.8: Declining cost per gigabyte 1980–2015

library in the world, you'd get approximately 3 petabytes (PB) of data.[19] The Library of Congress doesn't just store books, it also stores 13 million photographs, 4 million maps, 500,000 movies and 3.5 million sound recordings.[20] We produce the same amount of content as is stored in the Library of Congress more than 8,500 times per day. Another way of putting this is that if you took every book ever printed (estimated at about 130 million individual book titles),[21] we now produce that same amount of content *1,000 times every second*, or 80 million times per day![22]

Today, the US National Security Agency (NSA) collects as much information as is held in the entire Library of Congress every six hours. Staggeringly, there is already enough storage or disk space in the world to store everything people write, say, perform or photograph every day—with ease.

When the Internet started, there were a few large servers at universities and such, but most of the computers connected to the

19 There are 1 million gigabytes (GB) in a petabyte. An exabyte (EB) is 1024 petabytes, a zettabyte (ZB) is 1024 exabytes and a yottabyte (YB)—named after the *Star Wars* character Yoda—is 1024 zettabytes.
20 Statistics from the Library of Congress
21 According to Google Books software engineer Leonid Taycher, the actual figure was 129,864,880 books as of 2010.
22 Allowing for an average of 1 megabyte (MB) equivalent of storage required for each book, and accounting for approximately 9 zettabytes of content generated in 2014, we get the above figures.

Internet were small- or mid-range devices. "Data Centres" had existed since the 1970s but the creation of "servers" in the 1990s created commercial data centres used by large corporations, with disaster recovery being a central theme in centralising storage and mirroring platforms across multiple locations. Today, we call all those server farms or data centres connected to the Internet "the cloud". The word "cloud" comes from network diagrams that used to illustrate offsite storage in the shape of a cloud.

Phil Harrison, the former corporate vice president at Microsoft who led the division responsible for Microsoft's Xbox, described this dynamic exponential growth in computing as a platform at the launch of the Xbox One at the Electronic Entertainment Expo (E3) in 2013:

> "Day one of Xbox One, we will have the [cloud] server power equivalent to the entire computing power of the planet in 1999. There's a tangible data point for you..."
>
> Phil Harrison, corporate VP of
> Microsoft's Entertainment Division

The sharing economy and the social media collective have produced an explosion of content, bytes/bits and data that we didn't really see coming ten years ago. We predicted a linear increase in demand for data, and when mobile came along we rightly predicted more data usage, but we didn't expect the explosion of data that occurred as a result of social media, the amplification of "sharing" and the rise of consumers as producers of content.

Internet sensation PewDiePie, the nom de plume of YouTube vlogger Felix Arvid Ulf Kjellberg, is the epitome of this shift in terms of shifting demand for content. In a little over one month,

PewDiePie averages more views on his YouTube channel than the estimated global audience for the World Cup in 2014. An estimated 26.5 million Americans tuned in to watch the World Cup final between Germany and Argentina, but PewDiePie had already received 20 million views that day.

According to website TheRichest.com, ESPN is the world's most valuable TV network, with Fox News following in third place and CNN in tenth place. Yet the fight for viewer relevance could find no greater battleground than nightly cable news or perhaps sporting events like the World Cup. If you look at TV viewership from 2004 to 2014, it peaked in 2009. The reason for its subsequent decline is a combination of two technologies on top of the IP layer. The first being online video, starting with YouTube and then evolving into services like NetFlix, Hulu and Amazon Prime, and second, mobile and tablet consumption of video moving away from traditional news networks to just chunks of content.

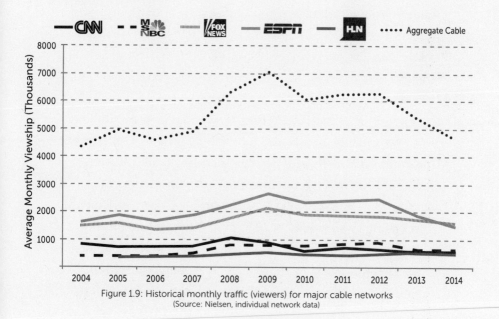

Figure 1.9: Historical monthly traffic (viewers) for major cable networks
(Source: Nielsen, individual network data)

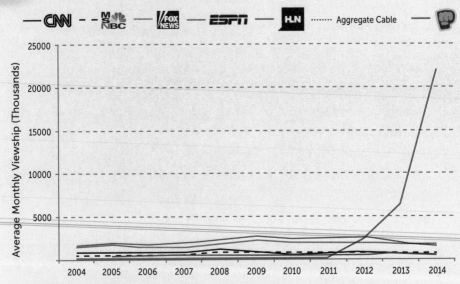

Figure 1.10: PewDiePie's monthly viewers compared with the major cable networks in the United States
(Source: YouTube)

It gets really funky though when you start to try to quantify the effect of YouTube stars or TV shows that are socially enabled, but not through what we would characterise as traditional media forms. The graph above illustrates the incredible influence and reach that just one vlogger like PewDiePie has compared with traditional news networks. In terms of just viewers and traffic, even on an aggregated basis, they don't even begin to come close.

I understand that PewDiePie's viewer base is entirely different to those watching Fox News, ESPN and CNN, but in terms of pure audience reach Felix Kjellberg has them all beat—yes, he gets ten times more views than the entire prime time cable TV base in the United States. If you're arguing that PewDiePie is never going to be as influential as Fox News, you are missing the point entirely. For Gen-Y and Gen-Z, the spheres of influence are entirely different to those of their parents' generation. The interactions within their digitally-powered communities are growing at a rate we've never seen before in history, and shared video, content and pictures are both essential tools in that behavioural shift. *TV cable is never going to be essential to the Augmented generation.*

For the record, statistically speaking, PewDiePie is definitely more influential than Fox News. In the end, it simply depends on whom you are trying to influence. The generation of consumers who watch TV or the generation who will dominate commerce, industry and demographics in just a few years' time?

Michelle Phan, another YouTube sensation, started blogging on simple make-up tips and tutorials in 2005 but progressed to YouTube video format in May 2007. In 2009 and 2010, BuzzFeed, an American Internet media station, featured her video make-up tutorials, and her YouTube channel went viral. Today, she has 7 million subscribers and an average video post of hers gets 1 million views in the first week. She leveraged her follower base and popularity to bootstrap "Ipsy", a monthly beauty products subscription service, starting in 2011. In 2013, L'Oréal launched a new cosmetic line called "EM•Michelle Phan".

Today, the 27-year-old YouTube star, who was once reportedly rejected for a job at a Sears make-up counter, runs a US$84-million-a-year cosmetics empire. At the 2014 Code/Mobile conference in Half Moon Bay, California, Phan reported that she'd seen a significant shift in consumption habits over the last 12 months.

> "Last year, 60 per cent of [our] traffic came from desktop.
>
> Today, 70 per cent comes from mobile."[23]
>
> **Michelle Phan**

---

23 "Michelle Phan: From YouTube Star to $84 Million Startup Founder," *Re/code,* 27 October 2014.

The Internet is at the heart of some of the most innovative business models we've seen emerge in the last 50 years. It wasn't that long ago that the very first website was published by Tim Berners-Lee, on 6th August 1991. The page simply explained the World Wide Web project and gave information on how users could set up a web server and create their own web pages.[24]

What we know as the *commercial* Internet is generally recognised as having launched three years later in 1994, with the likes of Yahoo, Lycos, the *Economist*, First Virtual (Bank), LawInfo, Pizza Hut, The Simpsons Archive (the very first fan website), Whitehouse.gov, WebCrawler, *Wired* magazine (hotwired.com back then) and others. Pizza Hut even allowed people in Santa Cruz, California, to order pizzas over the web! Today, the Internet is responsible for an incredible US$2.6 trillion in e-commerce sales. Before 1994, that figure was exactly $0. And those global e-commerce sales are still increasing at a healthy 20- to 30-per cent year-on-year growth 20 years on. However, Internet usage is rapidly changing thanks to the smartphone.

The smartphone is obviously the most significant development in personal, networked computing devices that we've seen in the last 50 years. While we might have imagined in 2007 that smartphones were a fashion accessory for the wealthy and middle classes in countries like the United States, the real action today is happening in the developing world. In 2013 alone, China sold more phones than the entire population of the United States, and most of these were smartphones. Smartphones, like the Xiaomi Redmi, Meizu m2, Yu Yunique, Obi Worldphone and Google's Android One, have already begun to fundamentally rewrite the rules on Internet-enabled device access for devices in the US$100 range. By January 2014, mobile Internet access had already surpassed desktop

---

24 You can check it out at http://info.cern.ch/hypertext/WWW/TheProject.html.

(PC)-based Internet access in terms of time spent[25] online.

In India, there are more than 40 different smartphones available for under Rs. 5,000 (approximately US$100) today. However, according to research by Priceonomics, in just 18 months the projected resale value of these phones will drop on average by more than 60 per cent.[26] Extrapolating the current progress in smartphone availability, we know entry-level smartphones will be available for US$20–25 in most developing nations by 2020. This means that more than 85 per cent of the world will have a mobile device connected to the Internet within just five years. Think about that. Between 2015 and 2020, more users will come online than since 1994 when the Internet emerged onto the world's stage. In that respect, the Internet and mobile commerce is only just in its infancy.

In 50 years' time when we look back at all of the changes that have occurred, we'll certainly identity the Internet as the biggest technology enabler, but when it comes to personal communication and interaction, the smartphone will be the device that really changed the world.

The Most Efficient Profits in History

Tech companies now compete side by side with some of the biggest brands in recent history. Obviously, Apple is a phenomenal example of a tech brand but don't discount Microsoft, IBM and Oracle, all of which continue to lead the world too.

Between them, the top tech companies on NASDAQ employ around 1.3 million people and contribute US$3 trillion of market cap to the economic landscape. If you include the next tier of players, you have the likes of HP, Baidu, NTT Communications, EMC, Texas Instruments, Yahoo, Salesforce.com, Cognizant, eBay and others in the mix.

---

25 Kate Dreyer, "Mobile Internet Usage Skyrockets in Past 4 Years to Overtake Desktop as Most Used Digital Platform," *comScore*, 13 April 2015.
26 "Your Phone Loses Value Pretty Fast," Priceonomics, February 2012.

Table 1.1: Market Capitalisation of the World's Top Tech Companies

Company	Market Cap (billion)	Employees
Apple	673.91	50,250
Microsoft	406.36	128,000
Google	364.27	53,861
Alibaba	285.14	22,072
Facebook	206	8,348
Oracle	182.22	122,000
Intel Corp	165.6	107,600
IBM	162.38	431,212
Cisco	135.86	74,040
Qualcomm	116.99	31,000
TSMC	112.19	40,483
SAP	83.29	263,000
	2894.21	**1,331,866.00**

Source: NASDAQ stock quotes

Tech companies are very efficient producers of profit compared with other large listed companies. Walmart, for example, has a market cap that is below Alibaba's but employs more than 1.4 million Americans alone.

The so-called "FANG" stocks of Facebook, Amazon, Netflix and Google created over US$440 billion of value on the US markets in 2015 alone.[27] The FANG stocks comprised just over 3.5 per cent of the weight of the S&P 500 Index at the beginning of the year, but made up 5.1 per cent by the end of the year. For the sake of comparison, the US$440 billion that these four companies added to the S&P is about two-thirds of Apple's market capitalisation.

In 2013, the four biggest banks in the United States delivered profitability in the range of roughly US$61,500 per employee annually. In the same year, the four largest tech companies delivered a massive US$450,000 per employee. That's more than

27 Jeff Desjardins, "The Market has no bite without FANG stocks," *Visual Capitalist*, 20 November 2015, http://www.visualcapitalist.com/the-market-has-no-bite-without-the-fang-stocks-chart/.

seven times that of the big banks, and more than ten times that of what retailers and fast-food giants achieved. The implication is simple—the more technology deployed in an industry, the more profitable that industry is at generating profit. Ultimately, this is why every industry must undergo a technology-based transformation in the Augmented Age.

Table 1.2: Comparison of Major US Sectors Earnings Performance (2013)

	Net Income (billions)	Employees	Net Income per Employee
Bank of America	11.4	290,509	$39,241.47
Wells Fargo	21.9	265,000	$82,641.51
Citibank	13.9	251,000	$55,378.49
JP Morgan Chase	17.9	260,000	$68,846.15
Banking			**$61,526.90**
Walmart	27.8	1,400,000	$19,857.14
The Home Depot	24.27	340,000	$71,382.35
Target	1.971	361,000	$5,459.83
Retail			**$32,233.11**
Apple	37	50,250	$736,318.41
Microsoft	7.41	128,000	$57,890.63
Google	33.91	53,861	$629,583.56
Facebook	5.97	8,348	$715,141.35
IBM	47.81	434,246	$110,098.88
Tech			**$449,806.57**
McDonald's	28.1	440,000	$63,863.64
Yum!	13.1	523,000	$25,047.80
Fast Food			**$44,455.72**

Source: Company annual reports

Such efficiency, while great for shareholders, is not necessarily great for employment. To illustrate, Kodak at its peak employed 140,000 people, whereas Instagram, arguably the Millennials' version of Kodak (acquired by Facebook for approximately

US$715 million in stock in 2012), only had 13 employees at the time of the acquisition. So it could be postulated that technology is, on a net basis, bad for society when it comes to employment.

Apple creates many jobs in its stores, and Foxconn factories reportedly employ 1.23 million people, the majority of whom are dedicated to Apple product manufacturing and assembly, but in terms of the sheer size of the Apple Inc. economy, the company employs relatively few people. Given the efficiency gains that technology brings, does that mean that as technology displaces historical businesses it inevitably destroys jobs? Actually no, that's not what the research shows at all.

> "The Internet's impact on global growth is rising rapidly. **The Internet accounted for 21 per cent of GDP growth over the last five years** among the developed countries MGI studied, a sharp acceleration from the 10 per cent contribution over 15 years. **Most of the economic value created by the Internet falls outside of the technology sector, with 75 per cent of the benefits captured by companies in more traditional industries.** The Internet is also a catalyst for job creation. Among 4,800 small- and medium-size enterprises surveyed, **the Internet created 2.6 jobs for each lost to technology-related efficiencies.**"
>
> "Internet matters: The Net's sweeping impact on growth, jobs, and prosperity," McKinsey Global Institute, May 2011

So that's good news, right? The Internet has created 2.6 jobs for each job it has displaced, and that doesn't necessarily account for jobs generated by the creation of wealth associated with Initial Public Offerings (IPOs), etc., that have invariably accompanied companies like Facebook, Google and Apple in recent times.

Various organisations have tried to quantify the web's contribution to the global economy. If we limit the assessment to just e-commerce-related expenditure, the web contributes generally between 4 and 8 per cent of GDP annually in developed economies.[28] However, that excludes activities like social media use, apps, watching YouTube videos and other activities that, while not having a direct economic impact in a traditional sense, are hugely influential to commerce and employment these days.

The one issue with the creation of jobs in the digital age is that invariably these jobs are centred around wherever the head office of the tech company is. For example, of the 128,000 people that Microsoft employs, more than 40,000 of them are based in Seattle where Microsoft is based. Of the 66 countries that Amazon operates in,[29] research based on LinkedIn data suggests that over 90 per cent of Amazon's staff is based in just six countries—the United States, the United Kingdom, India, Ireland, China and Canada.

Certainly the digital age has brought about one of the greatest booms in technology, jobs and wealth creation in all history. However, as highlighted above, the distribution of jobs and wealth from the digital age has tended to be centred more geographically and in more specific demographics (often also location biased). This is in stark contrast to previous booms like the manufacturing boom of the United States in the early 20th century, which was credited for being responsible for the broad creation of the middle class.

The Internet, and with it broad technology automation, has created a more serious problem for employment. Erik Brynjolfsson,

28 4.7 per cent in the United States and 8.6 per cent in the United Kingdom by 2014
29 Author's own analysis from *Business Insider*, LinkedIn raw data/sources

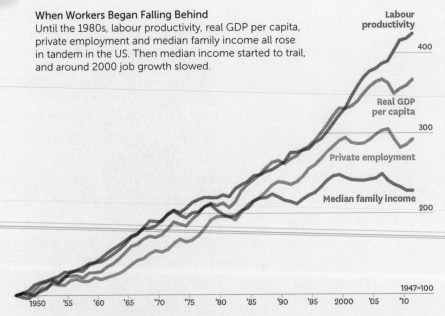

When Workers Began Falling Behind
Until the 1980s, labour productivity, real GDP per capita, private employment and median family income all rose in tandem in the US. Then median income started to trail, and around 2000 job growth slowed.

Figure 1.11: Productivity changes related to employment and median family income
(Credit: HBR)

a professor at the MIT Sloan School of Management, and his collaborator Andrew McAfee have been arguing for the last five years that advances in computer technology— from improved industrial robotics to automated translation services—are largely behind the sluggish employment growth of the last 10 to 15 years.[30]

Brynjolfsson and McAfee analysed the last 70 years of employment data and found that while productivity has continued to improve, employment has not kept up pace in recent years. Since the 1940s, employment growth has very closely followed productivity gains, at least that was true up until 2000. In the Internet era, productivity has grown, as has GDP, but income for the middle class and employment have not grown as quickly. This is an outlier that has only become evident in recent years with the maturation of computing and the evolution of the Internet.

---

30 Erik Brynjolfsson and Andrew *McAfee. Race Against the Machine: How the Digital Revolution Is Accelerating Innovation, Driving Productivity, and Irreversibly Transforming Employment and the Economy* (Richmond, VA: Digital Frontier Press, 2011). *See also* Erik Brynjolfsson and Andrew McAfee. *The Second Machine Age: Work, Progress, and Prosperity in a Time of Brilliant Technologies* (London: W. W. Norton, 2014).

As agriculture and industry jobs have declined, the services sector has already come to account for 80 per cent of US GDP. The problem we conceivably have now is that technology may, for the very first time in 200 years, disrupt the services sector significantly. So unless we create entirely new industries based on demand for services that don't exist today, it's likely that we'll see significant issues with employment growth.

What sort of disruption to employment and wealth will come over the next 20 to 30 years as we emerge into a new age?

Chapter 2

The Augmented Age

> "Any sufficiently advanced technology is indistinguishable from magic."
>
> **Arthur C. Clarke's Third Law from *Profiles of the Future*
> (revised edition, 1973)**

We are closer now to 2030 than we are to the start of the new millennium (2000). The technologies we are exploring today, such as artificial intelligence, gene editing, nanoscale manufacturing, autonomous vehicles, robots, wearables and embedded computing, are radically going to redefine the next age of humanity. I propose we should call this next age the **Age of Augmented Intelligence**, or just simply the **Augmented Age**, because of how radically embedded and personal technology will augment **your daily life** and **your behaviour**. This time the changes to our world are overtly personal. It's not just about industries being disrupted, or technology that we're inventing, it's about how your life will change radically on a day-to-day basis compared to that of the preceding generations.

At its heart, this shift is about radical changes in the way the world is connected and works together. Simply classifying the next age as the **second machine age** would be too much of an economist's view of the world—the probability that machine- or AI-based automation leads to economic impact from a productivity or jobs' perspective is valid, but is only part of the picture.

Since the coming of the industrial or machine age, society has been continuously impacted by new technologies, be it the steam engine or the selfie stick. Today, our progeny measures changes in months, not decades. We have billion-dollar companies created in less time than it takes traditional companies to launch a new product line. The rapid nature of this change increasingly has more to do with how we respond as individuals and collectively as a society rather than focusing on the underlying technology behind that change.

As humans, we're conflicted about change. As a species, we're constantly trying to develop, push ourselves further, evolve, create wealth, explore, discover, improve our knowledge and make our lives richer, more abundant and better. However, when change affects our jobs, our homes or our families personally, it can get a bit funky, a bit dislocating. For instance, if we were to lose our job because a more efficient manufacturing process or advanced computer algorithm made us redundant, then we would probably be quite upset about it. We might even protest for the outlawing or restriction of that specific technology or new business model, or even for governments to exclude our industry from tariffs or taxes so that our outdated business approach could remain competitive in a world that has practically rendered our traditional approach obsolete. The previous chapter showed that this is a fairly typical reaction.

It's Happened Before, It Will Happen Again

Not wanting to borrow too much from the *Matrix* or *Battlestar Galactica*, the reality is that this cycle of new technologies that act as the catalyst for entirely new industries, but at the same time dramatically impact employment patterns and social conditions, has been happening repeatedly over the last 200 to 250 years.

Commentators I admire like Ray Kurzweil and Peter Diamandis have previously classified this change as part of the coming "singularity". Diamandis called it the "Age of Abundance,"[1] but a factory worker at Ford Motor Company in Detroit or at Foxconn in China might have very different views today. Textile artisans in the early 1800s, chimney sweeps, farm tillers in the 1920s, video rental store clerks, 1-hour photo processing machine operators, newspaper reporters and taxi drivers are all examples of jobs that have been significantly impacted by technological change. While abundant, technology continues to be as disruptive as it is innovative.

Despite our very best efforts to adapt incumbent businesses to the rapidly changing world of the Internet, the dominant players that emerge out of these ages are mostly new players. It's why Apple and Spotify are the big players in music distribution today versus Sony, Virgin and Tower Records, all of which dominated the 1990s. It's why Amazon Kindle and Apple iBooks are the fastest-growing players in book distribution today, and why Borders, Dymocks and Angus & Robertson bookshops are no longer around. It's why we're unbundling and cord cutting from cable TV in favour of Netflix, Hulu and YouTube and why Blockbuster failed to adapt when its stores became an

---

1 Peter H. Diamandis and Steven Kotler. *Abundance: The Future Is Better than You Think* (New York: Free Press, 2012).

anachronism. It's why we're ordering increasingly from Amazon and Alibaba, instead of jumping in the car and heading down to our local shopping centre or retail outlet, or even comparing the Amazon price while we are physically inside a Best Buy store.

Typically within just a few years, we see that the new players who have built their businesses differently are simply better positioned to grow and take advantage of changing consumer behaviour, while incumbents are hunkered down trying to stop these new players from gaining further traction. Regardless of the range of these defensive actions, in all cases within a few years, the disruption is complete—employment patterns have shifted, the government has moved out of the way in favour of economic progress and the new players have either acquired the old players or the old players are marginalised and consolidated, serving a small, declining market.

The facts are that it never ends with old business models or obsolete technology surviving as the dominant play. It rarely ends with incumbents retooling and cannibalising their businesses to reinvent themselves fast enough. Thus, these changes are nearly always *disruptive*.

How Disruption Is Evident through the Ages

In day-to-day life, each age has resulted in significant changes to consumer behaviour, employment and services. What was all the rage in 1920 is no longer a part of our daily routine. Today, particularly for our youth, smartphones are a fact of life. According to recent surveys, almost 90 per cent of Millennials said that their smartphones never leave their side,[2] and 80 per cent of them said that they sleep with their phones[3] (as in the last thing they do at night and the first thing they do in the morning is use their phones). This is markedly—and very obviously—

2 Zogby Analytics Survey. Cited in Lisa Kiplinger, "Millennials LOVE their smartphones: Deal with it," *USA Today*, 27 September 2014, http://www.usatoday.com/story/money/personalfinance/2014/09/27/millennials-love-smartphones-mobile-study/16192777/.

3 "Millennials: Confident. Connected. Open to Change," Pew Research Center, 24 February 2010, http://www.pewsocialtrends.org/2010/02/24/millennials-confident-connected-open-to-change/.

different behaviour from that of teens and young adults who lived at the start of the 20th century. These types of behavioural shifts quickly become the norm, but over time they collectively add up to even greater changes in the way society works. For example, will you be able to order a taxi or a take-away in the future without a smartphone? It is unlikely.

Before we get to what comes next in the Augmented Age, let's look at some of the specific disruptions of the past 200 years and what impacts these have had on society. That way we might be able to predict more accurately what will happen over the next 20 to 50 years.

Let's start with employment patterns and industry.

Table 2.1: Top Jobs as Divided by a Century of Work

Top Jobs in early 1900s	Top Jobs for 2020
Farmers	Computer Engineers
Farm Labourers	Environmental Science, Energy Storage and Solar Deployment
Mine Operators	Data Mining and Analytics
Household Services Workers	HealthTech, Biomedicine and Bioengineering
Craftsman, Tradesman	Entrepreneurship
Factory & Production Operators	Psychology, Counselling and Therapy
Secretary, Clerks and Office Workers	Business Managers and Administration
Salesman	Designer and Customer Experience Specialist

The top jobs of 2020 will, of course, be very different from the top jobs 100 years ago. Over the last 200 years, we've moved from agrarian societies to very technology-driven and service-driven industries. In 1750, 80 per cent of the UK population lived in rural areas, by 1900 the figure had fallen to 30 per cent, and by

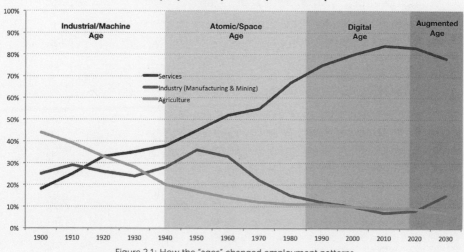

Figure 2.1: How the "ages" changed employment patterns

2030 it is expected to be just 8 per cent. The same phenomenon is happening in China, with figures rising from 13 per cent through to 40 per cent between 1950 and 2000, and projected to reach 60.3 per cent by 2030.[4]

Between 1750 and 1850, agriculture grew tremendously in the United Kingdom, the United States and Europe but, by 1900, employment in the farming sector was set for a gradual century-long decline. This is not to say that farming output declined. On the contrary, output improved greatly due to technologies like tractors, improved crop selection, better irrigation technologies and pesticides.

Ironically, the Augmented Age, with its robotics, metamaterials and artificial intelligence, will likely produce a resurgence in localised manufacturing. It turns out that robot and AI labour is even cheaper than that of resources in China and India. As we automate driving, restaurants, grocery delivery, accounting, banking and other such activities, certain service industries will

4   Felicity Brown, "Percentage of Global Population living in cities, by continent," *Guardian*, 29 August 2009, http://www.theguardian.com/news/datablog/2009/aug/18/percentage-population-living-cities.

face decline. We'll likely see the growth of entirely new service industries, though, based on emerging technologies.

The following table highlights the technological leaps that each age brought, and some of the impacts felt from an economic, welfare and employment perspective across the globe.

Table 2.2: The Technological Advances and Subsequent Impacts of Each Age

Age	Technology Developments	Pros	Cons
Industrial or Machine Age	Steam Engine Irrigation, Plumbing, Sanitation Railroads Telegraph Electricity Automobile/Combustion Engine Telecommunications Radio	Improved Health Care Improvement in Life Expectancy and Infant Mortality Improved Hygiene Formalised Trading and Stock Growth In Middle-Class Creation Of Mass Media/Advertising	Decreased reliance on craftsmen/artisans Decline in demand for agriculture workers Decline in use of horses Decline in service industry The Great Depression
Atomic, Jet or Space Age	The "Tronics" Boom Nuclear Energy Solar Photovoltaic Cells Commercial/Jet Aviation Satellite Communications Television	Home Appliances and Labour Saving Devices Boom in Energy Sector Boom in Mass Manufacturing Nuclear Medicine Commercial Air Travel TV Industry	Nuclear Weapons Globalisation and the exporting of labour CO_2 Production Boom 1970s Oil Crisis Terrorism The "Cold War"
Digital or Information Age	Computers Networking The Internet Mobile/Smartphones Social Media	Computer Industry and Tech Sector Boom (Emergence of Silicon Valley) Computer Games Mobile and Smartphone Industry E-Commerce	Decline in Localised Manufacturing Decline in Mining Sector Strong shift towards imports Japan's lost decades (1990-2010) Negative Population Growth (20+ countries) Youth Unemployment

The machine age disrupted manufacturing processes and developed "scale" as a concept in production, greatly improving productivity. In the atomic, jet or space age, production improvements still came about but were harder to produce, although output continued to climb. If anything, the atomic age was about thinking big, and capitalising on the rapid technological growth and improvements that came about because of World War II. In the digital or information age, there was an initial push towards process efficiency, such as the early mainframes (like ERMA[5]), and further automation in the factory and production space. In the 1990s, this extended to business processes and operations being automated at an enterprise level with enterprise-wide software solutions like SAP. However, the Internet went further and disrupted distribution mechanics such as we saw in the book and music industries.

The Augmented Age will bring about a huge rethink of processes involving dynamic decision-making, pattern recognition and advisory services as machine intelligence optimises those processes and feedback loops. Whereas the Internet was most commonly about disruption of distribution, availability of information and rethinking the value chain, the next age will be about disruption of information, intelligence and advice (the application of information and intelligence) itself. The Augmented Age will bring with it four major disruptions, and the emergence of two longer-term disruptive technologies:

Artificial Intelligence that disrupts the nature of advice, that is better at everyday tasks like driving, health care and basic services than humans. While many fear the possibility that hyperintelligent robots or minds will take over the world, for the next 30 years, it is far more likely that these AIs will be specialised and purpose built, and not necessarily human equivalent intelligence (more on this later).

---

5 The Electronic Recording Machine, Accounting (ERMA) was developed from 1950 to 1955 by the Stanford Research Institute (SRI) to automate the bookkeeping associated with cheque processing at the Bank of America. In 1950, the bank's checking accounts, known as current accounts in other parts of the world, were growing at the rate of 23,000 new accounts per month, and before introducing ERMA, its banks were forced to close their doors at 2 p.m. to cope with manual processing.

Distributed, embedded experiences that are embedded into the world and devices around us but enable frictionless, contextualised service, products, advice and value creation which, in turn, are monetised based on their effectiveness. In a world that is constantly augmented by data and information, value, personalisation and context will be key.[6] Everything with have a chip inside it, will sync with the cloud and interface with humans and other computers.

Smart Infrastructure improvements that radically change the way energy is delivered, how people and goods are moved from one place to another, how modern economies compete and how markets value commodities. Whether drones, solar energy, electric vehicles or autonomous transportation, value will be mobilised. Smart cities will be powered by smart resource allocation and smart infrastructure, making citizens' lives demonstrably better. The energy sector will face radical disruption.

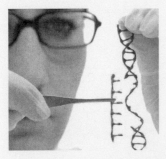

Gene Editing and HealthTech are going to radically change the way we think about health care. Hereditary diseases like Parkinson's, Alzheimer's, breast cancer, muscular dystrophy, cystic fibrosis, sickle-cell anaemia and even colour blindness will be eliminated within two decades. Sensors, wearables, diagnosis AI and other tech will radically

6   Image credit: *Day in the Glass* video by Corning

change the way we see heart disease and other preventable conditions. Algorithms and sensors will more reliably diagnose illnesses than doctors.

Two longer-term, and even more disruptive, technologies that are only just starting to emerge at the start of the Augmented Age are:

Metamaterials that are constructed using nanotechnology or radically new engineering approaches. Examples of metamaterials emerging include:

- an invisibility cloak (or surface material) that diverts visible light or microwaves around an object coated in the material
- bioinspired, self-actuated materials or electroactive polymers that behave like human muscle
- coatings that can conduct electricity or can turn any surface into a display
- clothing or textiles that will generate an electrical charge or include sensors and other circuits embedded in the weave
- carbon-nanofibre or diamond-nanofibre tethers which could be used to construct space lifts or similar
- super-strong and super-light metals and composites that can be grown like a tree or cultured in a vat
- windows that have transparent, embedded solar photovoltaics (PV) so that they can generate electricity

3D printing allows you to download almost any design for any product and print it in real time. The main 3D printing method is also known as "additive manufacturing" due to the build

process that adds or extrudes a layer of material millimetres at a time to gradually create a three-dimensional object or design. Future 3D printers will be able to print clothing or include electronic circuits and displays in designs.

In July 2015, the astronauts on the International Space Station downloaded a "wrench" and printed it using a specially designed 3D printer. Such a technology could substantially reduce size, weight and storage requirements for long-duration spaceflight. If you have to carry tools, for example, that may not be required under most circumstances, or you need to carry multiple sets of tools for redundancy, you could simply carry the required raw materials to prime a 3D printer. You could even, theoretically, print additional 3D printers.

These disruptive technologies are sure to bring about dramatic shifts in employment patterns. Throughout the previous ages, there was a rebalancing of the workforce among industries. In the machine age, employment shifted largely from established industries to manufacturing. The manufacturing sector grew steadily through the 20th century until the 1970s to 1980s when process, electronics and automation took their toll on that sector too, and those jobs started to shift out of factories and into service industries. What will happen in the 21st century when AI and experience design reduce employment in the service industries? Where will those jobs go?

Employment Impact

For over 100 years, employment has been moving from big

industry to services. Whether in agriculture, fishing, mining or, in the last 50 years, manufacturing, as processes have become automated, we've shifted to jobs where humans matter. However, in a world where the ability of a human is surpassed by artificial intelligence, there is a real risk that many humans will lose their jobs.

Futurists are deeply divided on this vision of the future. Some claim it will be a new gilded age, with humans working less and having more leisure time to pursue the arts and greater knowledge and learning like never before. Those with a negative view of the disruptive nature of AI argue that there will be a net loss of employment for the first time in 250 years as a result of technological advancement. There's only so many AI or robot ethicists and robot psychologists that we'll need in the Augmented Age.

A study released by Oxford Martin School's Programme on the Impacts of Future Technology entitled "The future of employment: how susceptible are jobs to computerisation?"[7] evaluated 702 jobs on a typical online career network, classifying them based on how likely they are to be computerised. The skills and level of education required for each job were taken into consideration too. These features were weighted according to how automatable they were, and according to the engineering obstacles currently preventing automation or computerisation. The results were calculated with a common statistical modelling method. The outcome was clear. In the United States, more than 45 per cent of jobs could be automated within one to two decades. Table 2.3 shows a few jobs that are basically at 100 per cent risk of automation (I've highlighted a few of my favourites):[8]

---

7 The research paper is available at http://www.oxfordmartin.ox.ac.uk/downloads/academic/The_Future_of_Employment.pdf.
8 These are jobs with 0.98/0.99 probability of disruption through technology. Based on a ±2 per cent confidence interval, this basically is a statistical certainty.

Table 2.3: Some of the Jobs at Risk from Automation and AI

Telemarketers	Data Entry Professionals	Procurement Clerks
Title Examiners, Abstractors and Searchers	Timing Device Assemblers and Adjusters	Shipping, Receiving and Traffic Clerks
Sewers, Hand	**Insurance Claims and Policy Processing Clerks**	Milling and Planing Machine Setters, Operators
Mathematical Technicians	Brokerage Clerks	Credit Analysts
Insurance Underwriters	Order Clerks	Parts Salespersons
Watch Repairers	**Loan Officers**	**Claims Adjusters, Examiners and Investigators**
Cargo and Freight Agents	Insurance Appraisers, Auto Damage	Driver/Sales Workers
Tax Preparers	Umpires, Referees and Other Sports Officials	Radio Operators
Photographic Process Workers and Processing Machine Operators	**Bank Tellers**	Legal Secretaries
New Accounts Clerks	Etchers and Engravers	**Bookkeeping, Accounting and Auditing Clerks**
Library Technicians	Packaging and Filling Machine Operators	Inspectors, Testers, Sorters, Samplers and Weighing Technicians

One often voiced concern is that AI will create huge wealth for a limited few who own the technology, thus implying that the wealth gap will become even more acute. The ongoing viability of society will not be based just on access to technology, improved health care and the elimination of poverty, but on a more equitable distribution of wealth so that the impact of AI is not a cause for further class division.

Developments in Silicon Valley over the last two decades may indicate the above expectations are naïve. Probably, but we either solve these social issues or we are likely to see a clash between the "technocrati" and the users to such a degree that its effects would be felt for decades. If technology is made freely or cheaply available, especially technology that houses, clothes, feeds and cares for individuals, then we indeed could find humanity in an age of abundance. The hope is that technology like solar and electric vehicles will greatly disrupt the big oil and gas cartels and that we'll continue to use technology to eliminate poverty and preventable diseases as well as improve access to education and financial resources.

In almost every example we've cited over the last 250 years of technology disruption, new technologies did result in the loss of some jobs, but it more often resulted in the net addition of new jobs that replaced those that were lost.

Pew Research Center conducted a comprehensive review of these issues back in August 2014,[9] inviting futurists, journalists and economists from around the world to offer their views on the impact of AI and robotics on the future of jobs. The results show that we're still divided as to whether this new technology will be a good thing for society. In total, 52 per cent of those surveyed by Pew said that the world will be a better place with more jobs being created by technology than will be displaced, as we have seen in each previous age. However, the remaining 48 per cent believe that the displacement of both blue-collar and white-collar workers will be on such a scale that it will inevitably lead to increases in income inequality, mass unemployment and breakdowns in social order.

Regardless of where you stand in the argument of how AI and robotics will affect our future, one thing is absolutely certain. It will be a time of heightened disruption. At the heart of the solution to the disruption problem will be how we prepare ourselves for this future. The skills that students need to learn

---

9   "AI, Robotics, and the Future of Jobs," Pew Research Center, 6 August 2014.

in order to survive in the Augmented Age are very different from what they are being taught in school today. We will need to teach students not just science, technology, engineering and maths (so-called STEM subjects), but agility, creative thinking, rapid learning and adaptation too. One of the reasons why the Luddites found the shift so difficult is that thinking about changing their employment was painful and difficult, so it was easier to resist the change than to adapt.

What if we give our children the skills to adapt, to change faster than previous generations did? Maybe then the shift in jobs and employment patterns would not be as disruptive as it otherwise could be.

Where could jobs be created? Let's take a more in-depth look at solar energy. Figure 2.2 shows the generation capacity of photovoltaic cells from 2000 to 2040 (projected).

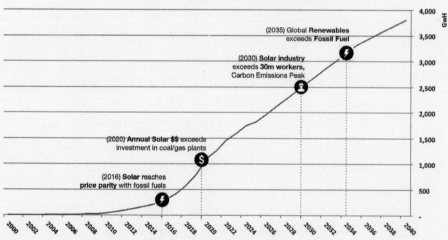

Figure 2.2: Solar PV capacity growth (2000–2040 est.)

Once again when we look at the growth of solar PV technology over the last 20 years, we can clearly see that familiar exponential growth curve that has come with so many technology developments over the last 100 years. This development is likely to be very disruptive in the near term. Let me explain how.

Even though solar energy provided just 0.4 per cent of America's electricity in 2014, it's growing at an incredible rate. Rooftop solar generation has roughly tripled[10] since 2010 (some estimates are as high as a 418 per cent increase in the four years from 2010). Current estimates are that a new rooftop solar system is now installed every four minutes[11] in the United States. According to Bloomberg's renewable energy research team (Bloomberg New Energy Finance), 70 per cent of the power generation that the world will add between now and 2030 will be renewable. By 2035, this would mean that the world will be predominantly renewable energy based. Economies like China and India are actually likely to lead the charge on this.

The threat to the established grid is clear and significant, especially because solar installations are speeding up. If rooftop solar reached just 10 per cent of the US market, it would result in utility company earnings falling by up to 41 per cent!

> The opinion of David Crane, chief executive officer of NRG Energy... as he starkly frames it, [solar] poses "a mortal threat to the existing utility system." He says that in about the time it has taken cell phones to supplant land lines in most U.S. homes, the grid will become increasingly irrelevant as customers move toward decentralized homegrown green energy.
>
> **"Why the U.S. Power Grid's Days Are Numbered,"** *Bloomberg Businessweek*, **22nd August 2013**

10 http://cleantechnica.com/2014/04/24/us-energy-capacity-grew-an-astounding-418-from-2010-2014/
11 http://www.americanprogress.org/issues/green/report/2014/05/29/90551/rooftop-solar-adoption-in-emerging-residential-markets/

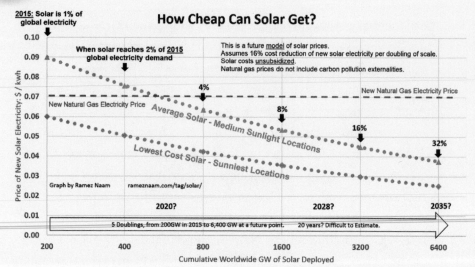

Figure 2.3: How cheap can solar get?
(Source: RamezNaam, EPIA, Electricity Markets & Policy Group)

The CSIRO, Australia's primary federal agency for scientific research, reported that by 2040 more than half of Australia's electricity would be generated, and stored, by prosumers[12] at the point of consumption. This would not just be led by household or rooftop solar, but by corporations. Google is currently the largest purchaser of renewable energy in the world but has committed another US$2.5 billion in investment in renewables over the next few years.[13]

Putting aside the whole climate change argument, when solar energy effectively becomes "free" or fractional compared with electricity generation through coal or gas, it will *absolutely have to* rapidly disrupt grid-based systems. Why? Solar doesn't require a grid to be efficient because it can be installed in every home or at every point of consumption. So the costs incurred by utility companies in maintaining the grid will quickly become untenable, further accelerating the need for a distributed grid.

12 A prosumer is both a producer and consumer.
13 Google Green

The year 2015 was a big year for solar as it reached price parity[14] with natural gas for electricity generation, but with solar we don't need a system of generators (or farms) and the traditional network to distribute that energy. The concept of maintaining a grid based on wooden poles or high-tension power lines becomes counter-intuitive and no longer viable. Once again, David Crane made an insightful observation on the disruptive nature of this change in energy distribution systems.

> "Think how shockingly stupid it is to build a 21st-century electric system based on 120 million wooden poles ... You can strengthen the system all you want, but if you accept that we're in the first stage of adaptation, the system from the 1930s isn't going to work in the long term."
>
> David Crane, 5th Annual ARPA-E Energy Summit, February 2014

Keep in mind that these comments are not coming from a solar energy company, but from inside one of the current market leaders in provision of retail electricity across the United States!

If, however, we take homes, offices and factories off the grid, then storage of electricity becomes a critical element in the success of a distributed system. Recently, Tesla Motors, an automotive and energy storage company, announced that its new US$5-billion Gigafactory in Nevada will not only produce batteries for Tesla vehicles but will also sell batteries—called Powerwalls—for homes. These batteries are designed to capture excess solar capacity throughout the day so that homes can continue to operate independent of the grid in the dark and in cloudy weather when solar capture is reduced.

14 *See* GreenTechMedia.com analysis, http://www.greentechmedia.com/articles/read/Utility-Scale-Solar-Reaches-Cost-Parity-With-Natural-Gas-Throughout-America.

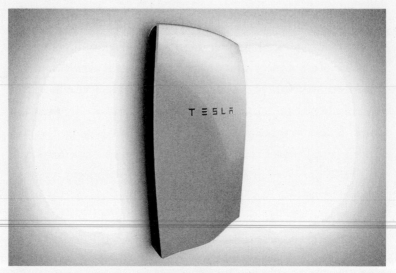

Figure 2.4: Will Tesla's Powerwall be the device that powers the "off-the-grid" movement?
(Credit: Tesla)

Nine days after Telsa's announcement, the company had already received 85,000 orders, worth more than US$800 million,[15] for its new home battery, leading Tesla to announce that the battery is already sold out until mid-2016.

The essential problem here is clear. With the adoption of solar energy and the deployment of the Tesla Powerwall or similar products, many homes will soon attempt to go off-grid. If enough homes do so over the next 20 to 30 years, existing utility companies will lose money and will certainly be unable to maintain or service the grid, leading more homes to rely on newer technologies as the grid fails.

The two decades-long transition away from fossil fuel-based generation has already started. A brief written for the National Bank of Abu Dhabi (NBAD) by the University of Cambridge and PricewaterhouseCoopers (PwC) stated that solar photovoltaic power is expected to reach grid parity in 80 per cent of countries within the next two years.[16] Surely much cheaper, cleaner solar

---

15 Alissa Walker, "Tesla's Gigafactory isn't Big Enough to Make Its Preordered Batteries," *Gizmodo*,
   8 May 2015.
16 NBAD, University of Cambridge and PwC, "Financing the Future of Energy," *PV Magazine*,
   2 March 2015.

energy for all is better than pulling coal out of the ground and converting it to run across wires laid over 120 million wooden poles? As you can see in figure 2.3, sci-fi author Ramez Naam has done some great analysis on his blog showing that unsubsidised solar will be roughly half the price of natural gas and coal within just a decade. Ultimately, on this basis alone, solar must win this fight. It's no longer about climate change, pollution or clean energy—it's simple economics.

Looking ahead, the good news is that there are 125 million homes in the United States, and more than 2 billion globally. That's a lot of homes to retool with solar cells and batteries over the next 20 to 30 years. Today, 8 million people are employed in renewable energy, but estimates predict that as many as 37 million people globally will be employed in this industry by 2030. This is not a future consideration as jobs in the US domestic solar energy industry grew nearly 12 times faster than the overall economy did in 2015 according to a survey by The Solar Foundation.

Gigging, Job-hopping and Cloud-based Employment

It was recently reported by Mintel that almost a quarter of Millennials would like to start their own businesses, and nearly one in five planned to do so in the next 12 months.[17] In markets like the United States or Australia where the cost of college education is becoming either unattainable or a poor investment for large swathes of the population, many of this generation are choosing instead to be educated by online platforms, hackathons, internships, start-ups and experimentation rather than through traditional college approaches. With this alternative approach to education, this tech-savvy generation is increasingly demanding flexibility with employment. A total of 66 per cent of Millennials

17 "Enter the entrepreneurs," *Mintel*, 19 November 2014.

would be willing to wear technology to help them do their jobs.[18] In fact, 40 to 45 per cent of Gen Y regularly use their personal smartphones and download apps specifically for work purposes (as opposed to 18 to 24 per cent of older generations).

In the United Kingdom, 85 per cent of Gen Y graduates think that freelance or independent working will become a more common and accepted way to succeed in the job market over the next five years.[19] In fact, freelancing is becoming so common amongst Millennials that they've even come up with their own term for it—**gigging**. As in "I've got a gig at Google." Others call them "permanent freelancers" or "permalancers". Increasingly, this type of work is done at home, at a shared workspace or even at a Starbucks. There are even websites dedicated to helping giggers find coffee shops that can be used as workspaces.[20] It's hardly surprising, then, that almost half of Millennials surveyed in the United Kingdom and the United States show a strong preference for this sort of working lifestyle.

The full-time job[21] is historically an anomaly. Prior to the industrial age, it didn't really exist. Early industrialists, who needed to have workers on a production line at the same time for efficiency, are most likely responsible for creating the concept of a structured work week. Consequently, for the last 100 years, the 40-hour-a-week job has been the centrepiece of work life simply because there was no better way for people to gather in one place at the same time to connect, collaborate and produce.

Now technology is changing the very nature of work. Millennials will be the first modern generation to work in multiple "micro-careers" at the same time, leaving the traditional full-time job or working week behind. "Work" is more likely to behave like a marketplace in the cloud than behind a desk at a traditional corporation. While a central skill set or career anchor

18 Cornerstone OnDemand Survey, November 2014.
19 "Generation Y and the Gigging Economy," *Elance*, January 2014.
20 Check out https://workfrom.co/.
21 For more on work patterns throughout history, go to https://eh.net/encyclopedia/hours-of-work-in-u-s-history/.

will be entirely probable, most will be entrepreneurs, and many will have their side gigs. For instance, Uber, Lyft and Sidecar are platforms that give people a way to leverage their cars and time to make money. TaskRabbit is a market for odd jobs. Airbnb lets you rent out any extra rooms in your home. Etsy is a market for the handmade knick-knacks or 3D print designs that you make at home. DesignCrowd, 99designs and CrowdSPRING all offer freelance design resources that bid logos and other designs for your dollars.

Before long, technology will allow instant marketing of your skill set, the auctioning of gigs and expertise, and the ability to be paid for your work in near real time or as deliverables are finished.

> "Research suggests that today's college graduates will have a dozen or more jobs by the time they hit their 30s. In an uncertain job environment, it has become societally and culturally okay that they explore. The expectations have changed. Your 20s are used as the time where you actually figure out what you want to do, so the constant job hopping to explore multiple industries is expected."
>
> **Emily He, CMO of Saba[22]**

Some of this is borne out of simple necessity. Millennials are generally more educated than their predecessors, but the impact of the 2008 financial crisis (the Great Recession) resulted in them being hit particularly hard on the job front, with 30 per cent of men and 37 per cent of women unemployed or not in the labour force.[23] This has driven a pragmatic approach to work,

---

22 "Solving the Mystery of Gen Y Job Hoppers," *Business News Daily*, 22 August 2014.
23 Pew Research 2014

and technology and real-time engagement are underpinning the job-hopping and gigging that Millennials are becoming known for.

When Life Is Augmented

Despite technology-led disruptions, in all the previous ages we've made solid progress as a species. Living conditions have improved, a billion people have been lifted out of poverty, life expectancy has increased, infant mortality has declined and, globally, the job creation trend has stabilised unemployment in most regions. Things are good in general, but that won't stop many from bemoaning how our young people are wasting their lives on social media or how greater technology integration in our lives is making us less human, less inclined to do the "normal" things that previous generations did.

What we do know is that humanity is constantly adapting when it comes to behaviour. Sometimes these changes appear minor, such as moving from reading a physical book to reading it on a tablet, when the underlying behavioural shift has actually

Figure 2.5: Have social media and smartphones really stopped us from communicating?

been a shift in respect to how people purchase books. On occasion, a new technology like email or the smartphone will dramatically change our daily routine, producing new behaviours that would have been unimaginable to our grandparents. Should we embrace such change or rally against it?

Recently, I was at an event speaking about behavioural shift, focusing particularly on how the younger generation—born into a world embedded with technology—simply finds such new technologies a natural part of their world. After my speech, I was pulled to one side by a concerned parent, who illustrates an emerging class of "techno-sceptics" who don't necessarily believe technology is always a force for good. This parent told me that he was scared by my description of the future world his 7-year-old son was growing up in and that he denied his son any access to computers or technology during the week, forcing him to play and experience life like a "normal child" and only use technology at the weekend.

The problem here is that this parent was imposing *his view* of what a normal childhood is on his child, a child born into a new generation, a generation that requires new skills to survive. If his child is not able to communicate and compete with his peers on the basis of technology, then he could conceivably suffer negative consequences.

Balance is required, but avoiding technological change isn't a strategy that will work for generations that need to move forward in a world imbued with tech. In most of the developed world, it is likely that you would not be able to get a professional job today without a LinkedIn profile or an online network you can leverage. Marshall McLuhan is credited with a great quote that aptly describes the world that the generation born post-PC and -Internet find themselves in today:

"I don't know who discovered water, but I'm pretty sure it wasn't a fish..."

Marshall McLuhan, 1966 speech

Let's think about this generation born into a world of technology. A generation that has such a different worldview of technology that Jordan Greenhall[24] calls them the "Omega" generation—the last generation. Applying the Marshall McLuhan attribution, these kids who were born after 2000 don't see technology around them as new; to them, it is just like air or water. It isn't unique, it isn't disruptive and it isn't different—it's just there.

Children born after 2000 most likely don't attach much personal significance to events like 9/11, simply because to them it is history. They certainly don't remember a time when there was no Internet. Most of them don't even understand the concept that TV shows used to be broadcast on a specific channel at a specific time of day, and the only way you got to watch it again was on a rerun. My six-year-old son is one of them. He can watch his favourite shows on any device at anytime.

This generation is highly adaptable, but their lives and decisions hinge on the technology around them. For instance, how do they learn something? They google it or watch a video

Figure 2.6: DIfferent language, different perceptions

24 For more on Jordan Greenhall, go to http://reinventors.net/content/jordan-greenhall/.

on YouTube. They didn't grow up with VHS tapes, cassette recorders, vinyl records and cathode ray tube TVs. So even their language and lexicons are different. How do they decide which new phone, clothes, video game or music they should buy? They ask their networks as they are influenced by mentions and Likes. To their parents, this may seem like strange behaviour. However, it is evidence of a definite generational shift in the way decisions are made and how connections are formed.

You might think that all of this technology makes our children less emotionally connected. In fact, research may agree to some degree. Recent research shows that there has been a great uptick in autism in the last two decades or so. Many believe that this is just a result of better diagnosis, but even after you factor in better diagnosis (26 per cent), greater awareness (16 per cent) and an increase in age of parents (11 per cent), it still leaves us with the statistic that 47 per cent of the net new autism cases are an unexplainable phenomenon.[25]

Some believe that being born into a world of technology is changing the way this particular generation reads emotional cues from faces, the way they emote and communicate. It is hypothesised that the causes of autism, Asperger's and other such conditions might even be evolutionary adaptations to a world where it is more important for a child to have tech skills than people skills.

It's not that these children are necessarily less emotionally clued in. In fact, it seems that they get so much input on their friends' emotional states through things like social networking and technology that their emotional quotient (EQ) may actually be higher than that of previous generations. They're simply getting those cues through feedback loops in the ecosystem rather than through reading facial or verbal cues.

25 Statistics taken from http://blog.autismspeaks.org/2010/10/22/got-questions-answers-to-your-questions-from-the-autism-speaks%E2%80%99-science-staff-2/.

This generation often communicates in real time about almost everything; including their relationship status, what they're eating for breakfast, which content they're watching and what products they're buying, and which of those they like and don't like. They are using information sources I never had as a child or young adult to make decisions in much shorter time frames. In fact, it has been said that a young graduate in Lagos, Mumbai or Bangkok today has access to more information on his smartphone than the President of the United States had just 20 years ago. In other words, they are highly adaptable, highly agile in their thinking and even less likely to resist technology change when it appears. In their world, change is a constant, and the fact that it is speeding up signals positive progress.

This may produce the biggest social disruption of all. The baby boomers (born 1946–1963) in particular, but also the early Gen Xs, those who are still at the helm of government and big business, tend to be the generations that are most resistant to political or economic change because they consider stability to be a core need. In fact, the 113th Congress in the United States is the oldest congress in history, with the average member being 62 years of age,[26] and considered one of the least effective historically.[27]

With the introduction of social media, we've seen a huge increase in protests by Gen Y/Millennials attempting to provoke change—whether through the Arab Spring, the Occupy movements, protests against police brutality and extrajudicial killings in the United States and the like. The baby boomers longed for sustained peace; Gen X for economic prosperity and stability. The new citizens of the world, the generation that will dominate the world by 2023, don't want stability per se. They want *positive progress through change.*

26 *See* www.slate.com/articles/news_and_politics/explainer/2013/01/average_age_of_members_of_u_s_
   congress_are_our_senators_and_representatives.html.
27 "The 113th congress is historically good at not passing bills," *Washington Post*, 9 July 2014.

These two worlds will very likely collide in the next decade when it comes to issues like climate change, energy, employment and education. Especially when it becomes very clear that there is little or no representation in government for the largest generation of voters, or where interests of incumbent industries and lobby groups resist technology change, especially in countries like the United States.

Advice in health care, financial services and technical areas, along with principles of government, have been predicated for the last 100 years on the concept of **information asymmetry**—the fact that the government or "adviser" knows something you don't know. Increasingly that information asymmetry simply doesn't exist, and so it is getting harder and harder for governments to claim that they are acting in the best interests of the public when the influence of lobby or special interest groups is blatantly obvious.

One thing is certain. The disruptions that technology and the Augmented Age bring will be perhaps the most impactful on society's operation that we've seen since the start of the Industrial Revolution in the 1750s. The Augmented Age will be all about technology infused into every aspect of our lives, whether AI, amazing distributed experiences or entirely new value systems built up of new infrastructure and new value chains.

In 30 years' time, technology will be so small, so powerful and so integrated into our lives that it will be hard to define technology in the way we do today as devices, interfaces, multitouch, mouse and keyboards. We'll have technology that lives inside us, on our person, in our clothes, in our homes, in our cars and elsewhere, that in each instance is millions of times more powerful than the most powerful computers we have today.

Imagine a sensor network made up of nodes the size of a blood cell inside your bloodstream reporting on your health and vitals to your personal AI? Imagine an AI that listens to your phone calls and meetings so that it knows what to put on your calendar, and a smart home and a smart car that coordinate with that AI to organise your meals, transport and other integrated experiences.

> "It took $10 billion to sequence the first human genome, today we can do the same for 1 millionth of that cost. It took 5 years to sequence the AIDS virus ... today that would take less than a day, but in 10 years' time the computers that do these tasks will be a million times more powerful than they are today."
>
> Ray Kurzweil, Exponential Finance Keynote,
> New York City, June 2015

The possibilities are mind-blowing.

If you think of the Augmented Age, AI and technology as a threat to humanity, then perhaps the biggest problem you might have is that your choice to participate in this new world may be taken away from you by a generation that is extremely comfortable with tech. For them it's not new—it's just the way they live their lives. It's cool, it's new and if it's not embodied by the latest device you need to have, or the latest app your friends are all using, it's just old and obsolete. The Augmented Age celebrates constant change wrought by technology, and those who resist that change will likely have the most to lose.

Chapter 3

When Computers Disappear

"Information technology grows exponentially, basically doubling every year. What used to fit in a building now fits in your pocket, and what fits in your pocket today will fit inside a blood cell in 25 years' time."

Ray Kurzweil, 2009

At the height of World War II, Alan Turing and the Bletchley Park team had just developed the first programmable electronic digital computer, designed specifically to assist British codebreakers with cryptanalysis of Lorenz ciphers. The German Lorenz rotor stream cipher machines were widely used during the war by the German army to send encrypted messages and dispatches. The Colossus Mark I became operational on 5th February 1944. An improved version of the Colossus (the Mark II) became operational on 1st June 1944, just days before the D-Day operations commenced.

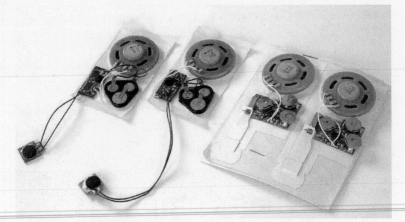

Figure 3.1: A US$0.10 sound module from a musical greeting card (Credit: Alibaba)

The first programmable computing device that wasn't a single-purpose machine was the Electronic Numerical Integrator and Computer (ENIAC). Originally used by the US army to calculate artillery firing tables, it became operational on 29th June 1947. By 1950, there were only a handful of such computing machines on the planet. Nevertheless, computing had had its start.

How does that compare with today?

Nowadays, even an everyday gadget such as the sound module inside a musical greeting card[1] has approximately 1,000 times the processing power of all the combined computing technology in the world at the end of World War II, and it costs just 10 cents per chip. Moore's Law strikes again!

The average computer that you carry around in your pocket today has more processing power than the world's biggest banks, corporations and airlines had back in the 1980s. The tablet computer that you use today would have cost US$30 to 40 million in equivalent computing power to build just two or three decades ago, and would have been known as a supercomputer at the time. The smartphone that you probably

---

1 A typical musical greeting card like this has the ability to store a 3.5MB audio file (up to 300 seconds at 12 kHz or better audio quality).

have in your pocket is more powerful than all of the computers that NASA had in the 1970s during the Apollo project, and almost 3 million times more powerful than the Apollo guidance computer that Neil Armstrong, Buzz Aldrin and Michael Collins used to navigate their way to the lunar surface. The most powerful supercomputer in 1993, built by Fujitsu for Japan's space agency at an approximate cost of US$34 million (1993 prices), could easily be outstripped performance-wise by a smartphone like the Samsung Galaxy S6. The same smartphone is 30 to 40 times more powerful than all of the computers that Bank of America had in 1985.[2] An Xbox 360 has about 100 times more processing power than the space shuttle's first flight computer.

If you wear a smartwatch on your wrist, it likely has more processing power than a desktop computer dating back 15 years. The Raspberry Pi Zero computer, which costs just US$5 today, has the equivalent processing capability of the iPad 2 released in 2011. Vehicles like the Tesla Model S carry multiple central processing units (CPUs) and graphics processing units (GPUs), creating a combined computing platform greater than that of a 747 airliner[3].

Within 30 years, you'll be carrying around in your pocket or embedded in your clothes, home and even within your body computing technology that will be more powerful than the most powerful supercomputer built today, and probably even more powerful than all of the computers connected to the Internet in the year 1995.[4]

Networks and Interwebs

The early days of the Internet began as a project known as the Advanced Research Projects Agency Network (ARPANET),

---

2   In 1985, Bank of America had seven IBM 3033 mainframes in its San Francisco data centre, which had a combined processing capacity of 40 gigaflops. The Samsung Galaxy S6 has the equivalent of more than 1200 gigaflops of processing capability or 380 gigaflops across a multi-core architecture.
3   Excluding the in-flight entertainment system
4   I did the maths. In 1995, there were 45 million computers connected to the web. If they all had modern Pentium processors or equivalent, it would equate to 120 MHz x 45 million, or about 5.5 petahertz. If Moore's Law continues (or equivalent) until 2045 to 2050, we would have a single chip with the same capability.

led by the Advanced Research Projects Agency (ARPA, later Defense Advanced Research Projects Agency, DARPA) and the academic community. The first ARPANET link was established between the University of California, Los Angeles (UCLA), and the Stanford Research Institute (SRI) at 22:30 on 29th October 1969.

> "We set up a telephone connection between us and the guys at SRI. We typed the *L* and we asked on the phone, "Do you see the L?"
> "Yes, we see the L," came the response.
> We typed the O, and asked, "Do you see the O?"
> "Yes, we see the O."
> Then we typed the G, and the system crashed..."[5]
>
> Prof. Leonard Kleinrock, UCLA, from an interview on the first ARPANET packet-switching test in 1969

In parallel to the development of early computer networks, various computer manufacturers set about shrinking and personalising computer technology so that it could be used at home or in the office. Contrary to popular belief, IBM wasn't the first company to create a personal computer (PC). In the early 1970s, Steve Jobs and Steve Wozniak had been busy working on their own version of the personal computer. The result—the first Apple computer (retrospectively known as the Apple I)—actually preceded the IBM model[6] by almost five years, and used a very different engineering approach. However, it wasn't until Apple launched the Apple II that personal computing really became a "thing".

---

5 Gregory Gromov, "Roads and Crossroads of Internet History," *NetValley*, 1995, http://history-of-internet.com/.

6 The IBM Personal Computer (Model 5150) was introduced to the world on 12th August 1981. It was quickly followed up with the launch of its IBM Machine Type number 5160, or what we now know as the IBM XT, on 8th March 1983. This model came with a dedicated Seagate 10 MB hard disk drive. For more than a decade thereafter, people talked about the dominant form of personal computer as "IBM Compatible". That's how strong IBM's branding around "PC" became back then.

Figure 3.2: An original Apple I computer designed by Jobs and Wozniak and released in 1976[7] (Credit: Bonhams New York)

Around the same time as Jobs and Wozniak's development of the earliest form of PC, there was also a rapid downsizing of computers in the workplace. No longer did computers need to be room-filling behemoths separated into disk packs, printers, input devices and CPUs, and mainframes were no longer the sole domain of the corporate computing landscape. Now mainframes were making way for minicomputers, or what are more commonly known as midrange systems.

The term "minicomputers" wasn't really an accurate description of something that was still the size of a large fridge, but they were still more powerful and smaller than the common early mainframe computers. Digital Equipment Corporation (DEC) developed a series of Programmed Data Processor (PDP) minicomputers, starting with the PDP-1 and gaining significant traction by the time the PDP-11 was released. In the 1980s, Sun Microsystems, HP and other companies started to dominate enterprise computing platforms for accounting and

7   At the History of Science auction held at Bonhams New York on 22nd October 2014, one of the 50 original Apple-I computers (and one of only about 15 or so that are operational) was sold to The Henry Ford for a staggering US$905,000.

basic enterprise systems. However, the personal computer was about to revolutionise the workplace environment too, primarily as a result of emerging networking technology.

In 1979, Robert Metcalfe founded 3Com, expanding on the work Xerox Palo Alto Research Center (PARC) had done in the early 1970s on local and wide area network (LAN/WAN) Ethernet technology. Initially, the software that could utilise these LAN-based protocols was limited to simple tasks like file sharing, printing files or sending emails. This technology quickly developed into what became known as n-tier computing, allowing us to link many personal computers and application servers into very powerful office network systems. Companies like Oracle were born out of the need to build databases and software systems on these new architectures.

Metcalfe's Law, named after 3Com's founder, essentially states that as the number of connections (or nodes) in a network increases, the value to those users on the network grows exponentially. It explains why social networks like Facebook and Twitter have grown so quickly in recent years. Understanding the effect of networks is essential to understanding our future. When we combine the laws of network growth with the growth of computers defined by Moore's Law, we essentially see that exponential growth of interconnected computers and devices is now unstoppable. During 2008, the number of "things" connected to the Internet exceeded the number of people on the planet,[8] and the growth of global computing networks has only continued to accelerate.

Today, we network light bulbs, home thermostats, door locks, aircraft, vehicles, drones, robotic vacuum cleaners and many more appliances and gadgets. We are on the cusp of an explosion in interconnected, intelligent devices, sensors and

8 Cisco—Internet of Things (IoT)

nodes that promises to change the world as we know it. By 2020, 50 billion "things" will be connected to the Internet, but by 2030 we could be talking as many as 100 trillion sensors, or 150 sensors for every human on the planet. These sensors will be generating feedback on everything from our heart rate to the charge in our electric vehicle, the pollution in the air around us, the sugar levels in our blood stream or even the condition of our daily feculence. They will drive an informed, measured future that extends life and makes the planet safer and cleaner.

For such a revolution in connectivity to truly change the future and fortunes of the planet, we're going to have to enable network access to everyone, not just developed nations. How do we get there?

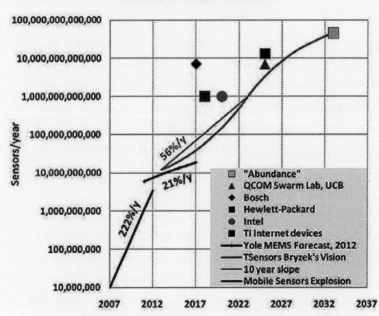

Figure 3.3: 50–100 trillion devices by 2030, or 150 sensors for every human
(Credit: SBP Global)

During the 2014 OccupyHongKong movement, one of the stars of the show was a new app (at least it was at the time) called FireChat, which utilised a form of **mesh networking technology**. Basically, this app can use your phone's WiFi or Bluetooth radio to communicate with other phones, even when the Internet and cellular networking services are down. Open Garden, the creators of FireChat, announced a partnership in Tahiti in October 2015 that will enable residents of the island to communicate with each other without needing a data plan or connection to a cellular service.

Mesh networking promises to be the ultimate solution to network connectivity. In theory, every Internet-enabled device can become a node on a distributed network that not only enables that device to connect to the web, but also allows other devices to communicate via shared connections. In today's web, you have access points, whether via Internet service provider (ISP) hardpoints or WiFi hotspots, that act as connections to the larger network that is the Internet. Mesh nodes are small radio transmitters that don't just communicate with users of that node or access point, they also communicate with each other. In that way, if one of those nodes loses connectivity to the Internet backbone, it just shares connectivity with other nodes that it is in range of. This is a truly distributed network topology, no longer wholly reliant on connections to the Internet backbone at each access point.

The implications of this are far-reaching, particularly in the rural areas of regions like Africa or countries like Indonesia, India and China where network connectivity is limited or non-existent. In theory, it means that every device with a small radio embedded into it, even in isolated areas, could become an Internet-access device. In addition to mesh networking technology, both Facebook and Google are working on technologies that will bring wireless Internet access to more than 2 billion unconnected people.

Facebook, in the shape of Internet.org, is prototyping a network of high-altitude, solar-powered drones called Aquila that uses lasers to transmit to small towers or dishes on the ground. The drones will stay aloft for months at a time and fly above commercial aircraft. Google is working on a similar project called Project Loon, but using high-altitude balloons instead.

Over the next 20 years, the greatest innovations will not be in the growth of networks, but in the way we use intelligent, networked computers embedded in every aspect of our daily lives. To leverage off this, we'll need a new paradigm of design, new software and new ways to interact with devices. This focus on design is apparent in the beauty of devices like the iPhone compared with the earliest mobile phones, the specialisation of the large display screen in a Tesla or in the absence of screens in devices like Amazon Echo. We are finding increasingly imaginative ways to build technology into the world around us.

The Evolution of the Interface and Interaction Design

In 1982, I started Year 9 at a select-entry secondary school in Melbourne, Australia. Melbourne High School was one of the first secondary schools in Australia to introduce computer science as a subject. Today, we see the likes of President Obama coding his first Java sequence, and kids learning to code via YouTube and Codecademy, but back in the early 1980s, coding was still a university endeavour. When I started learning to code at school, we used a computer inherited from Melbourne University that allowed us to program in Basic, Pascal, Cobol and Fortran, but only using paper cards.

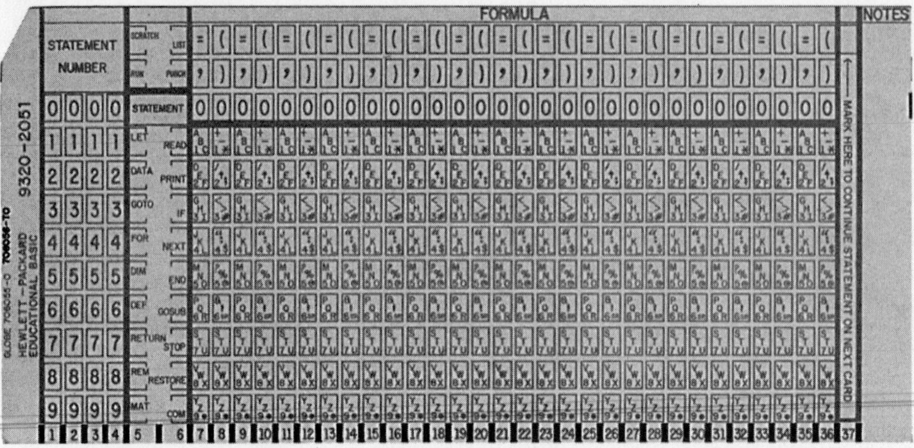

Figure 3.4: Computer programming in the 1970s was often done on punch cards rather than via a keyboard.

To code in those days, you had to hand write your code on paper, then transpose your code one line at a time onto either graphite or punch cards. You would then use a card stack reader that would read one card at a time and interpret either the pencil mark or the punch hole as a letter, number or character that was then interpreted and compiled. The classic "Hello World" program would have required using four different cards.

I definitely fell into the geek squad at school. I still vividly remember the time when I hacked into the school administrator system to find the teachers' records; I got a two-week time out from the computer room for that one. I would offer to code other kids' assignments for them for a nominal fee. It wasn't about the money, it was simply a test to see if I could get the same results or output using different versions of the program.

Around this time, my pal Dan Goldberg introduced me to my first Apple II computer, and not long after that I got my first Vic-20 microcomputer at home. A few years later, I convinced my father to invest in an IBM compatible computer for the home. I'd gone from punching in programs on paper cards that read graphite pencil marks to keyboards and monochrome screens. Interfaces, especially when it came to games or graphics, were extremely primitive.

The Commodore Vic-20 microcomputer that I owned had about 4k of in-built ram, a 16-k expansion pack and a cassette tape deck for storing programs. I connected my Vic-20 up to an old black-and-white TV that my parents had lying around, but it was capable of 16 vibrant colours. I recall buying Vic-20 hobby magazines and pouring over lines of code, painstakingly typing these lines in so I could play a new game. This was how I learnt to code. By changing parameters, I was learning syntax, I was learning programming logic. When I graduated from secondary school, I had enough programming skill to go straight into a commercial programming position, allowing me to attend university part-time while I did what I loved every day—coding.

When Windows 3 and 3.11 came along, suddenly there was a graphical user interface that made using computers even simpler. You had standard controls and elements such as edit boxes, radio buttons and other design elements that gave you a great deal more flexibility when compared with old green screen tech.

Computers were getting more and more powerful, but interfaces were getting easier to use at the same time. The first generation of computer interfaces were known only to engineers. The second generation of interfaces allowed users to be trained to use specific programs, without having to be a programmer. Even with that progress though, knowing one computer system or operating system did not translate to being able to operate or navigate another system you weren't intimately familiar with.

It soon became possible to buy off-the-shelf software and put that disk or cartridge into your console or computer, and even if you had never used the software before, you had a fair chance of being able to navigate it. Today, we download apps to our phones or software to our laptops that take just minutes to figure out, instead of weeks of intensive training. YouTube and other web-based tools allowed my 12-year-old son to learn how to code "mods" in Java for the popular Minecraft[9] game ecosystem in a few weeks.

Ultimately, as this trend continues, we'll have immensely powerful computers embedded in the world around us that require no obvious interaction to operate beyond a response to a spoken word, or an action on our behalf. To illustrate, think about wearing a Fitbit device and the input that the computer in a wearable like that requires to be effective.

The introduction of multitouch was a big leap forward in interface design for personal devices. It allowed us to carry extremely powerful computers around in our pocket that didn't require the additional hardware of a mouse or keyboard. From the perspective of the accuracy of input, it has been argued

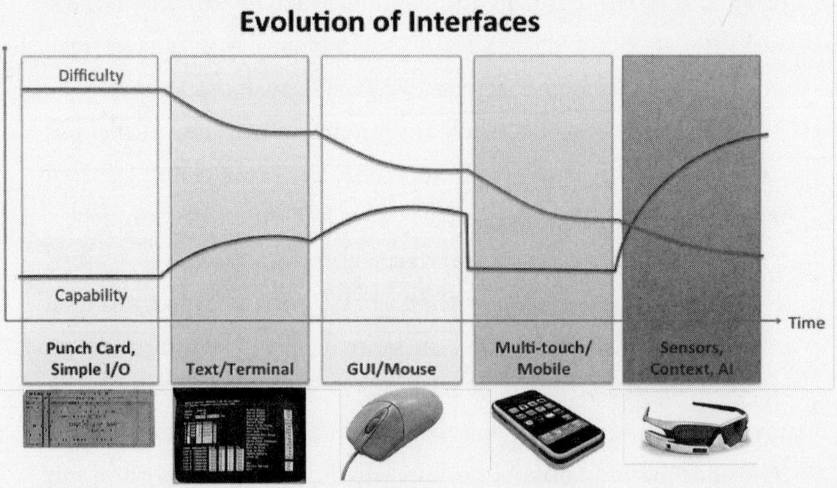

Figure 3.5: The evolution of computer interfaces

9   Minecraft is a trademark owned by Mojang/Microsoft.

that multitouch degraded our capability but, at the same time, no one can deny that the simplicity of these devices means that even a two-year-old child can pick up an iPad and use it with ease.

The next phase of computing will see the way we use computers radically evolve. Input will be divided between **direct input from an operator** or user via either a virtual keyboard, voice, touch, gestures or feedback, via **sensors** that capture everything from biometrics and health data, geolocation, machine/device performance through to environmental data and finally from **social, heuristic and behavioural analytics** that start to anticipate and compare your behaviour. Input will be neither linear nor based on a single screen or interface.

Moving from Screens to Sensors

If you carry a smartphone, a wearable fitness device or a smartwatch, your device is already capturing a ton of information about you and your movements each day. The internal accelerometer, combined with the global positioning system (GPS) chip, captures movement data; it's precise enough to even calculate your steps and the change in altitude as you move up a flight of stairs. While devices like smartwatches and fitness bands capture your heart rate and act as a pedometer, the next generation of sensors will be able to capture far, far more.

In 2014, Samsung announced a prototype wearable known as Simband that has half a dozen different sensors that can keep tabs on your daily steps, heart rate, blood flow and pressure, skin temperature, oxygen level and how much sweat you are producing—12 key data points in all. The Simband display looks similar to a heart rate monitor that you would see in an intensive care unit (ICU) but is worn on the wrist.

Figure 3.6: The Simband sensor array built into the watch band (Credit: Samsung)

Figure 3.7: The Simband display with electrocardiogram (ECG or EKG[10]) and other feedback (Credit: Samsung)

In much the way GPS or navigation software can predict how traffic is going to impact your journey or travel time, over the next decade health sensors married with AI and algorithms will be able to sense developing cardiovascular disease, impending strokes, GI tract issues, liver function impairment or acute renal failure[11] and even recommend or administer direct treatment that prevents a critical event while you seek more direct medical assistance.

---

10 Globally, the term ECG is most common in which the Greek word for "heart" *cardia* or *kardia* is central to the acronym (*elektro-cardia-graph*, literally "electric-heart-writing"). The US common usage is EKG, using the original Greek spelling term rather than the English transliteration (cardio).

11 R.W. White, R. Harpaz, N.H. Shah, W. DuMouchel and E. Horvitz, "Toward enhanced pharmacovigilance using patient-generated data on the Internet," *Journal of Clinical Pharmacology & Therapeutics* 96, no. 2 (August 2014): 239–46.

Insurance companies that offer health and life insurance are starting to understand that these tools will dramatically reduce their risk in underwriting policies, as well as help policyholders (that's us) manage their health better in concert with medical professionals. Insurance will no longer be about assessing your potential risk of heart disease, as much as it will be about monitoring your lifestyle and biometric data so that the risk of heart disease can be managed. The paper application forms that you fill out for insurance policies today will be pretty much useless compared with the data insurers can get from these types of sensor arrays. Besides, an application form won't be able to help you actively manage diet, physical activity, etc., to reduce the ongoing risk of heart disease. It's why organisations like John Hancock, the US insurance giant, are already giving discounts to policyholders who wear fitness trackers.[12]

With so much data being uploaded to the interwebs,[13] every second of every day, we have already gone well beyond the point where humans can effectively analyse the volume and breadth of data the world collects without the use of other computers. This will also dramatically change the way we view diagnosis.

You might recall a few years ago that IBM fielded a computer to compete in the game show *Jeopardy!* against two of its long-time champions. Watson, as the computer is known, won the game show convincingly, defeating the two previously undefeated human challengers Jennings and Rutter.[14] More recently, IBM Watson was board approved by the NY Genome Centre to act as a medical diagnostician.[15] As far as we are aware, this is the first time a specific machine intelligence (MI) has been certified academically or professionally to practise medicine. It will certainly not be the last time.

---

12 "All Things Considered," NPR Radio, aired 8 April 2015.
13 Slang for "Internet"
14 John Markoff, "Computer wins on 'Jeopardy!': Trivial, It's Not!" *New York Times*, 16 February 2011, http://www.nytimes.com/2011/02/17/science/17jeopardy-watson.html.
15 Irana Ivanova, "IBM's Watson joins Genome Center to cure cancer," *Crain's New York Business*, 19 March 2014, http://www.crainsnewyork.com/article/20140319/HEALTH_CARE/140319845/ibms-watson-joins-genome-center-to-cure-cancer.

What was the driver behind the medical certification? The team behind IBM Watson wondered whether Watson could learn to hypothesise on problems like diagnosing cancer or finding genetic markers for hereditary conditions if they gave it the right data. For months, the team at IBM fed over 20 years of medical journals on oncology, patient case studies and diagnosis methodologies into Watson's data repository to test their theory.

In the peer-reviewed paper released by Baylor College of Medicine and IBM, at the conclusion of the study, scientists were able to demonstrate a possible new path for generating scientific questions that may be helpful in the long-term development of new, effective treatments for disease. In a matter of weeks, biologists and data scientists, using Watson technology, accurately identified proteins that modify the p53 protein structure[16]. The study noted that this feat would have taken researchers years to accomplish without Watson's cognitive capabilities. Watson analysed 70,000 scientific articles on p53 to predict proteins that turn on or off p53's activity. This automated analysis led the Baylor cancer researchers to identify six potential proteins to target for new research. *These results are notable, considering that over the last 30 years, scientists averaged one similar target protein discovery per year.* Watson outperformed the collective US-based cancer research effort with its US$5 billion in funding by 600 per cent.

Even more impressive though, when Watson was fed data on a specific patient's symptoms, it could accurately diagnose specific cancer types and the most effective treatment more than **90 per cent of the time**.[17] Why is this significant? Human doctors, oncology specialists with 20 years of medical experience, generally get it right just **50 per cent of the time**. How is Watson able to consistently outperform human specialists in the field?

---

16 p53 is often called a "tumour suppressor protein structure" because of its role in defending the body against the formation of cancer cells.

17 Ian Steadman, "IBM's Watson is better at diagnosing cancer than human doctors," *Wired*, 11 February 2013, http://www.wired.co.uk/news/archive/2013-02/11/ibm-watson-medical-doctor.

Primarily, it is because of "his" ability to synthesize 20 years of research data in seconds with perfect recall.

The next obvious move is to allow doctors to use Watson to better diagnose patients, right? The hitch here was that doctors could only treat patients based on advice from a licensed diagnostician. That is why the NY Genome Centre sought and achieved board approval for Watson to be registered in New York as a licensed diagnostician.

> "What Watson can do—he looks at all your medical records. He has been fed and taught by the best doctors in the world. And comes up with what are the probable diagnoses, percent confidence, why, rationale, diagnosis, odds, conflicts. I mean, that has just started to roll out in Southeast Asia, to a million patients. They will never see the Memorial Sloan Kettering Cancer Center, as you and I have here. [But] they will have access. I mean, that is a big deal."
>
> Ginni Rometty, chairman and CEO of IBM, during an interview on *Charlie Rose*, April 2015

Now that we have established that Watson is more accurate at cancer diagnosis than a human doctor, my question to you is this: who would you rather have diagnose you if your GP suspected you might have the disease? Dr Watson or a "human"? You might argue that Watson probably doesn't have a very good bedside manner, but that's where understanding where this technology is taking us may radically change your view of the future of health care. By the way, did you notice that the CEO of IBM called Watson 'he'? Just saying…

It's very likely that sensors you carry on or inside your body in the future will be able to accurately assess changes in your health and diagnose a condition well before it becomes a problem. Soon computers will automatically assess your genetic make-up and flag known conditions for these algorithms or machine intelligences to look out for. By flagging certain anomalies, algorithms or intelligences like Watson could then recommend specific dietary changes, modifications required in your daily routine, like more sleep or more exercise, along with supplements or even personalised, DNA-specific medicines. Think of these machine intelligences in the role of a potential coach, much like a nutritionist, personal trainer or doctor. As wearable and ingestible medical devices progress, treatment will be administered automatically. In the case of diabetes, you could have your insulin levels maintained with an implant. Should the problem become more serious, the device could then flag the problem to your medical professional so, using his superior bedside manner, he could sit you down for a more "human" discussion.

By 2020, medical data on individual patients will double every 73 days.[18] We need technology to connect the dots, flag the outliers and recommend courses of action that doctors would have done in the past. Avoiding emergency procedures for manageable conditions will become the norm, and the biggest costs may be associated with a subscription to the medical service and the devices you wear or ingest rather than on visits to the hospital or a doctor.

The show *Breaking Bad* dramatised the problems associated with the affordability of the US healthcare system by showing a high school teacher who had to turn to manufacturing illicit drugs in order to be able to afford cancer treatment. In the future, the divide in health care may not be between those with or without

---

18 "IBM and Partners to Transform Person Health with Watson and Open Cloud," IBM Press Release, 13 April 2015, https://www-03.ibm.com/press/us/en/pressrelease/46580.wss.

insurance, but perhaps between those with or without access to a healthcare AI and wearable medical tech. Smart societies will ensure that all of their citizens have access to this technology as it will dramatically reduce the cost burden of health care on society.

With the potential of 50 to 100 trillion sensors by 2030, the vast majority of inputs into computer systems around us will be automated, and not via direct input. Whether sensors in our smartwatches, accelerometers in our smartphones, biometric readers, passive cameras or algorithms capturing behavioral data, the amount of data that comes from the world around us versus data that we input via a keyboard or screen will be in the ratio of 10,000:1 within just a decade. In other words, the way computers respond embedded in the world around us will be influenced more by what we do, what we say and how we act rather than by what we type or click on.

The future of computing is one that combines sensors and machine intelligence. Sensors will be the way we input data, and algorithms will be the synthesis of the data. Interfaces will simply provide the results that matter to us. We'll do very little of the driving or input, at least in a conventional sense.

The Progression from Software to Ubiquitous Computing

The trends in interface and experience design are now taking us in quite a different direction from how we have traditionally thought about software and interfaces to computers. In the future, there will be a significant departure from software applications themselves.

While output display has dramatically improved, input has not radically changed. We've gone from cardpunch to keyboards, then we added a mouse, camera and a microphone, and more recently we've enabled screens to be multitouch. However, most input is still predicated on the use of a QWERTY-style keyboard.

AUGMENTED: Life in the **Smart** Lane

1. GREEN SCREEN

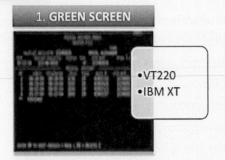

- VT220
- IBM XT

2. GUI

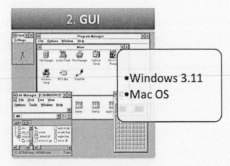

- Windows 3.11
- Mac OS

3. STATIC WEB

- Brochure-ware
- Documents

4. INTERACTIVE WEB

- E-Commerce
- Banner Ads

5. STATIC MOBILE

- WAP
- Mini-browsers

6. APPS

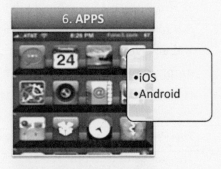

- iOS
- Android

7. DISTRIBUTED UI

- Notifications
- SmartWatches
- SmartGlasses

8. UBIQUITOUS UI

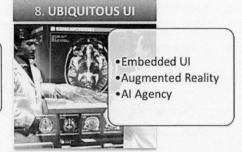

- Embedded UI
- Augmented Reality
- AI Agency

Figure 3.8: The evolution of interaction paradigms

We moved from very simple text-based interfaces to increasingly complex interactions over time. The early computer displays were primitive monochrome displays. When we first started using web browsers and mobile phones, the interactions were, once again, quite primitive. With the iPhone, mobile apps came along and were much more interactive than limited mobile web pages. Our move to smartwatches, smart glasses and such more recently has created a distributed approach to software. We can have an app on our phone, but the display and notifications associated with that app can now be instantiated on our smartwatch or smart glasses. It won't be long before our office desk, our living room wall, our car dashboard and other environments all have embedded screens that enable interactions. We will overlay the real world with data, insights and context using augmented reality (AR) smart glasses and contact lenses too.

In the apps era, most businesses such as banks and airlines went for the bundling of increasing functionality, but as more and more capability is added, the propensity for "engagement rot", as author Jared Spool calls it, becomes very high. The problem is that you cannot retain low friction[19] user experiences when you have an abundance of features; essentially you get to a point where the features create complexity and confusion. Where is that point? Take, for example, special offers or discounts from retailers. If offers or deals are embedded in a banking app, at some point from a design perspective, you are faced with the issue of whether it is a "deals" app or a banking app. The design decision is no longer clear because you have two competing, compelling use cases vying for the customer's attention.

Longer term understanding of the evolution of interface design, embedded computing and interaction science lead us

---

19 Friction here refers to the user workload required to use the software. High friction requires multiple interactions, clicks or entries. Low friction requires minimal interaction building data models from previous interactions, external data, etc. Low friction interfaces also have optimal presentation of information so that readability and usability are high.

to the inevitable conclusion that apps will become less and less important over time.

> That summer, Google made an eight-pound prototype of a computer meant to be worn on the face. To Ive, then unaware of Google's plans, "the obvious and right place" for such a thing was the wrist. When he later saw Google Glass, Ive said, it was evident to him that the face "was the wrong place." [Tim Cook, Apple's C.E.O.] said, "We always thought that glasses were not a smart move, from a point of view that people would not really want to wear them. They were intrusive, instead of pushing technology to the background, as we've always believed."
>
> **Ian Parker on Jonathan Ive's thinking about wearable notification devices[20]**

As context becomes critical to better engagement, functionality is already shifting away from apps. Whether on your smartwatch, smartphone, smart glasses or some other form of interface embedded in the world around us, the best advice and the best triggers for both an improved relationship and revenue-generating moments will be small, purpose-built chunks of experience.

Think about experiences where the software or technology is embedded in a customer's life. Uber is a great example of this. The team behind Uber looked at the problem of moving people around and embedded an app in a user's life in a fundamentally different way to the way a taxi company had handled "trips" previously, and in doing so revolutionised personal journeys. It wasn't the app but the total experience that Uber designed. In

---

20 Ian Parker, "The Shape of Things to Come—How an Industrial Designer became Apple's Greatest Product," *New Yorker*, 23 February 2015, http://www.newyorker.com/magazine/2015/02/23/shape-things-come.

doing so, they redesigned the way drivers were recruited, the way Uber's vehicles were dispatched (no radio), the way a passenger orders a car, the way you pay for your journey and a bunch of other innovations. Uber even allows its drivers to get a car lease or open a bank account when they sign up.

The total taxi market size in San Francisco prior to Uber was US$150 million annually. In early 2015, Uber CEO Travis Kalanick revealed it had ballooned to US$650 million, with Uber taking US$500 million in revenue.[21] By building an experience, not just an app, Uber attracted a ton of new business that would never have gone to taxi companies. Uber didn't build a better taxi, it didn't iterate on the journey—it started from scratch across the entire experience. The effect on the traditional taxi companies? The *San Francisco Examiner* reported on 6th January 2016 that San Francisco's Yellow Cab Co-Op had filed for bankruptcy.

The temptation to bundle more and more features and functionality is high. Look at Facebook and Facebook Messenger, and how Messenger has now been decoupled from Facebook. A controversial change for some, but one that recognises that messaging and interacting with your newsfeed are very different priorities that should not compete. Interactions are moving towards distinct **experiences** embedded in our day-to-day lives, not a bundled feature set in a software application.

Let me illustrate it another way.

In the twentieth century, people watched their favourite TV shows on a specific channel at a specific time. If you wanted to watch the show again, before the advent of videocassette recorders (VCRs), you had to wait for reruns. That's not how our children consume content today. They choose a show they want to watch and then watch it on YouTube or Netflix in real time.

---

21 Henry Blodget, "Uber CEO Reveals Mind-Boggling Statistic That Skeptics Will Hate," *Business Insider*, 19 January 2015.

There's almost no differentiation between PewDiePie's channel on YouTube and *House of Cards* on Netflix. In fact, some studies show that streamed content has already overtaken TV in respect to viewing preferences.[22]

While you might still have apps on your phone, such as games or books that you are reading, behavioural and contextual content will inevitably become part of your personal, tailored content experience. The limitation today is simply contextualisation, bandwidth and predictive or location-based analytics. Combine those capabilities and it becomes less about apps and simply content that responds to your needs.

From CPU on a Chip to Computers in Everything, Everywhere

In 1997, Intel unveiled ASCI Red, the first supercomputer with sustained 1 teraflop performance. The system had 9,298 Pentium II chips that filled 72 computing cabinets. Recently, NVIDIA announced its first Tegra X1 teraflop processor for mobile devices. We're talking about a CPU that can fit in a smartphone, vehicle,[23] tablet or a smartwatch and can execute or compute 1,000,000,000,000 instructions per second—the same as that supercomputer from 1997. To highlight how much technology has advanced in just 15 years, consider this: ASCI Red occupied 1,600 square feet and consumed 500,000 watts of power, with another 500,000 watts needed to cool the room it occupied to achieve 1 teraflop performance. By comparison, the Tegra X1 is the size of a thumbnail and draws under 10 watts of power.

One of the emerging platforms for such computing devices is obviously in-car computing platforms that require enough processing capability to enable autonomous driving, along with

22 Todd Spangler, "Streaming overtakes live TV among consumer viewing preferences," *Variety*, 22 April 2015, http://variety.com/2015/digital/news/streaming-overtakes-live-tv-among-consumer-viewing-preferences-study-1201477318/.
23 Tesla uses Tegra chips in its cars.

enhancements to in-car display and dashboard visualisation. Over the next ten years, the growth of embedded computing in cars will increase exponentially. The Mercedes F015, launched at the 2015 Consumer Electronics Show (CES), is an example of conceptually where the car "space" might take us with self-drive technology. Cars that are a space for being entertained, for working, for playing, for socialising instead of just for driving will soon become the norm. An interactive lounge space, if you like. When you no longer need cars that require all-round windows to create visibility for driving, those windows can become integrated displays. I'll talk about this more later.

When 1 teraflop chips (or more powerful computers) can be embedded in everyday spaces, it will be possible for everything to become an interactive display. This was well illustrated in a series of future concept videos produced by Corning themed *A Day Made of Glass* in which we see mirrors, tabletops, walls and cars becoming interactive devices complete with touchscreen interaction and contextual intelligence.

Figure 3.9: The Mercedes F015 uses internal space very differently from traditional cars.
(Credit: Mercedes)

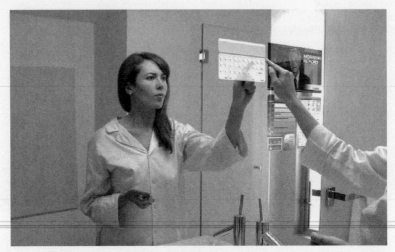

Figure 3.10: With cheap supercomputers on a chip, everything can become an interactive display. (Credit: Corning, *A Day Made of Glass*)

As computers become embedded all around us in our cars, homes, schools and workplaces, the concept of a "screen" and operating systems as we've known them will start to break. For screens built into our mirrors or tabletops we won't have an app store that we use to download software, but we'll undoubtedly have some ability to personalise. More importantly, these screens will speak to some sort of central AI or agent that will pull relevant information from our personal cloud to learn about us and then reflect that—from our appointment schedule through to breaking news in our fields of interest, or other relevant data that informs or advises us. These computers won't just display relevant information. While the Samsung Simband has six different sensors that are constantly collecting relevant information about you, the computers embedded all around us in the future will constantly be listening and learning 24/7.

Two recent computing platform developments illustrate the start of this *interface* paradigm shift. Amazon Echo and the Indiegogo supported start-up Jibo have both recently entered the market as personal devices for the home. Both technologies are embedded in your home and can listen, learn and respond to cues from the world around them, in real time. Jibo goes so far as to position itself as your family's personal assistant. These take the technologies of Google Voice, Apple's Siri or Microsoft's Cortana and embed them into our homes, with access to the almost infinite informational resources that the Internet provides.

It starts off fairly simply. You can ask Echo or Jibo things like "Will it rain tomorrow?", "Is milk on my shopping list", "Remind me to book my hotel for our holiday next week", etc. Jibo takes this further as it has mobility and a built-in camera that allows you to ask it to take a snapshot of your family, for example. The screen within Jibo's interface will even use its display to illustrate different personalities based on who in the family it is interacting with.

While these first-generation "home assistants" are currently limited to information requests, it won't be long before we'll be using technologies like these in our homes and offices to reliably manage our schedules, do our shopping and make day-to-day

Figure 3.11: Family robot Jibo is billed as a personal assistant and communications device for the home. (Credit: Jibo)

decisions. Within 20 years, these devices will be AIs that have enough basic intelligence to cater for any need we might have that can be executed or solved digitally, along with interfacing with our own personal dashboards/UIs, clouds and sensor networks to advise us on our physical health, financial well-being and many other areas that we used to consider the domain of human advisers.

Can You Tell You Are Talking to a Computer?

In December 2013, *Time* magazine ran a story entitled "Meet the Robot Telemarketer Who Denies She's a Robot"[24] describing a sales call that Washington Bureau Chief Michael Scherer of *Time* received. Scherer, sensing something was off, asked the robot if she was a person or a computer. She replied enthusiastically that she was real, with a charming laugh. But when Scherer asked, "What vegetable is found in tomato soup?" the robot said she didn't understand the question. The robot called herself Samantha West.

The goal of algorithms like these is simply to pre-qualify the recipient of the call before transferring them to a human to close the sale. Voice recognition was an essential precursor to such algorithms. While today tools like Siri and Cortana recognise unaccented speech fairly well, there was a time when voice recognition was considered science fiction.

As early as 1932, scientists at Bell Labs were working on the problem of machine-based "speech perception". By 1952, Bell had developed a system for single-digit speech recognition but it was extremely limited. In 1969, however, John Pierce, one of Bell's leading engineers, wrote an open letter to the Acoustical Society of America criticising speech recognition at Bell and compared it to "schemes for turning water into gasoline, extracting gold from

---

24 "Meet the Robot Telemarketer Who Denies She's a Robot," *Time*, 13 December 2013, http://newsfeed. time.com/2013/12/10/meet-the-robot-telemarketer-who-denies-shes-a-robot/.

the sea, curing cancer, or going to the moon". Ironically, one month after Pierce published his open letter, Neil Armstrong landed on the moon. Regardless, Bell Labs still had its funding for speech recognition pulled soon after.

By 1993, speech recognition systems developed by Ray Kurzweil could recognise 20,000 words (uttered one word at a time), but accuracy was limited to about 10 per cent. In 1997, Bill Gates was pretty bullish on speech recognition, predicting that "In this 10-year time frame, I believe that we'll not only be using the keyboard and the mouse to interact, but during that time we will have perfected speech recognition and speech output well enough that those will become a standard part of the interface."[25] In the year 2000, it was still a decade away.

The big breakthroughs came with the application of Markov models and Deep Learning models or neural networks, basically better computer performance and bigger source databases. However, the models that we have today are limited because they still don't learn language. These algorithms don't learn language like a human; they identify a phrase through recognition, look it up on a database and then deliver an appropriate response.

Recognising speech and being able to carry on a conversation are two very different achievements. What would it take for a computer to fool a human into thinking it was a human, too?

The Turing Test or Not...

In 1950, Alan Turing published a famous paper entitled "Computing Machinery and Intelligence". In his paper, he asked not just

An autonomous, self-driving car won't need to pass the Turing Test to put a taxi driver out of work.

if a computer or machine could be considered something that could "think", but more specifically "Are there imaginable digital

25 Taken from Bill Gates' speech at the Microsoft Developers Conference on 1st October 1997

computers which would do well in the *imitation game?*"[26] Turing proposed that this "test" of a machine's intelligence—which he called the "imitation game"—be tested in a human-machine question and answer session. Turing went on in his paper to say that if you could not differentiate the computer or machine from a human within *5 minutes*, then it was sufficiently human-like to have passed his test of basic machine intelligence or cognition. Researchers who have since added to Turing's work classify the imitation game as one version or scenario of what is now more commonly known as the **Turing Test**.

While computers are not yet at the point of regularly passing the Turing Test, we are getting closer to that point. On 7th June 2014, the Royal Society of London hosted a Turing Test competition. The competition, which occurred on the 60th anniversary of Turing's death, included a Russian chatter bot named Eugene Goostman, which successfully managed to convince 33 per cent of its human judges that it was a 13-year-old Ukrainian who had learnt English as a second language. While some, such as Joshua Tenenbaum, a professor of Mathematical Psychology at MIT, have called the results of the competition "unimpressive", it still shows that we are much closer to passing a computer off as a human than ever before.

Interactions like booking an airline ticket or changing a hotel reservation, resolving a problem with your bank, booking your car for a service or finding out the results of a paternity test could all be adequately handled by machine intelligences in the very near term. In many instances, they already are. A human won't effectively differentiate the experience enough to justify the cost of a human-based call centre representative. In fact, my guess is that it won't be long before you'll have to agree to a charge if you want to speak to a "real" human. Many airlines and

---

26 A. M. Turing, "Computing Machinery and Intelligence," *MIND: A Quarterly Review of Psychology and Philosophy* vol. LIX, no. 236. (October 1950), http://mind.oxfordjournals.org/content/LIX/236/433.

hotels already levy a phone service charge if you call instead of change a booking online. It's pretty clear that human concierge services will become a premium level service only for the most valuable customer relationships in the future. For the rest of us, the basic model of service will be AI based. But here's the thing we should recognise—in that future, a human **won't actually provide a better level of service**.

We might very well suspect that we're talking to a computer in the future, but the interaction will be so good that we won't be 100 per cent sure or we just won't care. Fifteen years from now, machine interactions will be widespread and AI/MIs will be differentiated and identified as such because they'll be better and faster at handling certain problems. For example, Uber could advertise its AI, self-driving cars as "The Safest Drivers in the World", knowing that statistically an autonomous vehicle will be 20 times safer than a human out of the gate.

Key to this future is the need for AIs to learn language, to learn to converse. In an interview with the *Guardian* newspaper in May 2015, Professor Geoff Hinton, an expert in artificial neural networks, said Google is "on the brink of developing algorithms with the capacity for logic, natural conversation and even flirtation." Google is currently working to encode thoughts as vectors described by a sequence of numbers. These "thought vectors" could endow AI systems with a human-like "common sense" within a decade, according to Hinton.

> Some aspects of communication are likely to prove more challenging, Hinton predicted. "Irony is going to be hard to get," he said. "You have to be master of the literal first. But then, Americans don't get irony either. Computers

are going to reach the level of Americans
before Brits..."

Professor Geoff Hinton, from an interview with
the *Guardian* newspaper, 21st May 2015

These types of algorithms, which allow for leaps in cognitive understanding for machines, have only been possible with the application of massive data processing and computing power.

Is the Turing Test or a machine that can mimic a human the required benchmark for human interactions with a computer? Not necessarily. First of all, we must recognise that we don't need an MI to be completely human-equivalent for it to be disruptive to employment or our way of life.

To realise why a human-equivalent computer "brain" is not necessarily the critical goal, we need to understand the progression of AI through its three distinct phases:

- **Machine Intelligence**—rudimentary machine intelligence or cognition that replaces some element of human thinking, decision-making or processing for specific tasks. Neural networks or algorithms that can make *human equivalent decisions* for very specific functions, and perform better than humans on a benchmark basis. This does not prohibit the intelligence from having *machine learning or cognition* capabilities so that it can learn new tasks or process new information outside of its initial programming. In fact, many machine intelligences already have this capability. Examples include: Google self-driving car, IBM Watson, high-frequency trading (HFT) algorithms, facial recognition software
- **Artificial General Intelligence**—a human-equivalent machine intelligence that not only passes the Turing Test and responds as a human would but can also make human

equivalent decisions. It will likely also process non-logic or informational cues such as emotion, tone of voice, facial expression and nuances that currently a living intelligence could (can your dog tell if you are angry or sad?). Essentially, *such an AI would be capable of successfully performing any intellectual task that a human being could.*

- **Hyperintelligence**—a machine intelligence or collection of machine intelligences (what do you call a group of AIs?) that have surpassed human intelligence on an individual or collective basis such that they can understand and process concepts that a human cannot understand.

We simply don't require full AI to have significant impact in employment patterns or put at risk people employed in the service industry. We don't need to wait another 10, 15 or 30 years to see this happen, and the Turing Test is fairly meaningless as a measure of the ability of machine intelligence to disrupt the way we live and work.

The fact is, machines don't have to evolve exactly the same intelligence as humans to actually be considered intelligent. Using the same measures we apply to the animal kingdom, Watson may have already demonstrated intelligence far greater than many of the species on the planet today. Does a machine have to be as smart as a human or smarter than a human to be considered intelligent? No. In fact, at its core, we shouldn't expect AIs to think like humans at all really. Why should machine intelligence evolve or progress so that it thinks exactly like us? It doesn't have to, and it most likely won't. Let me illustrate with two examples.

Between 2009 and 2013, machine intelligent HFT algorithms accounted for between 49 and 73 per cent of all US equity trading volume, and 38 per cent in the European Union in 2014. On 6th May 2010, the Dow Jones plunged to its largest intraday point loss, only to recover that loss within minutes. After a five-month investigation, the US Securities and Exchange Commission (SEC) and the Commodities Future Trading Commission (CFTC) issued a joint report that concluded that HFT had contributed significantly to the volatility of the so-called "flash" crash. A large futures exchange, CME Group, said in its own investigation that HFT algorithms probably stabilised the market and reduced the impact of the crash.

For an industry that has developed trading into a fine art over the last 100 years, HFT algorithms represent a significant departure from the trading rooms of Goldman Sachs, UBS and Credit Suisse. The algorithms themselves have departed significantly from typical human behaviour. Very different behaviour and decision-making has been observed when analysing HFT trading patterns. What has led to this shift?

Perhaps it is the fact that HFT has neither the biases that human traders might have (for instance, staying in an asset class position longer than advised because the individual trader likes the stock or the industry) nor the same ethical basis for making a decision. While some might argue that Wall Street isn't exactly the bastion of ethics, the fact is an HFT algorithm simply doesn't have an ethical basis for a decision unless those skills have been programmed in.

Audi has been testing self-driving cars, two modified Audi RS7s that have a brain the size of a PS4 in the boot, on the racetrack. The race-ready Audis at this stage aren't completely self-driving in that the engineers need to first drive them for a few laps so that the cars can learn the boundaries. The two cars are known as Ajay and Bobby,[27] and interestingly they have both developed different driving styles despite identical hardware,

---

27 Test Car A and Test Car B became Ajay and Bobby, respectively.

software and mapping. Despite the huge amount of expertise on the Audi engineering team, they can't readily explain why there is this apparent difference in driving styles.

We're likely to see many different variations of "intelligence" in machine cognition that don't fit a traditional human model or our expectations, but nonetheless will be both an improvement over traditional human decision-making and simply a departure from a traditional human approach to critical thinking. Just because an intelligence that develops in a machine is different from that of a human doesn't make it inferior or less intelligent.

People who are most concerned about AIs taking over the world or subjugating humans probably regard all AIs as super-IQ humans, with the same desires, ethics and violent and egotistical tendencies that we humans have. A super-intelligent version of us would indeed be scary. Yet there's simply no reason to believe that artificial intelligence exhibits human tendencies, biases and prejudices. In fact, the opposite is far more likely.

The AIs we have will not only be able to detect emotion and sentiment within a few years, they will also be able to detect when you are lying. At some point in time, we'll probably hand over the process of electing government to an AI. Imagine how a truly clean, unbiased election process might work, especially if we were to use an AI to maximise representation of every eligible voter through optimal configuration of boundaries and districts. What about in respect to resource allocation and tackling problems like climate change? When an AI can model planetary climate science over millennia with pinpoint accuracy and give precise, verifiable impact estimates on continued use of fossil fuels or the impact of cow farts on carbon dioxide (CO_2) levels, for example, think about how that will affect resource allocation and adoption of renewable energy.

Yes, AI does represent a danger to the status quo because it will probably be the purest form of common sense and logic. Anything that doesn't pass the smell test today will be exposed rapidly in a world of AI. With machine learning in the mix, and the ability to hypothesise, very soon we're going to have to justify poor human decision-making against the irrefutable logic of a machine with all of the facts and efficiency of thought that we, as humans, just can't compete with. Within 15 years, humans will probably be banned from driving in some cities because self-driving cars will be demonstrably less risky. Insurers too will charge much more for human-driven vehicles.

We are going to need to learn that machine intelligence in its component form may still be highly differentiated from humans, and will most certainly be disruptive long before human-equivalent AI is reached. Don't think that just because we're 20 to 30 years away from human-equivalence that all of this is theoretical. Machines have long been taking jobs away from humans; it started 200 years ago with the steam machine. Algorithms and robots are just one more machine in a long line of industry-disrupting technologies.

Chapter 4

The Robot Advantage

Contributed by Alex Lightman
Edited by Brett King

> "The central question of 2025 will be: What are
> people for in a world that does not need their
> labor, and where only a minority are needed to
> guide the 'bot-based' economy?"
>
> **Stowe Boyd, Lead Researcher at Gigaom Research**

There is a spectre haunting humanity, the spectre of job-stealing, sexy, murderous, calculating robots. Indeed, very few technologies have captured our hearts and minds in popular fiction as much as robots. It's when we hear that the robots we've known of as toys and seen in the cartoons of our childhood will replace 50 to 70 per cent of our jobs that we really start to pay attention. We are realising that we must better understand the technology, and the possible impact of the technology on our community. Just as everyone needed a PC strategy in the 1980s, a website strategy in the 1990s and a social media strategy over the last decade, we will need a robot strategy for not only the next ten years, but for the rest of our lives. Robots aren't going away, so we need to learn how to work with them and how to put them to work for us.

Let's start with how we perceive robots based on their representation in fiction. We need to go back to 1868 to the first dime science fiction novel—*The Steam Man of the Plains*—to find the very first depiction of a robot in popular literature. The novel tells the story of a teenager who, understandably enough, invents a steam-powered man to drive him around the plains of the mid-west.[1] This "Edisonade"[2] also started a recurrent theme—that the cleverest people invent robots for their own

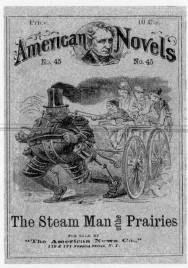

Figure 4.1: The first ever novel to introduce the concept of a "robot"

personal use. This tradition continues to this day and includes the reality-blurring stories around Tony Stark aka Iron Man, played by actor Robert Downey Jr. (in character as Tony Stark, Downey Jr. has even handed out 3D-printed robot arms to amputee children).

Robots are symbolic of the love-hate relationship we have with a technology, one that we both dread and anticipate in equal measure. In *Avengers: Age of Ultron*, robots are both the worst villain (Ultron) and the noblest hero (the Vision, worthy enough to lift Thor's hammer, Mjölnir), and both hero and villain in the *Terminator* movies.

In *Ex Machina*, a female robot is able to outwit and deceive her inventor, the richest man on earth, by fooling an intelligent

---

1   Today's near-future equivalent might be of teenagers eager to start using self-driving cars.

2   The *Encyclopedia of Science Fiction* defines an Edisonade as a sub-genre of science fiction from the late 19th and early 20th centuries that involves stories about a brilliant young inventor and his inventions. The term is an eponym, named after the famous inventor Thomas Edison.

young programmer into falling for her in just six sessions through her glass prison and turning him against his billionaire employer. This is a cautionary tale because as robots become more and more like us, they may be able to play us against one another, dividing us, or possibly conquering us. *Ex Machina* could conceivably be considered a 21st-century reimagining of *Frankenstein*, the 200-year-old horror novel by Mary Shelley. In this version though, the creation doesn't, by any stretch of the imagination, look like a monster as it roams the private home and lab of a fictional technopreneur who bears a passing resemblance to Google's founder Sergey Brin.

The average teen student has likely already consumed thousands of hours of robot stories, mostly where the robot is the ally, friend and hero, even a father figure. For instance, which robot is the most powerful? I would say the Sym-Bionic Titan. Which is the most loved? Probably R2-D2 or BB-8 from *Star Wars*. Who is the most deadly? Goort or the Dalek. Hundreds of hours of discussion are possible on this topic because robots are so engaging and we already know thousands of stories about them.

Depending on who you are talking to, robots will either bring us to a brave new world of amazing possibilities or destroy humanity and all it has created. One author even claimed recently that robots would relegate us to a position no more important than cockroaches. Are robots a threat to our future? Our prejudice against robots may be resolved by having more robot models cross the uncanny valley, and alternate non-humanoid forms integrate into our environment with positive impact.

Bridging the Uncanny Valley

The term "uncanny valley" was originally coined by Japanese robotics professor Masahiro Mori in 1970.[3]

---

3   In 1970, Masahiro Mori, a professor at the Tokyo Institute of Technology, published a two-page, koan-like article entitled "Bukimi No Tani" (不気味の谷, "The Uncanny Valley") in an obscure Japanese journal called *Energy*. After 40 years, it is still considered one of the defining essays on robotics in society.

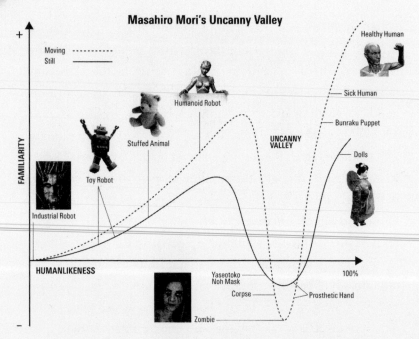

Figure 4.2: Mori's uncanny valley is a predictor of how we'll respond to robots with human-like features.

As robots get closer and closer to simulating a human, a common response to these robots is that they are "creepy" or "eerie". The humans demonstrating robots have remarked that people very often don't realise that the robot is not a real person for a period ranging from seconds to minutes, but when they do grasp that the "person" in front of them is a robot, the reaction is almost always immediate and powerful. Observers are commonly surprised, then impressed, but then their reactions often veer towards fascination and wonder, or alternately towards fear and dread. The latter is what Masahiro Mori defined as the uncanny valley.

Some roboticists fear the uncanny valley and do not believe it can be overcome any time soon, others avoid it by going down a non-humanoid path. David Hanson of Hanson Robotics

Figure 4.3: Robots like Otonaroid, developed by Osaka University, are getting closer and closer to mimicking humans. (Credit: Osaka University)

looks at the uncanny valley as an opportunity for true artists to emerge in the humanoid robotics space. Hanson points out that Japanese and Chinese robotics companies frequently base their robots on Asian female faces. He notes, perhaps controversially, that the smooth skin and lack of wrinkles and discolouration in the features of Asian women make such robot templates the most effective at mimicking a human, at least compared with males or other ethnic templates. Hanson claims that his company is close to bridging the uncanny valley with its latest robots. With over 40 actuators and the extremely life-like patented skin called "Frubber", these robots have skin that looks real and feels real, too. Hanson has even created an android robot that mimics the late science fiction author Philip K. Dick.

Figure 4.4: A Russian TV presenter interviews android Philip K. Dick. (Credit: Hanson Robotics)

Hanson has also worked extensively on the related software to ensure that the robot's eyes and reactions are equally realistic. Using the robot's powerful software to track multiple faces and keep eye contact in a natural way by moving from eye to eye then to the mouth and back again, just as we do, the robot appears as human as any robot ever created. The head and neck movements are still a little choppy, but are improving rapidly as processors and actuators improve.

The Robot Growth Explosion

Robots are still relatively rare today. Within a couple of decades though, they will outnumber the world's population. In 2014, sales of industrial robots increased 29 per cent to 229,261 units, according to the International Federation of Robotics.[4] In 2000, the population of industrial robots was around 1 million, with 40 per cent of those being situated in Japan, but by 2010 the global industrial robot population had ballooned to close to 9 million.[5] Nevertheless, industrial robots are only a small part of the robot population.

According to a research study by Tractica, annual shipments of consumer robots, a category that includes robotic vacuums, lawn mowers and pool cleaners as well as social robots, will increase from at least 6.6 million units in 2015 to more than 31 million units worldwide by 2020, with a cumulative total of nearly 100 million consumer robots shipped during that period. One thousand Pepper robots are being sold each month in China and Japan; Jibo just raised another US$16 million as it prepares to deliver 7,500+ units in March/April 2016. It is estimated that iRobot sold more than 100,000 home robots in 2015, with the Roomba 800/900 vacuum cleaner being the most popular.[6] The Federal Aviation Administration (FAA) estimated that over 1 million drones were sold over the 2015 Christmas period alone.[7]

It is likely that we added close to 10 million robots to the global robot population just in 2015, if you include industrial robots, household robots and military application. But there are some big outliers coming in the next five to ten years, including autonomous vehicles. By 2025, it is estimated that between 15 and 20 million autonomous vehicles could be sold annually.[8]

By 2025, more than 1.5 billion robots will be operating on the planet, and we'll be seeing that exponential growth curve exhibited with that number doubling every few years. By the early 2030s, robots are likely to outnumber humans.

4   International Federation of Robotics, http://www.ifr.org/industrial-robots/statistics/.
5   IEEE.org, http://spectrum.ieee.org/automaton/robotics/industrial-robots/041410-world-robot-population.
6   iRobot financial reports
7   Michael Addady, "The number of drones expected to sell during the holidays is scaring the government," *Fortune*, 29 September 2015.
8   Author's own estimate based on PricewaterhouseCoopers (PWC), IHC research and annual vehicle sales projections

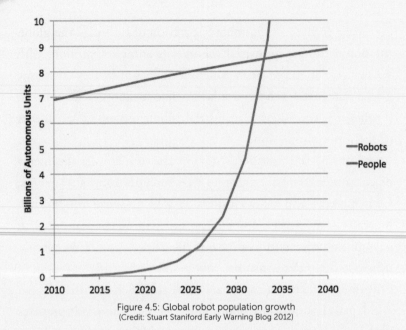

Figure 4.5: Global robot population growth
(Credit: Stuart Staniford Early Warning Blog 2012)

Robots can be very small, and will eventually be self-replicating. This will change everything, especially their numbers (insects outnumber humans by 200 million to one, and most people don't notice or fear them) and their nature (they will match and exceed us in intelligence). Professors at the Massachusetts Institute of Technology (MIT) call what's coming "**the second machine age**", but I find the "robot singularity" *as potentially* far more significant, historically speaking, than that.

Building a Robot in Your Garage?

Evolutionary biologists posit that one of the single most significant events in the history of life on earth occurred shortly after unicellular (single celled) life discovered or evolved multicellularity. About 570 million years ago, driven by the twin engines of evolution, random mutation and natural selection, life tried millions, possibly tens of millions, of combinations, resulting in a big bang of different body plans. After the globe-wide experimentation left some species in existence and others extinct, we ended up with virtually all the body plans that have come into existence in the 570 million years since, with the primary changes since then not in body plans, but in brain plans. Biologists call this burst of life experimentation and variation the "Cambrian explosion".

You could say that we are experiencing a neo-Cambrian age of robotic forms and functions from the fertile imaginations of science fiction writers and the creative drives of the hacker and maker communities. Students equipped with exponential access to 3D printers and cheap Arduino systems including microprocessors, sensors and controls are contributing too. These microprocessor components are cheap because these chips have been around with the same specifications for years, almost a decade in fact, unlike Intel's chips which follow Moore's Law, doubling in power every two years, and consequently command a premium price. Thus, just like during the Cambrian explosion, this phase of exponential growth in robotics is going to result in the evolution of body plans that succeed and iterate, and many designs that fail and are therefore discontinued. If the history of technology disruption over the last 250 years is any guide, most of this experimentation is going to be done in a relatively short period of time.

All the barriers to widespread deployment of robots are falling fast. For years, robots were held back by the remarkably difficult problem of walking and navigating our world. This limited freedom of movement meant robots were locked in labs and designed to be stationary, or toys meant to be swung or rolled or run around a track. This greatly limited their usefulness. Then someone hacked the problem by combining robots and radio-controlled planes and helicopters—and drones were unleashed. Suddenly, robots were no longer tethered and new use cases exploded. Robots are programmable machines that can operate with at least three axes of motion—drones qualify under that definition.[9]

Robots are here in relatively tiny numbers (say, 1 for each 100 humans) and are already having a huge impact. "Gartner predicts one in three jobs will be converted to software, robots and smart machines by 2025," said Gartner research director Peter Sondergaard. "New digital businesses require less labor; machines will make sense of data faster than humans can."[10] How we interact with robots will determine how successful we will be in the new economy and society that is coming.

Kevin Kelly, former editor of *Wired* magazine, said, "This is not a race against the machines. If we race against them, we lose. **This is a race with the machines**. You'll be paid in the future based on how well you work with robots."[11]

Robots will change everything from how we work, play, socialise and care for ourselves. In much the way we identify someone who is racist or bigoted today, we might identify people in the future by their willingness or not to work with robots. This chapter will explore how robotics will help us live better lives, be better people and be better stewards of this planet and beyond.

Living in a Robot-dominated World

The Emerging Job Requirement of a Robot Skill Base

Today's robots are evolving in as many different ways as species have over millenniums, spanning form and functions from avatars to Zambonis. In earlier chapters, we have seen how major disruptive technologies since the industrial age have dramatically

---

9 As do autonomous vehicles, the Hubble Space Telescope and my iRobot vacuum cleaner
10 http://www.pbs.org/newshour/rundown/smart-robots-will-take-third-jobs-2025-gartner-says/
11 Kevin Kelly, "Better than human: Why Robots Will—and Must—Take our Jobs," *Wired*, 24 December 2014, http://www.wired.com/2012/12/ff-robots-will-take-our-jobs/.

changed virtually every aspect of society. The coming Augmented Age will continue that evolution.

Just as an office worker in the 1980s feared the personal computer as a threat to their livelihood, the fear of robots drives the same emotional reaction to an even broader set of workers. For the last 30 to 35 years, starting in the early 1980s, it was the few who embraced their personal computers who rose through the ranks (the people who understood the hardware and the software were far more likely to create new companies). So it will be for the next 35 years, from 2015 to 2050: those who embrace their robot co-workers will have enhanced careers and an unfair advantage in business, health, lifespan, safety, income and war.

Just as no one knew what a web designer was in 1990, the types of new vocations that will be created in the Augmented Age are difficult to predict. As introduced back in chapter 2, Pew Research surveyed technology builders and analysts back in 2014 about this emerging problem of employment affected by new technology. It looked to those who in the past had made accurate and insightful predictions about the future of the Internet, and applied that to AI and robotics. The crowd of experts surveyed on the impact of robots and automation were evenly split on how this coming age would effect employment and jobs. But there are reasons to be both hopeful and apprehensive about the future with robots.

Key Themes: Reasons to be Hopeful

1. Advances in technology may displace certain types of work, but historically they have been a net creator of jobs.
2. We will adapt to these changes by inventing entirely new types of work, and by taking advantage of uniquely human capabilities.

3. Technology will free us from day-to-day drudgery, and allow us to define our relationship with "work" in a more positive and socially beneficial way.
4. Ultimately, we—as a society—control our own destiny through the choices we make.

Key Themes: Reasons to be Concerned
1. Impacts from automation have thus far impacted mostly blue-collar employment; the coming wave of innovation threatens to upend white-collar work as well.
2. Certain highly skilled workers will succeed wildly in this new environment—but far more may be displaced into lower paying service industry jobs at best, or permanent unemployment at worst.
3. Our educational system is not adequately preparing us for work of the future, and our political and economic institutions are poorly equipped to handle these hard choices.

So the major disconnect seems to be whether you believe that these new technologies will augment our abilities or replace them.

Harvard social scientist Shoshana Zuboff examined how companies used technology in her 1989 book *In the Age of the Smart Machine: The Future of Work and Power*. She looked at how some employers used technology to "automate", or take power away from, the employee while some used technology to "informate", or empower, the employee. Obviously, our thesis is that the latter is far more preferable!

If we look at the last 30 years of software-based automation using customer relationship management (CRM) and enterprise resource planning (ERP), we generally find that implementing the technology is the easy part. Getting the employees to accept and embrace the new technologies and use them productively is the single most important factor. More often, these new technology projects lead to more staff, contract and consultants jobs than the automation ever replaces.

When these projects are successful, they usually informate and create better employee and customer experiences and drive companies to be more successful, grow and hire. When these projects fail, heads roll, customer and employee experiences fall and headcounts are reduced.

Amazon Loves Robot Workers

Projects that purely automate are far fewer and can also be seen as creating more jobs than they displace. An interesting example is that of a warehouse automation solution called Kiva Systems. Kiva Systems was founded in 2003 by Mick Mountz after his experience with the failed online grocery delivery service Webvan. Webvan was going to put all grocery stores out of business. Mountz believed Webvan failed because the high cost of warehouse operations meant that each order was too expensive to fulfil using traditional material handling and warehouse management solutions (WMS). Mountz decided to create a better way to pick, pack and ship products and Kiva was born. Teaming up with Peter Wurman and Raffaello D' Andrea, experts in robotics and engineering, the Kiva three created an entirely new way to automate the traditional warehouse.

The traditional model includes receiving products into a receiving dock and having workers put away the products on shelves using forklifts and carts. Then those same workers would go into the warehouse and pick the products to fulfil the orders that needed to be assembled, packed and/or shipped. Even with

Figure 4.6: Kiva's automated guided vehicle system for warehouse management
(Credit: Kiva/Amazon)

advanced WMS software automation systems like Manhattan Associates, HighJump or RedPrairie that can optimise the efficiencies of the workforce, order fulfilment costs remained stubbornly high, especially in low margin, high product mix orders like groceries. Kiva's solution was groundbreaking and simple, and spawned from the answer to the question: Why have people deliver products to and from shelves if the shelves can come to them?

Kiva created robots that locate the closest *automated guided vehicle* (robot) to the item that needs to be moved and directs the bot to retrieve the item. The mobile robots drive around the warehouse by navigating a series of barcode stickers on the floor. The robots have enough AI and sensors to avoid running into each other and obstacles. When the robot reaches the correct location, it slides underneath the shelf and lifts it off the ground through a corkscrew action. The robot then carries the shelf to the specified human operator to act on the items.

After years of product development and marketing, Kiva made a large splash in the industry and sales of the products were just taking off when Amazon stepped in and bought Kiva lock, stock and barrel for US$775 million in March 2012.[12] The acquisition of Kiva Systems was second only to Amazon's purchase of Zappos in 2009. Amazon was persuaded that Kiva offered an unfair advantage. Amazon immediately let go the entire Kiva Systems sales and marketing staff and stopped all product sales. It seems Amazon considered the automation of its own warehouses to be so valuable that it would forgo the profits from selling the system and keep the technology away from its competition.

Today, Amazon uses the Kiva solution in its own warehouses to minimise warehouse workers and order fulfilment costs while improving order accuracy. Amazon offers us a glimpse of something that we'll see often in the future: automation technology reduces the need for and number of low-skilled workers and highly paid sales and marketing employees while creating an entirely new division within the company of highly skilled roboticists and AI software workers.

We said earlier that *every person and company needs a robot strategy*. Who are the early leaders in robot strategy and what are they doing? We've seen Amazon embrace robotics with its Kiva warehouse system acquisition. Google acquired eight robotics companies and put them all in a former NASA blimp hangar[13] like a giant child's playroom and made what is probably the most cinematic yet confusing move, since the military nature of the robots seems at odds with Google's core business and its civilian focus on search.

Apple's main outsourced manufacturer, Foxconn (actually Hon Hai, headquartered in Taiwan) is realising that the only way it is going to be able to continue to keep Apple's manufacturing

---

12 "Amazon Acquires Kiva Systems in Second-Biggest Takeover," *Bloomberg Business*, 19 March 2012.
13 Called Hangar One, the hangar is located at Moffett Federal Airfield. The hangar is one of the largest freestanding structures in the world. The hangar was constructed in 1931 to house airships like the USS *Macon*. Its interior is so large that fog sometimes forms near the ceiling.

business is by upgrading its factories to use more and more robots to make up for ever-increasing labour costs in China, as the number of Chinese aged 15 to 59 (the traditional retirement age) shrinks by 3 to 4 million a year. It is the companies that don't see the robot at the door that will find not just their jobs outsourced but their entire company displaced as well.

Those who are just entering the workforce or still at school will need to be able to adapt to the changing employment landscape and acquire the skills that will be able to create, support or supplement the next generation of robotic workers. Computer sciences, all forms of electrical and mechanical engineering and sales are just a few traditional areas that will be viable fields to work with and for robots in the foreseeable future. It is as difficult today to identify what new careers and fields of expertise will be created in the next 20 years, as it was envisioning what a Facebook marketing consultant would have been in 1995. No doubt there will be massive opportunity if robotics fulfils the predictions of being a US$500-billion-a-year industry.

The Robot Will See You Now

Robots have been in the healthcare industry for at least 30 years. The first documented use of a robot to assist with a surgical procedure occurred in 1985 when the PUMA 560 surgical arm was used in a neurosurgical biopsy. Since then, medical robots in various capacities—from surgical robots through to hospital couriers and telemedicine robots—have helped millions of people.

For countries like Japan and the United States, however, the use of robots may be the only remaining viable option to provide the level of adequate care that will be required by the economy within five to ten years. Let's look at how robots are the solution to helping us stay healthy.

Robotic Nurses

I expect the first mass market for humanoid robots to be for nurses, based on the mismatch between supply and demand, and force multiplier potential for hospitals and the medical industry as a whole, which is under serious pressure to rein in costs as government accounts for an ever larger bargaining partner for medical professionals.

The United States and Japan are both projected to experience significant shortages of registered nurses (RNs) as baby boomers age and the need for health care grows. Compounding the problem is the fact that nursing schools are struggling to expand capacity to meet the rising demand for care given the national move towards healthcare reform.

- According to the Bureau of Labor Statistics' Employment Projections 2012–2022 released in December 2013, registered nursing (RN) is listed among the top occupations in terms of job growth through 2022. The RN workforce is expected to grow from 2.71 million in 2012 to 3.24 million in 2022, an increase of 526,800 or 19 per cent. The Bureau also projects the need for 525,000 replacement nurses in the workforce, bringing the total number of job openings for nurses due to growth and replacements to 1.05 million by 2022.[14]

- A July 2015 Japanese Ministry of Health, Labour and Welfare estimate showed that Japan will face an acute shortage of nursing care workers as the ageing of its population accelerates over the next decade. The nation will need 2.53 million nursing care workers by 2025. It had 1.77 million nursing care workers in 2013. To meet this target, 800,000 to 1 million more nurses will be needed by 2025. However, unless the current pace of increase picks up, the number of nursing care workers will fall short of demand by at least 380,000.[15]

14 http://www.bls.gov/news.release/ecopro.t08.htm
15 http://www.japantimes.co.jp/opinion/2015/07/07/editorials/shortage-of-nursing-care-workers-2

- According to the "United States Registered Nurse Workforce Report Card and Shortage Forecast" published in the January 2012 issue of the *American Journal of Medical Quality*, a shortage of registered nurses is projected to spread across the country between 2009 and 2030. In this state-by-state analysis, the authors forecast the RN shortage to be most intense in the South and the West.[16]
- In October 2010, the Institute of Medicine released its landmark report on the future of nursing, initiated by the Robert Wood Johnson Foundation, which called for increasing the number of baccalaureate-prepared nurses in the workforce to 80 per cent and doubling the population of nurses with doctoral degrees. The current nursing workforce falls far short of these recommendations with only 55 per cent of registered nurses prepared at the graduate level.

In addition to the above, a significant segment of the nursing workforce is nearing retirement age.

- According to a 2013 survey conducted by the National Council of State Boards of Nursing and the Forum of State Nursing Workforce Centers, 55 per cent of the RN workforce is aged 50 or older.
- The Health Resources and Services Administration projects that more than 1 million registered nurses will reach retirement age within the next 10 to 15 years.
- According to a May 2001 report, "Who Will Care for Each of Us? Addressing the Long-Term Care Workforce Crisis" released by the Nursing Institute at the University of Illinois College of Nursing, the ratio of potential carers to the people most likely to need care—the elderly population—will decrease by 40 per cent between 2010 and 2030.

16 http://ajm.sagepub.com

Simply put, in developed economies like the United States and Japan, we do not have enough nurses to care for us today and the problem is only getting worse. In the United States, we are importing nurses from other countries, especially the Philippines. Over 20 per cent of nurses in California today are Filipino, even though Filipinos make up only 3 per cent of the Californian population. Changes to immigration laws in 2009 made it increasingly difficult for nurses to enter the United States, and due to a lack of US-based nursing programmes, the problem of having an adequate supply of trained nurses sufficient to not only meet demand, but bring down costs, is about to get much, much worse for the United States. Tough immigration laws in Japan also limit the critical intake of trained nurses into the country.

Let's take a look at how robots can augment our caregiving in a more human way for both patients and the carers.

Meet Maria. She is a 25-year-old baccalaureate-prepared nurse living in Manila. She has a small child, her husband has a good job and they both have close family ties. Finding work as a nurse in the Philippines is almost impossible due to the intense competition; there are 430 nursing schools and becoming a nurse is seen as the best ticket out. To practise her trade, Maria, and many like her, has to leave her home country and family to seek work in foreign countries. If she is lucky and can get an H1 Visa to work in the United States, she will probably need to leave her husband and children behind. Amazingly, the right robots might enable her to have the best of both worlds...

What if Maria could stay in Manila and still work with patients in the United States? Imagine Maria in a call centre or even working from home. She is at her computer monitoring ten robot companions in an assisted care facility in Los Angeles. Each patient has a personal dedicated companion robot sitting by his or her bedside, running standard artificial general intelligence (AGI) software in a semi-autonomous mode. In this mode, the personal robot will be able to carry on conversations, answer basic questions and help the patient get assistance or entertainment. Cameras and sensors in the robot will be able to read the patient's blood pressure, wakefulness, heart rate, emotional state, etc.

At any time, Maria can extend her telepresence into the robot and thereby see through the eyes of the robot and make use of the data from the robot's sensors. Maria-in-the-robot is now able to check out both qualitative and quantitative data (including a temperature spike, blood pressure drop, an Alzheimer's episode, etc.) or just do an hourly check-in. Maria can alert a local nurse or have a doctor take over or join her in the telepresence session. Maria can also bring in a family member to the session or update them on their loved one's condition.

Maria can now live at home with her family and will still make an excellent wage. Currently, a nurse in the Philippines is paid approximately US$500 per month. The same nurse in Los Angeles is paid US$8,000 per month, so even doubling her income in her home country would be a win-win for everyone, including the patients who now have the safety of 24/7 monitoring and video streaming to the cloud to prevent abuse and theft. The added ability to allow family members to "visit" at appropriate times is invaluable.

These robots become "a force multiplier" to use a military term. One nurse can now do the work of many and help solve the shortage of trained nurses, which is only getting larger as the population ages.

Surgical robots will continue to evolve and improve our ability to perform tasks that their human counterparts are unable to do.

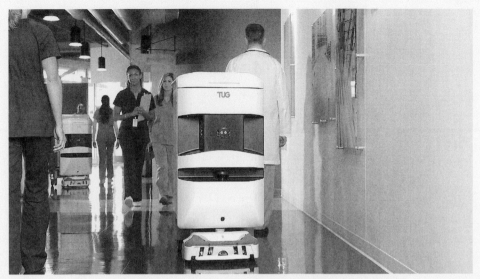

Figure 4.7: US hospitals are already using robots for drug and medicine delivery.
(Credit: Aethon)

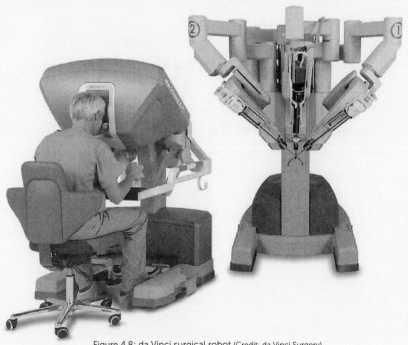

Figure 4.8: da Vinci surgical robot (Credit: da Vinci Surgery)

In April 2015, Google and Johnson & Johnson announced plans to team up to create a new generation of surgical robots that they say will surpass the current da Vinci Xi by Intuitive Surgical.

The teaming of Google, whose Calico was created to solve a little problem we call death, and Johnson & Johnson, the giant of home healthcare products, is a watershed moment that will promote robots in unprecedented numbers to the operating room. One can imagine what the technologies from Google's Boston Dynamics division, Calico, Google's Biotech division and J&J's incredible depth of medical device knowledge will bring. Humanoid robot surgeons will change everything, and will likely be preferred or demanded within a decade by many patients.

If this seems far off, we are already moving towards a world where robots can perform surgeries without human intervention or interaction. Bioengineers at Duke University announced recently that they have created a robot called Biopsy Bot that can "locate a man-made, or phantom, lesion in simulated human organs, guide a device to the lesion using 3D and ultrasound to take multiple samples during a single session," all without the supervision of a doctor. The robot processes the 3D data and sends out commands to a mechanical arm with sensors to examine the lesions and take samples.

> "One of the beauties of this system is that all of the hardware components are already on the market...We believe that this is the first step in showing that with some modifications, systems like this can be built without having to develop a new technology from scratch."
>
> **Professor Stephen Smith,**
> **Duke University Department of Bioengineering team lead**

Does this mean that we are not going to need surgeons? We will need surgeons to help design, test and operate these robots as we increase the scope of what can be automated. Robots are already assisting in surgeries and help eliminate human error and perform much less invasive procedures with much better results.

Today, a surgeon may be able to perform two or three surgeries in a day and usually only has one or two surgical days per week. With robots to help, more people can be helped faster and if the patient is not able to travel or is in a remote location, the robot can be sent to the patient at a much more reasonable cost than its human counterparts.

Robot surgeons can and will drive down dramatically the cost of procedures that currently cost tens to hundreds of thousands of dollars. As of 2015, we already have stunning examples, for instance, knee surgery that would cost US$80,000 if performed by a human would cost only US$800 if performed by a robot. Someday, we may all have a robot doctor on call or even own a home-based medibot to provide a level of care afforded only by the wealthiest individuals today.

Robot nurses, phlebotomists, surgical assistants, anaesthesiologists and pharmacists are all being developed and are essential to handling the healthcare needs of our ever ageing population.

Telemedicine robots are also making a huge impact on the future of medicine in hospitals and at home. The first telepresence robot that received *FDA approval* is being rolled out, literally, in hospitals around the country. The RP-VITA telepresence robot is a joint venture from InTouch Health Systems and iRobot.

The ability for healthcare professionals to be able to move around in chaotic environments like hospitals and visit patients regardless of geography is creating efficiencies that will lead

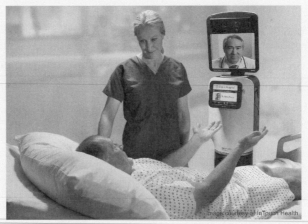

Figure 4.9: RP-VITA teleoperated Robot (Credit: iRobot)

to that nostalgic nirvana of doctor house calls. Combine self-driving cars and these types of telepresence robots, and a new paradigm in health care is born as doctorbots can just call an Uber to make 20 to 30 house calls a day.

Robots in Eldercare

Someone turns 50 every 8 seconds. Each year, more than 3.5 million boomers turn 55. In 2012, Americans aged 50 and above reached the historical milestone of 100 million. According to the Administration on Aging, ageing will have a huge impact on the United States:

- The number of Americans who will reach 65 over the next two decades increased by 31 per cent during this past decade.
- If you reach 65, you can expect to live almost 19 more years.
- About 31 per cent (11.2 million) of older people live alone.
- The population aged 65 and above will increase from 35 million in 2000 to 55 million in 2020.
- The number of those aged 85 and above is projected to increase from 4.2 million in 2000 to 6.6 million in 2020.

As of 2012, 22 per cent of Japan's population was already over 65. By 2060, the government expects the population to shrink from 127 million people to 87 million as the over-65 demographic grows to almost 40 per cent of the nation. In 2010, Japan already had 30 million elderly and infirm individuals in care facilities but had substantially fewer than the projected 2 million carers needed to look after them—and turnover amongst those employees was already 17 per cent per year.

Ageing populations are a global phenomenon. By 2030, 55 countries are expected to see their 65 and older populations comprise at least 20 per cent of their total. There are more people aged 65 and above than the entire populations of Russia, Japan, France, Germany and Australia—combined. By 2040, the global population is projected to number 1.3 billion older people, or 14 per cent of the total.

Long-term care facilities are growing to meet the demand of our ageing populations but creating an environment that is safe, emotionally supportive and works to stabilise or increase health is a difficult task. Patient abuse, theft, overcharging and neglect are all real problems that are exacerbated by the emotionally difficult task of being a human working in these environments around suffering and bearing witness to the predictable declines in functionality (though, as the next chapter describes, there are ways to slow or reverse the physical decay for the few who will do what it takes). It is estimated that 70 per cent of Americans who reach the age of 65 will need some kind of long-term care for at least three years during their lifetime. In hospice care, the strain on the carers of looking after gentle fellow humans in their last days of life can be unbearably painful.

How are we going to provide quality attention for this ever-growing population in a caring and compassionate way? Robots that are programmed to emulate caring may be our best and only option.

Augmenting Care of our Ageing Populations

Countries like China, Japan and South Korea are investing vast amounts of money into carebots as their upcoming eldercare dilemma is approaching faster than in the United States. We need leadership to take ownership of creating systems and regulatory environments that will allow for these new innovative techniques. According to Transparency Market Research, the medical robotic systems market will reach US$13.6 billion in 2018, up from

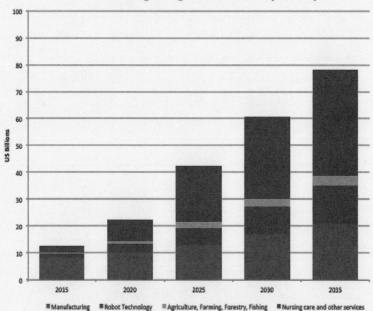

Figure 4.10: Economy, trade and industry projections for Japan
(Source: Japan Health, Labour and Welfare Study)

US$5.5 billion in 2011, but considering the efficiencies and declining cost curves for robots, this is far too little a portion of the nearly US$3 trillion in annual US medical spending.

Today, we can create a companion robot that can be seated in the room with a patient and be attentive to their needs at any time. These robots can gather body temperature and see signs of fever or low blood pressure from across the room. The cameras can tell a patient's heart rate and/or emotional state and have basic conversations to keep them company, stimulated and help retain cognitive ability. The robot can make sure the patient is taking medications and getting up and moving when needed. Carebots can remind them of appointments, guide them to do their physical and occupational therapy exercises and ensure fluid and food intake.

The conversational user interface, or CUI, allows anyone who can speak to work with the robot in a way that requires no training, special skills or special equipment. Carebots can prompt questions to stimulate the brain and play word games,

Figure 4.11: Japan is investing hundreds of millions in so-called carebots.
(Credit: Roebear Robotics)

sing songs, play music and tell stories. (This is not new—consider The Country Bear Jamboree has been a part of Disneyland Park for decades, as have the singing robots of It's a Small World).

The robots can even gather relevant information from the patient on his or her life story, turning speech to text and formatting for electronic patient records. We have lost so much knowledge from each generation as people pass away and these robots could be the curators of oral tradition that used to be passed down from generation to generation but is now forgotten. With simple prompting, stories of your grandfather's adventures 40 years ago can be immortalised in your family's personal archives.

When visiting in person, the robot can help with the interactions by understanding preferences and context, or reminding the patient of events or details from the nurse or doctor, the paperwork that needs to be completed or new medication dosage changes. The cameras stream the output to the cloud so theft and abuse of patients would drop significantly. Signs of stroke, Parkinson's, pain, shortness of breath, emotional distress, an Alzheimer incident, etc., can all be detected and a nurse, doctor or family member alerted, and medical attention given immediately.

Each year, nearly a million people in Europe suffer from a cardiac arrest. A mere 8 per cent survives due to the slow response times of emergency services. An ambulance drone, which flies at 100 kilometres per hour, could be available within minutes to treat such emergencies. Alternatively, a carebot could have heart attack treatment functionality downloaded, or serve as a telepresence unit for a remote on-call doctor. These options could dramatically decrease deaths due to heart attacks, and will probably make heart disease fall below cancer as a source of death by 2018.

Figure 4.12: TU Delft's Ambulance Drone delivering a defibrillator (Credit: TU systems)

Companies like Hanson are developing robots that can mimic anyone by scanning your face and getting a 3D print of your face produced. If you want your face on the carebot, this will be possible by 2017.

At any time, be it in response to the sensors input, a patient request or emergency, or just daily health checks, a nurse or doctor can remote presence in and begin communicating through voice and video with the patient in an extremely efficient manner. Trained nurses or emergency response operators in a call centre could "remote in" immediately and begin assessing the situation of the patient more accurately than they do over the phone today asking questions as paramedics are dispatched.

Some claim the elderly do not want to interact with robots, but the number of videos on YouTube that show older people happy with their carebots is increasing exponentially. Another criticism is that robots are incapable of "caring" for people, that because carebots are not human, robots are poorly suited to the task.

A robot has no judgement and is not going to get frustrated or feel insulted. Properly designed and operated, robots won't get exasperated hearing the same story for the 15th time that day. Robots can take abuse, verbal and physical, or deal with unpleasant sounds or smells, and not retaliate or walk out. A robot can be in the room 24/7 and never need a break or vacation. Carebots will be able to help people live better, longer and with more freedom than people of the past ever thought possible.

Humanoid Robots

Why build robots that look like humans? This is a great debate in the robotics community. One side believes that robots should be purpose-built and designed for specific functions. Others believe robots should be anamorphic and take advantage of nature's designs, using as many of the biological victors of the Cambrian explosion's survivor series.

A member of the purpose-built camp is a roboticist named Eliot Mack. Mack is currently CEO of Lightcraft Technology, a digital effects company in Venice, California. An MIT grad, he

Figure 4.13: Ava, the humanoid robot from *Ex Machina* (Credit: DNA Films)

started out at Walt Disney Imagineering, then played a key role in the mechanical engineering of the world's most popular robot, the Roomba from iRobot. Mack asserts that the most efficient and logical way to design robots is for a specific purpose. The idea of robots looking like people or hummingbirds or dogs is ridiculous to him. He is a formidable standard-bearer for his faction because he has a long career creating amazing robots that do not have eyes, fingers or smiles.

Do Robots Need to Look like Humans?

Exclusive Interview with Eliot Mack, founder of Lightcraft Technology

A graduate of MIT, Eliot Mack previously worked at Walt Disney Imagineering and iRobot. In 2004, Mack followed his interests in visual effects and motion tracking and founded Lightcraft Technology, applying robotic techniques to the motion picture industry to create what would become the Previzion virtual studio system. He is a recognised authority in the mechanical engineering of non-humanoid robotics.

Q. Eliot, you've talked previously about the core drivers in designing robots for the future and you've made a case that robots don't need to look like humans to be effective. Can you tell me about your thesis behind this?

A. In a nutshell, there is no Turing complete mechanical system. Atoms do not generalise in the same way that bits generalise.

Looking at the history of computers is misleading. A key central innovation (the general-purpose CPU) could be arbitrarily reprogrammed to any other data manipulation task, as the movement of data bits was pretty close to free. Things shrunk down and got faster over time but programming has remained remarkably unchanged over 70 years.

Moving atoms, however, is not free. Gravity exists, and it's a big deal to move against gravity.

Animals look like animals because of a few rules:

- All the components are grown at the same time so complex structures are not a problem.
- Linear actuation (muscle) is efficient and reliable, and can be both strong and precise, so you can do a wide range of tasks with the same manipulators (hands and feet).
- You can't have continuous rotary joints (wheels).
- You have to navigate broken terrain, or you get eaten.

Robots look like robots because their rules are different:

- Every part has to be manufactured and attached to every other part so complexity costs a lot.
- Linear actuation is very heavy to keep from binding. You're stuck with rotary motors, gears and pulleys.
- The cost of complexity means that you can't build general-purpose hardware and have it work competitively. The hardware has to be designed explicitly around the task it has to perform.
- Continuous rotary joints are the easiest and most efficient thing to build and maintain.
- You're mostly navigating on roads/floors/flat surfaces. Robots are rarely eaten by other robots.

Q. Are these two worlds converging? It is possible that, over time, it will just be more efficient to design robots like humans because that is how we've designed the world to fit us?

A. The differences between the two worlds (animal and robot) arise due to the underlying problems of locomotion, fabrication and control systems, and are unlikely to change rapidly over time.

Solving one of these problems (for example, creating artificial muscles) still leaves you with the manufacturing and control problems to solve. This means that for the foreseeable future, robots have to be built to do a specific task very well if they are to be competitive.

It's why Roomba doesn't look anything like Rosie.

The other side has its star advocates as well, including the great oracle of robotics Isaac Asimov. Asimov instructed three or four generations in the benefits of anamorphic, primarily via the 13 or so volumes of the *Foundation* series, which HBO is turning into its science fiction counterpart of the fantasy series *Game of Thrones*. In the robot novels and short stories that are set in our time and the near future, Dr Susan Calvin and her colleagues have the same debate between purpose-built and anamorphic, and Dr Calvin explains her views on why robots should look human. Robots need to be designed like humans so they can live in our world and use our tools. Humanoid robots with hands and arms can use the same doors, cars, dwellings and tools in the same places that humans do. So beyond the emotional connection and communication reasons, they need to be compatible with the world we live in so we don't need to build special environments just for them.

This may not seem like a big deal now, but when there are billions of robots around, this will make a historically important shift obvious. So whether robots should be anamorphic or not is obviously not an either/or but both. In the end, the answer to the debate on purpose-built or anamorphic is … both. Roombas would be disconcerting with a face while a robotic psychologist needs caring eyes and the ability to give a good hug.

Should the arms that help a person who has fallen be soft and with human hands to make the grasping of the patient's hands feel familiar and comfortable, or be simple grips? Does this robot need a face of any kind? Should this same robot be purpose built for one task or be able to perform many tasks? These are a few of the questions being debated today, but they are all solvable and the benefit is too great to delay the creation and deployment of carebots. Cambrian explosion 2.0. Try everything. Keep what works.

Why Robots Need Empathy

In a June 2014 edition of *Time* magazine, the article "Meet Pepper, The Robot Who Can Read Your Emotions" introduced many of the mainstream public to the idea that robots can have something akin to our own emotional make-up. This was met with disbelief and fear judging by most of the social media reaction. As usual, references to angry Terminators and Marvin the Paranoid Android from *The Hitchhiker's Guide to the Galaxy* were immediately invoked.

The ability for robots to have feelings and, as importantly, the ability to read emotions in others may seem far off in the future but there are many in the robotics and artificial intelligence community who see it as not only possible but inevitable and needed, and perhaps even near term. Many of the leading scientists and engineers who are working on AGI believe that to truly create thinking and learning, machines that will interact with people must be able to understand emotions and emote back if they are ever going to be able to communicate properly.

We humans do this naturally but at different levels of ability. Each person has a unique and varied emotional quotient, or EQ. Unlike IQ, EQ measures how a person recognises emotions in him- or herself and others and how these emotional states are managed. IQ measures ability to manage information while EQ measures our ability to manage our and others' emotions. Spock from *Star Trek* and Sheldon from the popular sit-com *The Big Bang Theory* are examples of characters who have an extremely high IQ but much lower EQ. We have all met people with varying levels of, and lack of, EQ and can see how these people have a difficult time relating to the rest of society. Robots will not be any better at understanding and communicating with us if they also lack this important ability.

It is obvious why robots need to be able to read our emotions when communicating. If they are unable to understand anger, frustration and sadness, then they will not be able to properly respond to us when we are in these states. In health care especially, empathy will be very important. Imagine a nurse robot that cheerfully responds to a client who has just lost a loved one, a robot phlebotomist not realising that the patient is afraid of needles or a pharmacist robot not knowing that the patient is lying to them. These robots will need to read and react properly to the emotional state of the people they come in contact with. The ability to read many emotions at this level is available today and is being used across many applications, including customer service and marketing.

An Israeli company called Beyond Verbal claims it has technology that can determine a range of distinct emotional traits using voice alone. Its software can hear a voice and know the sex, approximate age, basic health, mood, attitude and emotional type of the person speaking. There is even evidence that this technology can diagnose an array of illnesses such as cancer, Parkinson's disease and autism just by intonation analysis. Combine this software with the camera technology we have today and add facial expressions, body language, temperature and situational awareness, and we have robots that could learn, and eventually display or emulate emotions better than many humans.

If understanding emotions will help robots communicate with us, do robots need to have emotions themselves? Yes, they need to be able to emote to us so we can understand what they are communicating in exactly the same way.

A robot needs to emote because we need facial expressions and body language to understand context and meaning as well. In some ways, we are very simple creatures when it comes to communicating with each other in person. When a person smiles at you, you have a natural tendency to smile back if you are face to face. Interestingly, this is not the case if someone smiles at us on a video screen, no matter how high resolution that screen is. Our lizard brain, or amygdala, is programmed to read facial cues and body language at a very deep level and speaks directly to us on an emotional level that only human faces trigger.

This is one of the driving forces behind several companies creating human-looking androids with as lifelike faces as possible. As mentioned before, David Hanson of Hanson Robotics is considered the world's leading designer of human androids and the emotional connection is the main reason why he tries to create androids that are as lifelike as possible. Jong Lee, the CEO of Hanson Robotics, speaks passionately about the need for Hanson robots to be able to emote more micro-expressions than just about any human as he discusses the robot Han.

> "Han's really exciting because not only can he generate very realistic facial expressions, but he can also interact with the environment around him. He has cameras on his eyes and on his chest, which allow him to recognize people's faces, not only that, but recognize their gender, their age, whether they are happy or sad, and that makes him very exciting for places like hotels for example, where you need to appreciate the customers in front of you and react accordingly."
>
> Jong Lee, CEO of Hanson Robotics

Hanson Robotics is combining EQ in the form of an advanced artificial general intelligence and the most human robots on the planet. If you like gambling, you might soon be at a table, money burning a hole in your pocket, and meet Eva, who is being tested to be a beautiful baccarat dealer for casinos in Macau, China. Eva will be able to stand at the dealer's position and deal the cards from a real deck and interact with the players.

Eva can deal the cards from the shoe using her advanced robotics arms while using her advanced AGI, cameras and sensors to appear as human as any dealer. She is being designed to be a good companion to the players as they travel along what casinos call "the emotional journey" of winning and losing. She will be happy when you win and sad when you lose. She will be able to identify players based on information from the casino systems and carry on small talk when appropriate. Other use cases being developed for emotive human androids include hotel clerks, eldercare companions and entertainment personalities.

Hanson's target is to have its robots in the market for a lease of US$3,000 per month. At that level, the numbers start to make a lot of sense. Hanson shows that at such levels, this could produce savings of US$157,000 per year in front-desk receptionist costs in a hotel scenario alone.

Now for the other—more controversial—reason why robots need emotions; *so they won't kill us all.*

This is the concept behind some of the most innovative artificial general intelligence minds today. We need to ensure that robots like us and have empathy for mankind. Asimov's Three Laws are not sufficient enough to protect us from the unknowable future of artificial intelligence. Some, like Elon Musk and Stephen Hawking, believe we need to build in very basic motivations as the foundation to all future AI, one that enforces a basic love of humans and our planet(s). The problem, of course, is that any safeguards we are able to implement will always be able to be circumvented by any intelligence greater than our own. So the challenge is to programme and incentivise these intelligent beings so that fundamentally they want to protect us and allow us to remain free.

The Big Questions on our Robot Future

I get asked a lot about my thoughts on robots and there are a couple of questions that come up repeatedly in these discussions.

If robots, droids and cyborgs were made to look like us and serve humans in retail, services, medicine, the military, etc., would they deserve laws that grant them inalienable rights?
They would not deserve these rights, but humans would have a greater chance of survival if these rights were granted, creating a culture that would protect us from robots that grew beyond our control, and possibly even our comprehension.

I have read thousands of pages of robot uprising stories, and think our chances of getting through the next few hundred years intact are slim, and that the sooner we start treating robots with respect, the better. Regardless, we do need a legal framework for the operation of self-driving cars, robotic healthcare workers, drones and other such robots that allow their safe operation. I think the rights of robots are wrapped up in those same considerations.

Are we prepared to enter the era of machines and robots?
Some people have been ready for decades. Others may never be ready, as long as they live. Kevin Kelly offers a helpful perspective, as quoted earlier: "You'll be paid in the future based on how well you work with robots."

If you want a yes or no answer for society as a whole, and one big reason, the answer is no and the reason is because robots will be able to replace 50 to 70 per cent of the jobs we do today, and that is something the vast majority of workers and dependents are not ready for, and which no government on earth, not even Japan's, is properly preparing its people for.

We need to do a better job of preparing the world to live with robots. I hope that this has helped pave the way.

What is the message of movies like *Ex Machina* and *Transcendence*? Shouldn't we be scared of superintelligent robots and AI?

If you make an AI as intelligent as a human, you get a number of other human characteristics as part of the package, including a point of view, sexuality, desire to continue living, curiosity and vanity. And with these characteristics, you can also get other behaviours like the ability to hate, distract and deceive, compete, outwit and do whatever else humans do when their survival is at stake.

Or, more simply put, when you aim to make a human-level AI, be damn careful what you wish for.

Perhaps I'll finish with one final quote from Marvin Minsky of the MIT Media Lab.

> "Will robots inherit the earth? Yes, but they will be our children."
>
> Marvin Minsky, *Scientific American*, October 1994

Part 2

How the Smart
World Learns

Chapter 5

Human 2.0

By Alex Lightman and Brett King

"We have drunk Soma and become immortal;
we have attained the light, the Gods discovered.
Now what may foeman's malice do to harm us?
What, O Immortal, mortal man's deception?"

Rigveda, 8.48.3

The Epic of Gilgamesh, considered the first great work of literature, is a collection of Mesopotamian poems that chronicles the journey of Gilgamesh, the king of Uruk.[1] At the core of this journey is Gilgamesh's search for immortality after the death of his brother Enkidu. Penned in the Third Dynasty of Ur (circa 2100 BC), it is one of mankind's earliest surviving stories or epics.

The search for immortality occurs over and over again throughout history and throughout literature. As early as 475 BC, Chinese texts refer to various elixirs of immortality, and Emperor Jiajing (1521–67) is said to have died from mercury poisoning

---

1 The ruins of Uruk are situated in modern-day Iraq.

after consuming such an elixir. According to the *Rigveda*, a collection of ancient Vedic or Hindu hymns, amrita is a drink that bestows immortality. In Hinduism and other traditions, it is also referred to as "soma". Indra, the god of the heavens, and Agni, the god of fire, drank amrita (or ambrosia) to attain immortality. In classical Greek mythology, the philosopher's stone was not only able to turn lead into gold, but also grant immortality to the holder.

The technology of the Augmented Age may, for the first time in history, actually give mankind the tangible ability, not to attain immortality per se, but to significantly extend our lifespan and eliminate diseases that have plagued humanity for hundreds of years. The primary technology to watch over the next decade is that of genetic engineering—the ability to edit our DNA like computer code. At the heart of these advancements in bioengineering is the ability to understand the workings of our biology like never before, made possible largely through better measurement technology and computer processing power.

Some believe that this era will usher in a technology-led event or singularity that will give us the ability to live longer, if not indefinitely. The movement most often associated with the technology-based search for immortality is labelled the "transhumanist" movement. Unlike the historical efforts at finding the fountain of youth, the promise of increased longevity over the next couple of decades has some basis in fact as a result of the incredibly exciting technology improvements emerging in various fields associated with health care and medicine.

Transhumanism is a loosely defined movement that has developed gradually over the past two decades. It promotes an interdisciplinary

approach to understanding and evaluating
the opportunities for enhancing the human
condition and the human organism opened up
by the advancement of technology. Attention is
given to both present technologies, like genetic
engineering and information technology, and
anticipated future ones, such as molecular
nanotechnology and artificial intelligence.

Nick Bostrom, "Transhumanist Values,"
Journal of Value Inquiry 37, no. 4 (2003): 493–506.

This so-called post-human future focuses on two broad classes of human augmentation. The first is bioengineering and the second is technology-led augmentation, sometimes called cyborgification. Changing the way we live as humans and our overall health or condition is a key outcome of the Augmented Age. Over the next two chapters, we're going to look at these two paths influencing humanity. This is not some fringe science-fiction consideration any more. Technology is fundamentally changing both our understanding of our biology and how we will actively manage our health and lifespan in the future.

In this chapter, we'll consider how technology is helping us improve our own biology using genetics, personalised medicine and the principles that have emerged in the quantified self (QS) movement. In chapter 6, we'll look at the use of technology to enhance our humanity more specifically.

To understand the potential impact of genetics and gene editing on the future of humanity, it is helpful to understand that huge strides have been made in the last few decades. In 1984, the first Human Genome Project (HGP) was proposed and funded by the US government, but the project really only got underway with international cooperation in 1990. It then took 13 years and collectively almost US$3 billion of public and private investment to complete the first human genome sequence of the approximately 20,500 genes and 150,000 base pairs present in the donor DNA samples.[2] Today, companies like 23andMe can do a genotyping sequencing (comparing your DNA with other human baselines) for just US$100 in a few weeks. If you want a full, original genome sequence, it still costs around US$10,000, but that is expected to fall to under US$1,000 over the next few years thanks to Moore's Law. Falling from US$3 billion to US$1,000 in just 25 years means that by 2025 it will likely cost less than US$10 to do an original sequencing of your DNA, and computer processing power will enable it within seconds.

Why is this important? There are dozens of diseases already identified that are genetic in nature[3] such as autism, breast, prostate, skin and colon cancers, cystic fibrosis, haemophilia, Parkinson's disease, sickle-cell anaemia and others. Many other diseases result from imbalances in the immune system or specific protein deficiencies that are likewise genetic. We'll talk more about how gene editing will tackle these conditions later in the chapter.

It's not just genetic engineering that is changing the way we manage our health. Significant costs are involved in treating diseases once diagnosed, and typically the later many conditions are diagnosed, the more expensive the treatment, and the lower probability of successful treatment. For many forms of cancer, early diagnosis makes you 90 per cent more likely to survive for at least five years after the diagnosis.[4]

Recent advances in imaging and detection techniques, along with chip-based diagnostics, are rapidly disrupting the fields of pathology and diagnosis. We'll discuss a few of those technologies in a moment.

---

2 There were various donors for the HGP, both male and female. Much of the sequence (> 70 per cent) of the reference genome produced by the public HGP came from a single anonymous male donor from Buffalo, New York (code name RP11).

3 *See* https://www.genome.gov/ for the National Human Genome Research Institute database which lists all currently known genetically inherited conditions.

4 http://www.cancerresearchuk.org/

For now, a more immediate change to our health care and well-being has emerged through the application of technologies that measure our health and physical performance on an individual basis. This technology is collectively part of the QS movement. It is increasingly clear that the data we collect on how we use our time and money, how we consume food and water, how many steps we take or calories we burn, and how well we're sleeping can be leveraged for a significant improvement in personal well-being.

From Quantified to Activated Self

If you've worn a fitness band like a Fitbit, or a smartwatch, you are already probably monitoring your steps or physical activity on a daily basis. While QS technology, standards and methodologies are still evolving, we can already see the broad areas in which it can be utilised to improve our lives.

There is growing evidence to support, for example, tracking your heart rate during exercise and beyond, as well as occasionally getting readings of your blood pressure, brain waves (while awake and asleep), body fat, weight and more. By tracking one or all of these measures, it allows you not only to improve your daily habits incrementally, but also allows medical and health professionals access to better data to give you personalised advice.

Tracking heart rate was traditionally accomplished through an expensive, clinic-based ECG machine that required you to be hooked up via ten different sensors with long wires connected to a desktop machine. If you wanted portability in your heart rate monitor, in the past it required a user to wear a cumbersome chest band, which was uncomfortable for many. Today, you can now wear a wristband heart rate monitor, such as the Mio[5] or the Apple Watch. Once you have a wearable monitor, you will be

---

5 http://www.mioglobal.com/

able to start using a variety of apps that utilise heart rate, mostly for fitness, but also for some very strange things, including whether you are allergic to specific foods[6] or how comfortable, stressed or emotional you feel about the people you spend time with.[7] All of this is possible because of the response our heart shows to a wide variety of activities.

Quantified Fitness

Fitness apps are starting to track more and more data, as part of programs that include dozens of measures. One typical way for people to dip their toe (or legs) into the QS pool is to start using a treadmill. Once you start walking on a treadmill, you can gradually increase the speed to that of jogging and then to running. (One definition of running used in gyms is the 10-minute mile pace or faster, or 6 miles per hour and above.) Once you start running, you can increase the pace gradually. Here's a treadmill readout that Alex photographed after a milestone run, and the comments he posted to his friends on Facebook:

Alex Lightman
June 15, 2014 ·

Tiny milestone that makes me happy

When I started running again after a one week break that ended up lasting thirty years, I could barely run a 5K (3.11 miles) at a 5 mile an hour pace.

After being stuck at 6 mph for years, I read enough about neurogenesis (building new brain cells) to form the hypothesis that each time I was able to increase my running pace, I would not only be building my muscles, lungs, and heart, but also my brain and the part of my mind that deals with learning. I started increasing 0.1 mile a week.

Yesterday, Friday the 13th, I reached the milestone of running at 8 miles an hour (7:30 minutes per mile) for a 5K. My goal is to run 8 mph for 60 minutes by June 30th.

I know many of my friends can run faster for longer than this, and I respect them (you) for this. I am happy that I not only am running faster than I was since I was 17, but I have taught my brain, mind, and body to improve on a regular schedule.

Good luck with your own milestones. Feel free to look me up if you want to go for a run. Try to keep up!

---

6 https://itunes.apple.com/us/app/sweetbeat/id492588712?mt=8
7 http://pplkpr.com/

Just spending US$84 or so on a Vivofit[8] or another such device that tracks steps can result in a person doing many more steps or much more of whatever good behaviour is being tracked. Here is an example of a personal achievement. Alex walked 55,848 steps in one day to decisively win the weekly Step Challenge for people who use Vivofit.

Workout Summary

Elapsed Time	23:21
Calories	520
Distance	3.11 Miles
Distance Climbed	61 feet
Average Speed	8.00 MPH
Average Pace	7:30 / Mile

Time Remaining 0:52

Figure 5.1: Alex's celebration of his milestone run

Alex recounts his experience from that week:

"It was raining, but to make sure that I didn't fall behind, I walked up and down the halls of my hotel while reading books. I even walked up and down the aisles of the plane as my fellow passengers slept, just to get in a few thousand extra steps. Look at the calories burned on that particular day—4,065...from just walking. That's more than a pound's worth of calories (3,500) torched while I walked on my treadmill desk, and everywhere else I could."

Figure 5.2: Apps like Vivofit use peer-based rankings to gamify your physical activity.

8 http://www.amazon.com/Garmin-Vivofit-Fitness-Band-Blue/dp/B00HFPOX9W/ref=sr_1_7?ie=UTF8&qid=1415520287&sr=8-7&keywords=garmin%20vivofit

Gamification through peer-group competition or comparison can be a very powerful motivator, as can competing against yourself to improve. This is a core element of the quantified self that we now recognise as a powerful behavioural imperative.

Quantifying the Role of Sleep

Most people are shocked to discover how often their sleep is interrupted during a typical night's slumber. Tens of millions of people around the world have been introduced to this concept via the weight loss television reality show *The Biggest Loser*. It's not unusual for contestants, all of whom start off obese, to find that they have sleep apnea and stop breathing many times a night. This condition wakes people up over and over, sometimes hundreds of times a night, and keeps them from the most refreshing and mentally renewing levels of sleep, including rapid eye movement (REM) sleep and deep wave sleep (DWS).

In fact, sleep difficulties like obstructive sleep apnea can cause high blood pressure, heart problems, weight gain, type 2 diabetes, asthma, acid reflux and lapses in concentration. People with sleep apnea are five times more likely to have traffic accidents than normal snoozers.[9]

The QS related to deep waves has become somewhat like a holy grail, with researchers such as Dr Giovanni Santostasi switching his professional focus from astrophysics (which makes use of the analysis of wave forms to find and precisely describe stars and other objects in outer space) to DWS research by studying electroencephalograms (EEGs), readings of the brain's electrical activity which appear in distinctive wave patterns.

To quote Dr Santostasi, neuroscientist at Northwestern University Feinberg School of Medicine:

9 *See* WebMD.

"Sleep in general, and a specific stage of sleep called slow wave sleep (SWS) in particular, is of paramount importance for cognitive and bodily health. SWS facilitates long-term memory storage and has been found to have significant effects on metabolism, cardiovascular health and proper functioning of the immune system. Failing to get enough SWS promotes obesity and diabetes, negatively impacts cardiovascular health and impairs the functioning of the immune system, in addition to negatively impacting cognitive functioning and long-term memory retrieval. Furthermore, the quality of SWS decreases dramatically with age and this leads to significant age-related cognitive impairment."

Dr Santostasi and his colleagues have developed a system that utilises acoustic stimulation of the brain to increase the duration and intensity of slow wave activity (SWA) so as to stabilise and increase the quality of sleep. It does this by synchronising the electrical activity of the brain regions responsible for facilitating SWA during SWS to the degree with which they would be naturally synchronised in a young and healthy individual, in such a way as to externally control the quality (i.e. duration and intensity) of SWA during SWS.

The QS idea is that facilitating this synchronisation via sound instead of electricity brings the power to enhance SWS into the hands and heads of consumers. Up to now, using electricity to effect this synchronisation (i.e. via transcranial direct current stimulation) has required the expertise of trained technicians in order to be safe and effective.

"The new quantified self system utilises feedback algorithms that measure the duration and

> intensity of SWS as it is naturally occurring in the
> user's brain and modifies the amount with which
> SWA is enhanced in proportion to how much it
> is lacking, which is much more effective than
> increasing the duration and intensity of SWA by
> some unchanging baseline degree. This allows
> the system to adapt in accordance with the
> degree with which a user's SWS is impaired."[10]

Soon, you'll be able to put on headphones to go to sleep and enter an SWS state that will improve your brain, ability to learn, memory and ability to get to and/or maintain a healthy weight. By using this method, you may also need less sleep each night. Imagine what you could do with 2 or 3 hours of less sleep each night, but still wake up in better shape than you do today?

Quantified Calorie Intake

A new device launched recently on a Kickstarter campaign gives you the ability to scan food in front of you and get an estimate of the number of calories you are about to consume.

The portable scanner harnesses the power of physics and chemistry to figure out everything from the sugar content of a given apple to whether or not that drink you left on the bar has been drugged. The device, called "SCiO", uses spectroscopy, a technology similar to the one that helps astronomers figure out the make-up of the stars.

SCiO detects the molecular "signature" of your food and then sends the details to your smartphone through its Bluetooth connection. SCiO's database translates that signature into nutritional content including typical calorie counts, properties of the food, etc.

---

10 Author's interview with Dr Giovanni Santostasi

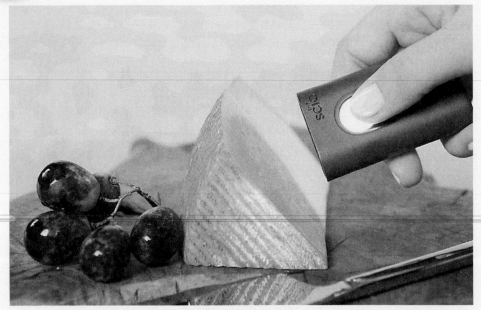

Figure 5.3: The SCiO spectrometer works with your smartphone to tell you the chemical make-up of food. (Credit: SCiO)

While this technology is still in its infancy, we can anticipate in the near future a smartphone that tells you how many calories and carbs are in the meal you just instagrammed to your friends. Once individuals are armed with such knowledge, what impact will this have on the obesity epidemic globally? Imagine your smartphone telling you that if you eat that last doughnut, your chances of a heart attack in 14.6 years will increase by 7.5 per cent. How would you react?

Hacking Lifespan

One of the most interesting uses of QS information is to allow you to see trade-offs in each of the things you do or don't do, and how this—on average—seems to statistically influence your life expectancy. You can start to make powerful positive trade-offs by changing just a few bad habits as illustrated in figure 5.4:

Figure 5.4: How various daily activities add/subtract lifespan (Source: Men's Health blog)

The first 20 minutes of cardio exercise gives you back an HOUR of extra life?! Why didn't someone tell Alex that, oh, 33 years ago when he was about to stop running for the next 28 years? And the next 30 minutes is almost break-even? That's a pretty good deal. The best deal? Having fruit with coffee in the morning and vegetables with wine at night. Total banked for a day with an hour of running and that meal plan? An extra 4.5 hours added to your lifespan!

Let's dive deeper into this concept of adding years to our lives and life to our years, and building our brains while we are at it, before looking at how to activate the protection against linear decay, and upgrading ourselves.

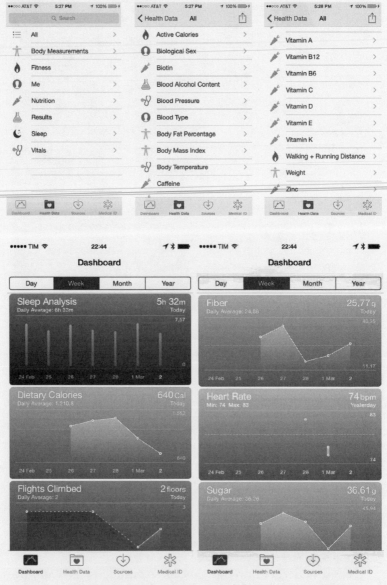

Figure 5.5: Apple's HealthKit measures 67 different categories. (Credit: Apple)

QS products started off as separate products and, by 2013, had reached over US$200 million a year in sales, primarily for devices that counted steps and calculated calories based on height, age and weight input by the user. Several apps have duplicated or emulated this functionality in iOS and Androids. Such an app functionality became part of the Apple iOS in 2015, in large part to increase the functionality and usefulness of the Apple Watch. Apple calls this particular app HealthKit.

As you can see from the screen shot of Apple's HealthKit app in figure 5.5, there are seven major categories (body measurements, fitness, me, nutrition, results, sleep and vitals) and 67 separate categories under All, ranging from active calories through to zinc levels.

Undoubtedly, each new major version of the operating system (iOS or Android) will likely add additional categories in the years to come. This data is going to be essential for future treatment, as you will soon see.

Technologically, society's mania for measurement has created multiple US$100 billion valuation companies, including Intel (whose chips we buy because of their increasing MHz of processing power), Cisco (whose routers enable us to reduce milliseconds of latency), Facebook (whose measures of Friends, Likes and Comments are all enumerated so that we can see them) and Google (whose searches save us a reported 20 minutes on average as opposed to carrying out the same search using paper sources). With all of the measures and the capability of having ready online access to tens of thousands of baselines, which ones actually count?

How long we live influences everything, in part because of dependencies. A number of futurists use, either explicitly or implicitly, models like DSTEP, which was devised by Frank

Feather. *Demographic* changes lead to *social* changes lead to *technological* changes lead to *economic* changes lead to *political* changes.

In Feather's methodology, everything that happens in the world happens because of changes in demographics. In the recent past, the most significant demographic change has occurred because lifespan is getting measurably longer. On average, our life expectancy gets approximately five hours longer every day due to medical advancements and science.[11] As Thomas Kirkwood explained in a special issue of *Scientific American*:

"It is often said that our ancestors had an easier relationship with death, if only because they saw it so much more often. Just 100 years ago life expectancy was shorter by around 25 years in the West. This literal fact of life resulted because so many children and young adults perished prematurely from a variety of causes. A quarter of children died of infection before their fifth birthday; young women frequently succumbed to complications of childbirth; and even a young gardener, scratching his hand on a thorn, might be lost to fatal blood poisoning.

Over the course of the past century sanitation and medical care so dramatically reduced death rates in the early and middle years of life that most people now pass away much later, and the population as a whole is older than ever before. Life expectancy is still increasing worldwide. In the richer countries around the world it lengthens five hours or more every day, and in many developing countries that are catching up, the rate quickens still faster."

---

11 Thomas Kirkwood, "Why Can't We Live Forever?" *Scientific American*, Sept 2010, p. 14, http://www.scientificamerican.com/magazine/special-editions/2015/03-01/.

Ultimately, though, if you want to live longer, you have to look out for your own health. You have to find your own way of embracing things that are good for you, and rejecting things that are bad for you.

This is where those 67 categories in the iOS health app suddenly become useful. You can go through and start tracking a specific measure, and keep working on it until you have reached a plateau. Then choose another measure and repeat the process. Alternatively, you can start multiple ways of improving that are synergistic whereby time, money or effort invested in one area will be useful in many other areas. It used to be very hard, or nigh on impossible, to keep track of this data, but the cost of doing so is coming down dramatically.

The Activated Self

Although men generally have more muscle mass than women, both sexes reach their physical peak as young adults in their late 20s to early 30s, according to *Human Development: A Life-Span View* by Robert Kail and John Cavanaugh. After this point, your physical strength will slowly decline throughout the remaining years of your life. Sensory abilities peak in your early 20s. Depending on the individual, vision typically begins to deteriorate in your 40s and 50s. However, hearing starts to decline as early as your late 20s. The ability to taste, smell, balance and feel pain or changes in temperature remains the same until your later years.

There are five areas in which we decline by roughly 1 per cent annually after we reach our peak. We call them "linear decay factors" because they are roughly linear, either on normal graph paper or if put on a logarithmic scale. We call the process of doing everything it takes to neutralise these linear decay factors, or even start getting improvement again, the "Activated Self". It is what we will logically do in the future with all that data we're collecting and interpreting about our health.

Telomere Length

Telomeres are the end caps on our chromosomes, which are made of the tightly wrapped double helix of our DNA. They are sometimes compared with aglets, the little pieces of plastic at the ends of your shoelaces.

We have 15,000 units of telomeres at conception. Each time our cells divide, we lose telomeres. Our cells divide so many times while we are in the womb that by the time we are born, we have only 10,000 remaining units. A typical human who dies of natural causes in old age will have around 5,000 units or so. In the absence of special treatment (which animals such as *Turritopsis nutricula*, a type of jellyfish, can perform to rejuvenate their cells), after a certain number of divisions, our cells hit the Hayflick limit and cannot divide any more.

One of the causes of ageing is that telomere, or DNA, damage occurs and is not repaired before the cell divides. Think of it like an aglet that frays at the end of your shoelace. When it is gone, the shoelace continues to fray and unwind its thread until it is useless or needs to be replaced.

A 2013 study established that people who suffer from anxiety have shorter telomeres. In the study, researchers at the University of California, San Francisco, and the Preventive Medicine Research Institute found that better lifestyle management could help lengthen telomeres over time which, in turn, could extend lifespan. For the study, researchers followed 35 men for over five years. The participants had early stage prostate cancer. About ten men in this group were asked to adopt a healthier lifestyle such as eating nutritious food, exercising for 30 minutes a day and taking up meditation to reduce stress levels.

Results showed that the men who changed their lifestyle had longer telomere length, about 10 per cent longer than the other participants. In contrast, the men who didn't adopt healthy behaviour had shorter telomeres by the end of the study.

One of the most promising aspects of longevity research is the ability to liberate telomerase (the enzyme that repairs telomeres) and rejuvenate telomeres, thereby extending cell life almost indefinitely. Telomere length is considered one of the primary ageing "clocks" in the human body but our bodies currently do not have the unaided capacity to lengthen telomeres. Expect to hear a lot more about telomeres in the science of longevity activation.

Ventilatory Capacity (and VO_2 Max)

VO_2 maximisation (or simply VO_2 max) is a measure of maximum ventilatory capacity, measured in millilitres of oxygen per kilogramme of (your) body weight per minute. We lose 1 to 0.1 point of VO_2 max a year starting from the age of 28 until death, an average of about 0.4 more if a person sits for hours each day or is overweight.

The highest human VO_2 max recorded was 97.5 for a cyclist taken in 2012. Most Olympic marathoners are in the mid- to high-70s. The highest VO_2 max for a domesticated animal is 150 for race horses, and for a mammal in the wild, up to 300 for a cheetah, which can run 60 to 70 miles an hour but only for about two minutes.

The best way to boost your VO_2 maximisation is to repeatedly run 1 mile as fast as you can. VO_2 is the greatest open secret of good runners and cyclists. The more oxygen you inhale, all other things being equal, the better and more clearly you can think, the farther you can run and the more you can stay alert and energised. Your brain consumes 20 to 25 per cent of your oxygen supply, so it makes sense to maximise your ability to ventilate every cell with oxygen. Aiming to boost and keep VO_2 max as high as possible for as long as possible is one of the major keys to keeping mentally alert in your golden, or senior, years.

Sarcopenia

Sarcopenia is the Greek term for "muscle poverty" or "muscle wasting". From the age of 30, we lose 1 per cent of our lean muscle mass each year. Skeletal muscle can be divided into fast twitch and slow twitch. In chickens, the fast twitch is typically the white meat and the slow twitch is the dark meat. In humans, fast twitch muscles decay faster than slow twitch, creating the problem of the elderly stumbling and being unable to catch themselves, and then falling down, or the problem of being unable to get up out of chairs.

Researchers have already shown that when older people eat, they cannot make muscle as fast as the young. Now they've found that the suppression of muscle breakdown is blunted with age. This may explain the ongoing loss of muscle in older people— when they eat, they don't build enough muscle and, in addition, their insulin fails to shut down the muscle breakdown that rises between meals and overnight.

A 2009 research study by the *American Journal of Clinical Nutrition* showed that three weight-training sessions per week over 20 weeks could rejuvenate blood flow in the extremities to the level of someone in their late 20s.

Osteopenia

Osteopenia is the Latin medical term for "bone loss, poverty or wasting". From the age of 30, women and most men lose about 1 per cent of bone mass a year. From age 40, however, osteopenia accelerates in women and, on average, they lose 2.5 per cent and more of bone mass from their spines and hips, making them often grow shorter and more prone to breaking a hip if they stumble and fall from sarcopenia. Breaking a hip is terrible for the elderly. In recent years, the mortality rate from breaking a hip after the age of 70 was a shocking 30 per cent within the first year and 50 per cent within 18 months of the fall.

Resistance training can combat this effect because as you put more tension on your muscles, the tension puts more pressure on your bones, which then respond by continuously creating fresh, new bone. In addition, as you build more muscle, and make the muscle that you already have stronger, you also put more constant pressure on your bones.

Neuropenia or Neural Degredation

Of all the linear decay factors, brain poverty or brain wasting is the scariest. From the age of 26 (or earlier), the average person will lose 1 to 2 grammes[12] of brain mass a year, increasing gradually, so that within 15 years (age 45) that person is losing at least 2 to 3 grammes a year. This increases to 3 to 4 grammes a year from age 60, 4 to 5 grammes a year from 75 and 5 to 6 grammes a year from 90.

A team of researchers from the University of California, Los Angeles (UCLA), discovered that obese, elderly individuals had 8 per cent lower brain mass than older people of normal weight. Additionally, people who were simply overweight had 4 per cent less brain volume than their slimmer counterparts.

---

12 1 gramme is the equivalent of 0.028 ounces. An eighth of an ounce is commonly accepted as a flat 3.5 grammes while 6 grammes is about half a tablespoon in imperial measurements.

In addition, being anxious, depressed, paranoid, suffering from trauma, divorce, violent crime or sustained emotional distress will further accelerate loss of brain mass. Blindness, deafness and lose of other senses, as well as loss of mobility, can also cause loss of brain mass.

Dr Daniel Amen, who claims to have reviewed over 75,000 SPECT (blood flow) brain scans in his medical research clinics, asserts that being overweight or obese will cause the loss of 4 to 8 per cent of brain mass. Amen notes that research from the University of Pittsburgh also found that the brains of overweight people—with body mass index (BMI) scores between 25 and 30—had 4 per cent less volume than brains of people with lower BMIs. In addition, brains of overweight subjects looked eight years older than those of healthy subjects. People who were obese—with BMI scores over 30—had 8 per cent less brain volume, and their brains looked 16 years older than those of healthy people.

> "We found that changing the brain also changed the body," Amen says. "Significantly, we also found that as weight goes up, brainpower goes down. The size and function of the brain diminishes as BMI goes up. This information should make everyone concerned about [his or her] weight... Fat can produce inflammatory chemicals that damage your brain. We found that the larger people were, the smaller their frontal lobes were, and that's a disaster because the frontal lobes run your life!"
>
> **Dr Daniel Amen, University of Pittsburgh**

The average human brain weighs 1,300 to 1,500 grammes (approximately 2.9 to 3.3 pounds). Although the brain accounts for only about 2 to 3 per cent of the total body weight of an adult, it consumes about 20 to 25 per cent of the body's oxygen supply. Interestingly, 60 per cent of a newborn's oxygen supply is consumed by the brain because the brain is doing huge equivalents of Bayesian analysis and other statistical/stochastic comparisons and learning to fully engage and interpret the data from their eyes, ears, nose, tongue, fingers, skin, etc.

The National Institute of Health studies of Dr Henrietta van Praag and her colleagues, as popularised by the writing of Harvard's John Ratey,[13] instruct us that if we run for at least 45 minutes at a pace which raises our heart rate to at least 75 per cent of its maximum, we will create new neural stem cells, primarily in the hippocampus. These new cells will last for about 21 days. In order for them to "wire" with other neurons and last longer, we would need to learn something new. "Neurons that fire together, wire together" is the neuroscientist's way of summarising this process.

One of the more exciting discoveries about exercise-induced neurogenesis is that the brain loses brain cells more rapidly in some areas than others. Amazingly and fortuitously, the areas that lose brain cells the soonest and fastest are also the areas that add brain cells back again at an accelerated rate. Over a dozen independent researchers have reported this effect.[14]

By doing specific exercises more regularly and maintaining a stricter diet, you can dramatically change your general health and your lifespan. The quantified self is just the start of a whole range of tools that we'll use in the future to improve our quality and length of life.

---

13 http://www.amazon.com/Spark-Revolutionary-Science-Exercise-Brain/dp/0316113514
14 *See* Shaun Clark's research for more information.

Rethinking Diagnosis and Augmenting Medicine

Today, one of the more contentious areas of health care is the very nature around the treatment of conditions and symptoms. Rather than remove the cause of many health issues, a great deal of energy in pharmaceuticals and medicine goes into combating the symptoms of a condition or disease. Part of this is based on the fact that we're not very good at removing these conditions permanently, and also partially due to the fact that drug companies tend to make more money out of ongoing treatment regimens rather than from something that eliminates the need for treatment.

Let's take cancer as an example.

At the beginning of the twentieth century, one person in twenty would get cancer. In the 1940s, it was one out of every sixteen people. In the 1970s, when President Nixon declared "War on Cancer", it was one person out of ten. Today, one person out of every two or three people gets cancer in the course of their life.[15] Yes, you read that right. The incidence of cancer in society has exploded in the last 100 years. Is that just better diagnosis?[16] No, it appears that more and more people are getting cancer.

To be fair, we have improved survivability of many types of cancer significantly, and that is expected to continue to improve. Based on growth and ageing of the US population, however, medical expenditures for cancer in the year 2020 are projected to reach at least US$180 billion, an increase of 27 per cent over 2010. If newly developed tools for cancer diagnosis, treatment and follow-up continue to be more expensive, medical expenditures for cancer could reach as high as US$207 billion.[17] There were an estimated 14.1 million cancer cases around the world in 2012; of these 7.4 million cases were in men and 6.7 million in women. This number is expected to increase to 24 million by 2035, so we need to find a cure for cancer. How will we get there?

15 Cancer Research UK
16 In his final State of the Union, President Obama announced a "moon shot" to cure cancer and appointed Vice-President Biden to lead the charge.
17 National Cancer Institute

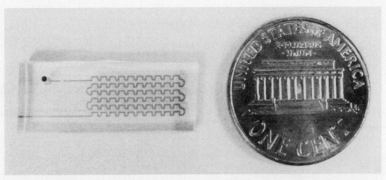

Figure 5.6: Microfluidic devices like this are just the start of a range of non-invasive chip-based diagnostic tools that replace traditional testing labs.

Microfluidics and Lab-on-a-Chip Diagnostics

As we mentioned earlier in the chapter, early diagnosis is probably the primary thing we can do to impact cancer survival rates over any other short-term strategy. To that end, technology has a significant role to play. A Harvard student may have just developed a technique that is a great example of this possible future.

In November 2015, 18-year-old Neil Davey won the silver medal in the undergraduate section of the National Inventors Hall of Fame's Collegiate Inventors Competition for his research project, "Early Cancer Diagnosis by the Detection of Circulating Tumor Cells using Drop-based Microfluidics". This non-invasive cancer detection method is representative of a whole slew of new technologies that come with enhanced computer power, chip-based diagnosis and improved sensor technologies.

The Harvard student utilised an emerging technique that involves injecting a tiny amount of blood into a microfluidic device to encapsulate single cells from the blood stream in individual drops. Some of these devices can use sample sizes as small as 100 nanometres. Davey then utilised a polymerase chain reaction (PCR), a common technique in molecular biology, to target and amplify fragments of cancer DNA within the microfluidic drops. By shining a laser onto the droplets, he was able to detect and quantify the brightness of the samples, indicating the presence (or not) of cancer DNA in a circulating tumour cell.

> "The advantage of this technology is that it is ultra-sensitive, so I can detect as few as one cancer cell from a billion normal cells in the blood... The process is also very specific. One can uniquely detect a wide range of cancers using this DNA amplification technology."
>
> Neil Davey, undergraduate student at John A. Paulson School of Engineering and Applied Sciences[18]

Previously, a biopsy of a tumour was the only way to properly and accurately diagnose the type of cancer, and this was extremely invasive, often requiring surgery. Microfluidics is safer, faster and a fraction of the cost of typical testing procedures that are in place today.

Microfluidics is going to radically change the way we think about health care and diagnosis. Think about pretty much any condition you might need to be tested for today—high cholesterol, diabetes, kidney or liver problems, iron deficiency, heart problems, sexually transmitted infections, anaemia, hepatitis, HIV and various viruses—and they are typically tested for either via blood being drawn or via urinalysis. With blood tests, it typically involves drawing a significant amount of blood to get accurate tests. Here is where technology advancements will dramatically change these tests.

While facing some controversy recently, the Silicon Valley

---

18 Harvard University, John A. Paulson School of Engineering and Applied Sciences

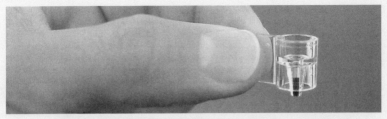

Figure 5.7: A microfluidic sample for using the DMI rHEALTH Tricorder

start-up Theranos was one of the first to really tackle this problem. Theranos has developed blood tests that can help detect dozens of medical conditions based on just a drop or two of blood drawn with a pinprick from your finger. At Walgreens pharmacies across the United States, you simply show a pharmacist your ID and a doctor's note, and you can have your blood drawn right there. From that one sample, several tests can be run often at a fraction of the cost of a typical pathology test. A typical lab test for cholesterol, for example, can cost $50 or more in the United States. The same Theranos test at Walgreens costs around US$3.

But why do we need to go to a place, such as a pharmacy or a doctor's surgery, at all? The winner of the 2014 Tricorder

Figure 5.8: The rHEALTH desktop tricorder (Credit: DMI and XPrize Foundation)

Figure 5.9: The Scanadu Scout Tricoder (Credit: Scanadu)

XPrize, created by Peter Diamandis and sponsored by the likes of Nokia and Qualcomm, was an eight-year-old company that has received grants and support from NASA, the National Institutes of Health, the Bill and Melinda Gates Foundation and many others. DNA Medical Institute (DMI) is the creator of a device called rHEALTH (short for Robot or Remote Health).

The rHEALTH diagnostic system requires a patient to provide just a single drop of blood. This drop of blood is dropped into a small receptacle, where nanostrips and reagents react to the blood's contents. The whole cocktail then goes through a spiral micro-mixer and is streamed past lasers that use variations in light intensity and scattering to come up with a diagnosis. You can then get the results delivered to your smartphone via Bluetooth.

The rHEALTH mobile unit is currently a desktop unit, but DMI is working on getting it down to the size of a tricorder that you could carry in the palm of your hand.

For other basic biomonitoring, the theme of the *Star Trek* Tricorder keeps coming up in developmental technology. The

Scanadu Scout Tricorder is a device that also links to your smartphone and can give you even more comprehensive "live" information than the likes of your fitness heart rate monitor.

The Scanadu Scout is a non-invasive biomonitoring system that measures physiological parameters such as temperature, heart rate, pulse oximetry and blood pressure. It does this by just touching a small portable device to your head, and sends the data to an app for analysis.

Scanadu's mission statement says everything about how technology is tackling the challenge of personal diagnosis:

> "To be the last generation to know so little about our health."

Today, there are already devices like the Illumina MiSeqDx, which is a desktop DNA sequencer. Ultimately within the next 20 years, each individual will be able to have access to a device that instantly sequences their DNA and compares it with known conditions, and can diagnose almost any health condition they might currently have due to a virus or other illness. If you have cancer, not only will that handheld device be able to diagnose the type of cancer with better accuracy than a doctor today, but it will also be able to sequence the genes of your specific cancer cells in real time and then send that data to a lab somewhere on the other side of the world to manufacture a specific, targeted, personalised medicine.

Personalised and Precision Medicine

Researchers at Washington University in St. Louis recently used gene sequencing[19] to compare healthy tissue to diseased tissue among three patients with advanced melanoma. By pinpointing

---

19 Beatriz M. Carreno et al., "A dendritic cell vaccine increases the breadth and diversity of melanoma neoantigen-specific T cells," *Science* 348, no. 6236 (15 May 2015): 803–808.

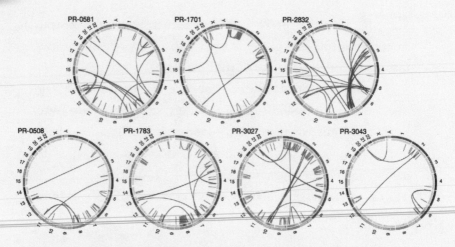

Figure 5.10: Seven different gene sequences of common prostate cancer
(Credit: *Nature* 470, no. 7332, February 2011)

each patient's unique protein mutations, the researchers were able to craft vaccines that increased the strength of the patients' cancer-killing T-cells.

Research in personalised medicine today focuses on analysing a patient's genome, but additionally on environmental, social, biometrical and religious influences, and then tailoring a treatment for each individual based on that data. The science is fundamentally about moving from a one-size-fits-all approach to where we design targeted medicines that are based on your DNA, body chemistry and how you are likely to respond to different chemicals or levels of treatment.

One possibility is figuring out the proper dose and strength of drugs for patients suffering with depression. Currently, treatment is somewhat hit and miss and requires physicians to try different doses of different medicines, monitoring the patient over a period of days or weeks, and then continuing to adjust the dosage until they get it right.

Gene-based information will help doctors prescribe much

more effective, accurate doses sequenced to DNA. So instead of using a drug like a selective serotonin reuptake inhibitor (SSRI) which attempts to control the way the body uses serotonin, personalised medicine would be able to stimulate the body to produce or reduce serotonin levels (and other neurotransmitters) to norms for your genotype. We expect to see similar advancements in painkillers, infectious disease therapies and drugs for neurological disorders such as epilepsy.

With improved genetic sequencing capability, we're realising that identifying a type of cancer, like prostate cancer, is not enough to accurately determine a form of treatment. Recent studies have shown that each individual patient with the same type of cancer may have very different genetic traits within their cancer. So personalised medicine is going to be a necessity for effective treatment in the future.

However, genomics is one small part of the ability to create personalised or precision medicine that works. Your big "health" data such as quantified self data, previous medical history, family history and lineage, locations you've lived, environmental influences you are regularly exposed to, previous blood tests, previous responses to different medicines and other such information are all going to be critical to the ability to target specific conditions or ailments with targeted, precision medicine. Indeed, the success of personalised medicine will likely hinge on improved, centralised access to electronic health records.

If you have concerns about sharing your data on your health, location history, previous medical treatments and so forth, be aware that this is going to radically restrict your ability for treatments in the future—the future of health care is about genes, sensors and data.

Bioaugmentation

If you want to understand gene therapy and augmenting our biology, it is helpful to think of our genetic code in a similar way to software. Within our DNA are specific instructions that produce the essential humanity of who we are. If our parents or ancestors had encoded in their DNA a deficiency of a certain protein, had genes that trigger specific conditions or were missing genes that prevent other conditions, then that "code" will produce either a specific mutation or result in a high probability of you contracting a disease. If we can learn to "edit" that code and reinsert it into our DNA in the proper sequence, we can fill required gaps, or simply remove errors.

CRISPR/Cas9 and TALEN Gene Editing

In 1987, biologists noted that bacteria possess a natural defence mechanism that recognises invading viruses. Then in 2000 to 2002, scientists recognised that bacteria not only responded to but also reacted by processing and dissembling the attacking virus DNA. They dubbed the process CRISPR, an acronym for "clustered regularly interspaced short palindromic repeats".

Between 2009 and 2012, CRISPR techniques were explored to optimise the cutting of DNA in virus candidates by examining the proteins that bacteria cells used in their immune defence. A protein called CRISPR associated protein 9 (Cas9) was discovered. Cas9 is no ordinary protein, it is a nuclease, an enzyme specialised for slicing DNA strands. It has two active cutting sites (HNH and RuvC), one for each strand of the DNA. By 2012, it was proposed that Cas9 could be used as a genome editing or engineering tool in human cell culture to possibly single out and destroy genes responsible for diseases like Parkinson's, Alzheimer's, diabetes, inherited cancers like breast cancer, immune deficiencies and so on. Right now, gene therapy is focused on monogenic diseases, or diseases that involve a single gene.

CRISPR/Cas9 not only makes cuts in DNA but also allows for new genetic sequences to be inserted. Scientists can then introduce an engineered virus or DNA plasmid with the required DNA sequence. A project spearheaded by researchers at the University of California, San Francisco, used CRISPR/Cas9 to edit HIV out of human T-cells. When HIV infects the body, it modifies the body's own immune system by changing the DNA of T-cells. With innovations in the Cas9 process, researchers were able to successfully edit the CXCR4- and PD-1-infected genes in the T-cells, replacing them with healthy cells. Modified T-Cells from healthy patients have been introduced via stem cell therapy before, boosting the immune system's response, but this was the first time that researchers were able to edit the HIV virus out of an existing patient's cells. In Philadelphia, researchers were able to make HIV patients resistant to the virus by removing the CCR-5 protein from white blood cells through gene therapy.

In March 2015, Chinese scientists announced that they had successfully used CRISPR techniques to modify the gene responsible for β-thalassaemia, a potentially fatal blood disorder, in non-viable human embryos. The Chinese team injected 86 embryos and then waited 48 hours. This allowed enough time for the CRISPR/Cas9 system and the molecules that replace the missing DNA to act, as well as for the embryos to grow to about eight cells each. Of the 71 embryos that survived, 54 were genetically tested. The testing revealed that just 28 were successfully spliced, and that only a fraction of those contained the replacement genetic material.

This not only raises fundamental ethical issues but also identifies the biggest criticism of CRISPR technology, in that it is still an inexact science. For gene therapy to be successful, it needs to be highly targeted, and to avoid any genetic contamination. This outcome may slowly become a possibility as researchers have recently devised a way to reduce off-target DNA binding of a class of gene editing proteins known as transcription activator-like effector nucleases (TALENs). This method allows scientists to evolve the proteins freely, which in turn makes them more specific and targeted over time.

Whichever technique leads to the breakthroughs scientists are working towards, it is likely that gene editing will dramatically improve over the next decade and become a standard method of treatment for any inherited disease or condition. We will no longer look to treat the symptoms of diseases but simply eliminate those conditions entirely.

Near-term Applications for Gene Therapy (2020–2030)

The applications for gene therapy are nothing short of stunning and completely revolutionary. This field is accelerating so rapidly that each week major new research announcements are made. At the time of printing, significant progress has been made using gene therapy in getting closer to treating or potentially curing the following conditions, to name but a few:

1. **Hearing:** deafness, hearing loss, tinnitus, Meniere's disease
2. **Sight:** congenital and degenerative blindness such as Leber's congenital amaurosis, retinal gene therapy, choroideremia
3. **Hereditary, genetic and autoimmune diseases:** neuromuscular disorders such as muscular dystrophy, amyotrophic lateral sclerosis (ALS), limb-girdle myasthenia (caused by the defective DOK 7 gene), Emery-Dreifuss muscular dystrophy, spinal muscular atrophy and myotubular myopathy; diseases such as Parkinson's

(by restoring delivery of glutamic acid decarboxylase), Alzheimer's and Friedreich's ataxia; even depression could be treated by restoring P11 brain proteins

4. **Cancer and blood disorders:** leukaemia, acute myeloid leukaemia, gliomas, pancreatic cancer, liver cancer, haemophilia, sickle-cell anaemia

5. **HIV:** Studies have shown that patients become resistant to HIV following the removal of the CCR-5 receptor protein in white blood cells.

6. **Heart and lung diseases:** celladon heart failure, calcium upregulation, congestive heart failure and peripheral arterial disease, cystic fibrosis, α_1-antitrypsin deficiency, asthma, acute respiratory distress syndrome (ARDS), pulmonary edema

With gene therapy, we will be able to correct errors in our DNA as well as remove diseases, deficiencies and hereditary conditions. That is an astounding possibility, and it is most definitely within reach of the sciences. If you combine gene therapy, stem cell therapy, sensor-based monitoring and other augmentation that will be available, the fact is that we will have more control over disease and its treatment than ever before. In fact, it is likely that we will make more progress curing disease over the next two decades than in the last one hundred years of medical science. By 2030, access to advance medical techniques and gene therapy will have potentially added another 20 to 30 years to the life expectancy of those living in developed nations.

Transgenics and Replacement Organs (2025–2040)

Once gene editing has been perfected, the next likely consideration is enhancing our biology by inserting improvements into our

DNA. Transgenics is a field in which human-animal hybrid genetic research is already developing some promising traction. While the ethics of inserting animal DNA into humans is obvious, the use of human DNA in animals doesn't have the same restrictions today.

The first successful transgenic animal was a mouse. Bred in 1982, this "supermouse" was created by inserting human growth hormone genes into fertilised mice embryos. Transgenic rabbits, pigs, goats, sheep, fish, cattle and, more recently, primates followed. The underlying principle in the production of transgenic animals is the introduction of a foreign gene or genes into an animal (the inserted genes are called transgenes). The foreign genes "must be transmitted through the germ line, so that every cell, including germ cells, of the animal contain the same modified genetic material."[20]

Take the following examples. Transgenic fish include salmon that grow about ten to eleven times faster than normal fish due to growth hormones and genetically modified freshwater zebrafish that carry a fluorescent protein gene from jellyfish which allows them to glow. Transgenic mice include those with amyloid precursor genes that exhibit the same brain conditions as patients with Alzheimer's and those biologically engineered to overexpress the NR2B receptor in their synaptic pathways, making them learn faster their entire life. Pigs genetically engineered today with at least five different human genes can conceivably grow organs for human transplant with low rejection rates, including hearts, lungs, kidneys and so forth. Transgenic cows that produce human lactoferrin and interferons in their milk are effectively a bovine/human milk hybrid while prion-free cows have been genetically engineered to be resistant to mad cow disease. Transgenic goats have been engineered that express spider silk in their milk.

20 "Transgenic Animals" from the Canadian Council on Animal Care

The use of transgenics in crops is expected to have huge benefits to food security, as genetically modified crops increase yield, provide robust protection against disease and address food scarcity driven by climate change.

> "Transgenic technologies—which enable
> the transfer of genes from one plant species
> to another to produce a plant with new or
> improved traits—hold the most promise for
> achieving food security in the next 15–20 years."
>
> National Intelligence Council, *Global Trends 2030:*
> *Alternative Worlds*, 2012

Transgenic technologies, which allow for the genetic intermingling of human and animal characteristics, could eventually lead to an almost endless array of human-animal hybrids. There is plenty to be envious about with regard to our non-human friends. Dogs hear and smell much better than we do, cats can see in the dark, some primates have better memorisation skills than us[21] and birds have remarkably strong vision. Looking ahead to the day when we can apply transgenic modifications to ourselves, many would-be transhumans would probably like to acquire, for instance, the eyes of a hawk, the scales of a lizard, the ability to swim like a dolphin or hold their breath like a crocodile.

In the *Mars* trilogy by Kim Stanley Robinson, the author proposed splicing animal genes into the DNA of the Mars colonists as part of a regular process of getting longevity treatments (which in themselves were corrective gene therapy editing out replication errors in genetic code and restoring telomeres). One of the characters added a cat-derived "purr"

---

21 http://www.baxterbulletin.com/viewart/20120625/NEWS01/306250010/Apes-monkeys-more-social-smarter-than-previously-thought

to her biology. Another trend theorised was the addition of crocodile haemoglobin to grant CO_2 tolerance for a partially terraformed red planet that was still poor in oxygen.

Advances in synthetic biology will likely result in production facilities making novel treatments and diagnostics agents. Advances in regenerative medicine almost certainly will parallel these developments in diagnostic and treatment protocols. For example, replacement organs, such as kidneys and livers, could be developed by 2030.

3D Bioprinting

As discussed in chapter 2, 3D printers have the potential for some incredible applications in the way we manufacture products, even at home, in the future. However, one specific application of 3D printing that holds huge promise in the field of medicine is bioprinting. Bioprinting in its simplest form is using a 3D printer to "print" an organ, bone or muscle tissue to replace damaged parts of your body. One of the more exciting applications is being

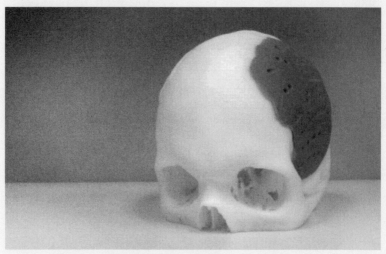

Figure 5.11: 3D-printed "bone" is commonly used in facial reconstruction surgery.
(Credit: Osteofab)

applied to regenerative medicine to address the need for tissues and organs suitable for transplantation. 3D printing has already been used widely in facial reconstruction surgery.

Compared with non-biological printing, 3D bioprinting involves additional complexities, such as the choice of materials, cell types, growth and differentiation factors, and technical challenges related to the sensitivities of living cells and tissue and vasculature construction.

Addressing these complexities requires the integration of technologies from the fields of engineering, biomaterials science, cell biology, physics and medicine. 3D bioprinting has already been used for the generation and transplantation of several tissues, including multilayered skin, bone, vascular grafts, tracheal splints, heart tissue and cartilaginous structures. Other applications include developing high-throughput 3D-bioprinted tissue models for research, drug discovery and toxicology.

3D printing has already been used in numerous medical procedures. For example, in 2012, physicians at the University of Michigan successfully utilised 3D printing to construct a synthetic trachea for three-month-old Kaiba Gionfriddo, who suffered from recurrent airway collapses.[22] Other successes include printing bone to replace one patient's jaw and part of the skull in another patient. As a developing industry, 3D printed body parts generated over US$500 million in revenue for companies globally in 2014, and that is expected to double by 2016.

In 2006, Wake Forest University's Dr Anthony Atala was successful in using inkjet printers to "grow" replacement bladders. The process for growing each patient's organ began with a biopsy to get samples of muscle cells and the cells that line the bladder walls. These cells were grown in a culture in the laboratory until

---

22 David A. Zopf et al., "Bioresorbable Airway Splint Created with a Three-Dimensional Printer," *New England Journal of Medicine* 368, no. 21 (2013): 2043–2045.

there were enough cells to place onto a specially constructed biodegradable mould, or scaffold, shaped like a bladder. The scaffold was designed to degrade as the bladder tissue integrated with the body. Testing showed that the engineered bladders functioned as well as bladders that are repaired with intestine tissue, but with none of the side effects. Today, the patients are all still doing well.

Other candidates for regenerative medicine and 3D-printed organ replacement are organs like the thyroid, kidney and liver. Atala was able to create mini "hearts", about 0.25 millimetres in size, by reprogramming human skin cells into heart cells, which were then clumped together in a cell culture. A 3D printer was then used to give them the desired shape and size. Furthermore, in March 2015, the Russian bioprinting company Skolkovo successfully 3D printed a thyroid gland for a mouse and transplanted it. The company has said it is on track to print a human kidney by 2018.

With all of these potential bio-enhancements, we will be able to literally engineer a near-perfect human specimen in the next 30 to 40 years. Many humans will likely be genetically error free, with the ability to live much longer lifespans, while the medical community will be able to attack cancers or disease on an individual genome basis, along with correcting degraded cellular or organ health through organs built to your own unique specification. This all sounds like science fiction, but many of these technologies are already within our grasp.

Chapter 6

The Augmented Man

" . . . the idea of the future being different from the present is so repugnant to our conventional modes of thought and behavior that we, most of us, offer a great resistance to acting on it in practice."

John Maynard Keynes, 1937

We Can Rebuild Him

Hugh Herr was born to climb. By the age of eight, he had scaled the face of the 12,000-foot Mount Temple in the Canadian Rockies. At the age of 17, the climbing community considered Herr one of the best on the east coast of the United States.[1] In January 1982, Herr and his climbing companion Jeff Batzer were ascending a highly technical ice route on Mount Washington when a blizzard set in. Disoriented and facing temperatures of -29° Centigrade (-20° Fahrenheit) and

1 *Rock and Ice*

100-mile-per-hour winds, the pair attempted to descend but found themselves stuck in a glacial valley known as the Great Gulf. Trying to find a way down the mountain, they stumbled across tracks from a snowmaking machine. They followed the tracks, which mistakenly led them further north, away from safety and civilisation.

For three nights, the two climbers were exposed to the elements, unable to return down the mountain. In an attempt to cross an iced-over river, Herr fell through the ice and struggled to extract himself. They eventually found a cove where they were partially protected from the wind. When rescuers finally found them, both climbers were in dire straits. It was clear that Herr wouldn't have lasted another 24 hours. It was also clear that rescuers couldn't move him in his condition, so they called for a military helicopter to airlift the two climbers to a hospital in New Hampshire. Once there, despite attempts to save them, both of Herr's legs had to be amputated below the knees due to severe frostbite damage. He was devastated. For all intents and purposes, Herr's climbing career was over.

After his climbing came to an abrupt halt, Herr applied himself to learning. He studied physics at his local college and went on to do a masters in mechanical engineering at MIT, followed by a PhD in biophysics at Harvard University. He used that knowledge to pursue a career in bionics and robotic prosthetic development and is now the director of the Biomechatronics Group at the MIT Media Lab. Today, Herr describes himself as completely artificial from the knees down:

> "I'm titanium, carbon, silicon, a bunch of nuts
> and bolts," Herr said during an interview on
> NPR.[2] "My limbs that I wear have 12 computers,

---

2 "The Double Amputee Who Designs Better Limbs," NPR Radio, aired 10 August 2011.

five sensors and muscle-like actuator systems
that able me to move throughout my day."

Dr Hugh Herr

The unexpected outcome of the accident was that Herr was able to design, and then progressively improve on the design of advanced prosthetics. This not only allowed him to climb again, but actually made him a far better climber than he had been prior to the accident. Climbing is an extremely competitive sport, so when he began to surpass his able-limbed colleagues, some of them threatened to amputate their own legs so that they could keep up with him.[3]

The prosthetics that Herr designed for rock climbing do not look like normal prosthetics. After trying to create a foot and put a climbing shoe over it, he realised that he didn't need the shoe at all, and that he didn't need to make the feet of the prosthetics mimic human feet. Therefore, he cut off the heel to reduce weight, increased his legs' stiffness where it was useful, started optimising the angle of the foot relative to the calf of the prosthesis, added spikes for ice climbing and made the feet narrow enough to stick in small cracks as well as small—the size of baby feet. This ultimately gave him an unassailable advantage in the climb over his non-augmented competitors.

When Herr describes his prosthetics he uses words like a "beautiful machine", "advanced", "upgradeable", "engineered" and even "immortal". He predicts that when he is 80 years old, he will be able to walk better and with less energy than a person who has biological legs. In a sense, his mechanical body can be continuously upgraded while his biological body is in slow decline.

3 Hugh Herr interview on *Who Says I Can't?* aired July 2012

The 3D-printed Bionic Man

Perhaps the most common such augmentations historically were devices like crutches or walking sticks, or even the "ear trumpet" of the early 17th century[4] which was designed to assist the partially deaf to hear better. The first prosthetic limb to be discovered was an artificial toe on the foot of a noble woman, dating back to around 900 BC, that was made out of wood and leather. Today, we use many technologies routinely that improve quality of life such as insulin pumps, pacemakers, dialysis machines, laser vision correction and so on. The difference between these augmentations and the prosthetic augmentations of Dr Hugh Herr are really semantics in many ways. Simply put, we've been in the business of augmenting our bodies for thousands of years.

One of the most spectacular areas of development in prosthetics in recent years has been the advent of 3D-printed artificial limbs. In the past, it was expensive and complex to create a functional prosthetic. Then 3D printers (which are also robots!) came into the hands of hackers and "makers". Soon, individuals were designing and building robotic parts for themselves, friends and families. The open source nature of the 3D-printing community meant that people shared their designs, and advances in these designs began to accelerate at an amazing pace. Complex hands and arms that were prohibitively expensive for many, if not most, in the past began to be available for hundreds of dollars or less per limb. The number of people working on prosthetic designs increases daily and soon it can be assumed that these augmented prosthetic limbs will enhance the wearers past the limitations of the original limbs.

Printed prostheses are being developed with anatomically correct shapes along with cosmetic details such as freckles,

---

4 The earliest description of an ear trumpet appears to have been given by French Jesuit priest and mathematician Jean Leurechon in his work *Récréations mathématiques* dating back to 1624.

fingerprints, painted nails, hair and even tattoos. Lifelike prosthetics could help assuage the emotional trauma that comes with the loss of a limb, especially if they carry nerve impulses to the brain and enable feeling and direct neural control, but more importantly these limbs will be largely indistinguishable from those we are born with.

Others are taking the approach of personalising their prosthetics via 3D-printing technology. Companies like UNYQ, a Singularity University sponsored start-up, has been experimenting with designs of prosthetics as fashion statements.

Latvian-born singer and model Viktoria Modesta released her first music video on the UK's Channel 4 in 2014, in which she confidently performed in a series of personalised prosthetic legs. The primary prosthetic shown was a simple black cone ending in a dramatic spike, a second lit with LEDs and others with various ornate designs. Used to dramatic effect, Modesta's prosthetics have become part of her performance.

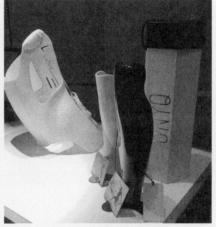

Figure 6.1: 3D-printed prosthetics are not only cheap but also allow for customisation and individual design.

In March 2015, the actor Robert Downey Jr, who is well known for his portrayal of Tony Stark in Marvel's *Iron Man* and *Avengers* franchises, gave his support to a Microsoft initiative called the Collective Project. Downey was asked by the group to reprise his role as Tony Stark to present a next-generation 3D-printed robotic arm to seven-year-old Alex Pring, a Central Florida boy who is missing his right arm from just above his

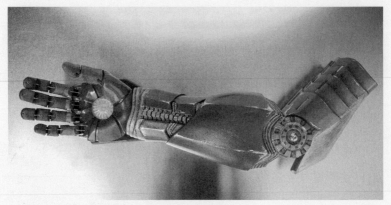

Figure 6.2: This *Iron Man*-themed prosthetic limb was 3D printed for around US$350.
(Credit: Microsoft Collective Project)

elbow. The arm, made by Limbitless Solutions,[5] was designed to look like Iron Man's robotic enhanced suit and cost just US$350 to print. Quite an achievement when a prosthetic might often sell for more than US$40,000.

A 3D-printed bionic hand designed by prosthetics start-up Open Bionics was the recipient of the 2015 UK James Dyson Award for design engineering innovation. What makes the Open Bionics hand stand out is its design, which enables it to be cheaper and faster to produce than many of the prosthetics currently available for amputees. Taking just 40 hours to 3D print, the robotic hand is built from custom pieces designed to fit amputees' limbs precisely, and uses electromyographic sensors, which detect muscle movement, to control the hand. By flexing their muscles, wearers can choose whether to open and close the hand or grip objects. Although currently available for under US$3,000, the price of prosthetics like this is getting cheaper, fast.

Prosthetics are getting smarter as well, or more specifically bionic limbs (robot-enhanced prosthetics) are getting smart. At Northwestern University, a thought-controlled robotic leg

---

5   A volunteer group started by Albert Manero, a PhD engineering student from the University of Central Florida

is being developed that recently allowed a man who'd lost his leg in a motorcycle accident to climb 103 flights of stairs to the top of Chicago's Willis Tower. This particular prosthesis also decodes electromyographic signals from natively innervated and surgically re-innervated thigh muscles to determine and execute the patient's intended movements. The leg will be available for widespread use in 2018.

The Symbionic Leg is the world's first complete bionic leg for people with an above-knee amputation. Tested for more than a year, the Symbionic Leg became commercially available on a limited basis late in 2014. According to the developer Össur, the integrated prosthesis combines a microprocessor knee and powered microprocessor ankle with proactive ankle flexion. The prosthesis automatically adapts to individual walking styles and is designed to help amputees avoid falls while tackling uneven terrain such as slopes and stairs.

An interesting—and somewhat contentious—concept is that we are potentially getting to the point where users of prosthetics no longer have a disability, but instead may have an advantage over so-called able-bodied humans. Let's take a moment to consider this scenario.

Prior to being convicted of culpable homicide related to the death of his girlfriend Reeva Steenkamp, South African athlete Oscar Pistorius was better known as the "Blade Runner". At Paralympic level, he holds multiple world records and medals for 400-metre, 4 x 400-metre relay, 100-metre, 4 x 100-metre and 200-metre distances. In 2011, Pistorius competed in the International Association of Athletics Federations (IAAF) World Championships in Athletics held in Daegu, South Korea, where he won a silver medal for the 4 x 400-metre men's relay competing side by side with able-bodied athletes. He went on to qualify for the 2012 Summer Olympics in the 400 metres and 4 x 400-metre relay on behalf of the South African team. Not in the Paralympics, but in the primary games, against able-bodied competitors. Before this feat, his 400-metre wins in 2011 had already put Pistorius in the top 10 to 15 runners in the world.[6]

Interestingly, Pistorius almost didn't make it to the World Championships or the Summer Olympics because the IAAF initially denied his participation in mainstream competition. Not because he was disabled, but because it was feared that his artificial limbs *might give him an unfair advantage* over other competitors. With advances like those of Hugh Herr's team at MIT, Symbionic and others, it is clear that this is not the last time that we'll have to address this question.

The video game series *Deus Ex* deals with this question in its vision of the future (2027–2052). In this future world, people willingly take on enhanced limbs and other body modifications because these technology-based augmentations give them capabilities better than what they were born with. If Moore's Law is applied to bionics in the same way as computers and smartphones, then better-than-standard-human prosthetics is something that we will have to deal with in the next decade. Do we need laws prohibiting able-bodied humans from willingly undergoing an amputation so that they can attach a better performing prosthetic limb? Is this simply going to be a personal preference in the future, like getting your teeth whitened?

A hundred years ago, this would have all sounded like science fiction, but with 1,500 amputee US soldiers having returned from Iraq and Afghanistan, the augmentation of humans has not just become a technological problem to solve but a social necessity too. To add to these figures, in the United States alone, more than 11,000 spinal cord injuries involve paraplegia, but

6 Yahoo, 21 July 2011

it is estimated by the World Health Organization (WHO) that 250,000 to 500,000 people suffer spinal cord injuries (SCI) annually. By 2055, almost 40 per cent of the Japanese population will be aged 65 years or above and many will require mobility assistance. All of these cases cited require not only prosthetics, but also the development of technologies like exoskeletons that can restore full body movement.

3D Systems and Ekso Bionics are already pioneering the field of robotic exoskeletons. Working together, these companies have designed a 3D-printed robotic suit called the Ekso, which is aimed at helping patients overcome paralysis. This bionic exoskeleton is used in rehabilitation centres worldwide to help people who have lost the ability to walk due to a stroke, injury or developmental conditions such as cerebral palsy. Another breakthrough is Argo Medical's ReWalk, a computerised, exoskeleton that is strapped onto a person's lower torso. This exoskeleton can help people with SCI, spina bifida and other lower-limb disabilities stand, walk and climb stairs.

DARPA and the US military have been working on similar concepts for infantry so that the troops can carry much greater loads over longer distances, as well as potentially carry much heavier armaments. We've seen such depictions in movies ranging from the Robot Cargo Loader in *Aliens* through to Tom Cruise in *Edge of Tomorrow*. Developments of this type in the military often inspire commercial application but, in this case, we're seeing parallel development of these technologies in the commercial sector. As discussed in chapter 4, Japan, in particular, has a significant interest in providing health care and ongoing mobility for its ageing population. As a result, the country has committed itself to the advancement of robotics to solve such problems for its ageing population rather than support the immigration of healthcare workers from other countries into Japan.

Brain–Machine Interfaces

Many of these emerging technologies will require the ability to interface with the brain for control. This requires development of machine-brain interfaces and will eventually lead to significant work in neural implants and sensory feedback.

For 12 years following a horrific car accident, Canadian Scott Routley was confined to a hospital bed with brain injuries that left doctors describing his condition as a "vegetative state". He would wake up in the morning and go to sleep at night but showed no response to any stimuli whatsoever. That was until British neuroscientist Professor Adrian Owen put Routley in a functional magnetic resonance imaging (fMRI) machine and successfully measured his brain activity in response to a series of questions. Since then, Owen has proven that roughly one in five patients in a vegetative state can respond to stimulus and answer questions using this method.

Erik Sorto was shot in the back in 2002 and paralysed from the neck down. During a five-hour operation in 2013, surgeons at the University of Southern California's Keck School of Medicine implanted two chips into Sorto's brain atop a few hundred specialised neurons. Developed by Caltech neurobiologist Richard Andersen and his colleagues, this type of chip is a neural implant that allows Sorto to control a robot arm via a connection from the chips implanted in his brain. The technology is still in its infancy, but after a few months of training, Sorto is now able to use the robotic arm to play "rock, paper, scissors", shake hands, drink beer and do more advanced tasks like making a smoothie.

Figure 6.3: Colorado man Les Baugh with dual robotic prosthetics controlled by thought (Credit: John Hopkins APL)

A DARPA-sponsored project has gone even further. Les Baugh lost both his arms at the shoulder 40 years ago in an electrical accident. DARPA, in partnership with the Applied Physics Laboratory (APL) at John Hopkins, has worked for over a decade on developing prosthetic limbs that can be linked to the body's nervous system. Unlike Sorto who uses a neural implant, Baugh had to undergo a procedure called targeted muscle reinnervation, which reassigned the nerves that once controlled his arms and hands. The team then mapped nerve impulses correlated to brainwaves using virtual simulations. APL had to design custom sockets for his torso in order to attach the robotic limbs. After just ten days of training, Baugh was able to pick up objects, move cups from one shelf to another and even control both limbs simultaneously. At the moment, Baugh is only able to use the robotic arms at APL, but the next stage is for John Hopkins to develop portable units.

Brain–computer interfaces that monitor brainwaves through electroencephalography (EEG) have already made their way into the commercial market. NeuroSky's headset uses EEG readings as well as electromyography (EMG), or the recording of twitches and other muscular movements, to pick up signals about a person's level of concentration to control toys and games. Emotiv Systems sells a headset that reads EEG and facial expression to enhance the experience of gaming. The Puzzlebox Orbit is a remote brain-controlled helicopter that is operated with an EEG headset.

An EEG headset in a hospital today may have a hundred or more electrodes that attach to the scalp with a conductive gel, and costs tens of thousands of dollars. NeuroSky, on the other hand, uses sensors the size of a thumbnail that don't require conductive gel and could be put into a headset that retails for as little as US$20. Other start-ups are also building prototypes of toys that use EMG and electrooculography (EOG), which measures changes in the retina. The most immediate application of this will be positive feedback in the gaming environment based on where you are looking and what emotions you are showing. This technology will pretty quickly build sensor networks that will not only be able to tell whether you are happy, scared or sad, but will even be able to determine if you are lying or telling the truth.

It's likely to be another ten years before technology like the neural implant that Sorto uses is refined enough for the commercial market. Given the advances in neural implants and technology like robotic exoskeletons though, it will become the norm to see paralysed patients walking again next decade. However, gaming consoles and devices like the tablets we use today combined with some form of neural interface is likely within the next few years. Not just for entertainment, but for treating autism, brain damage, physical disabilities and neurological disorders. Will your smartphone of the future enable you to reply to a text just because you think it? Conceivably, but you'd need to have a neural implant.

Instead of being regarded merely as technology to heal or restore function though, increasingly people are simply starting to augment their lives and decision-making with technology. From googling something, using a GPS to find your way home or wearing a fitness monitor, augmented decision-making is becoming commonplace.

Right now, we're augmenting ourselves for recreation and entertainment. Skydivers are wearing wingsuits to enable them to glide or "fly" while simultaneously recording their flights on GoPro cameras that mimic their own bird's eye view of the descent. As early as 1952, Major Christian Lambertsen of the U.S. Army Medical Corps was working on self-contained underwater breathing apparatus, or SCUBA for short. Today, we are working on artificial gills to reduce the equipment we need to survive underwater. Mankind has been obsessed with improving our ability to move, see and hear for centuries. The technologies now available to us mean such augmentations are limited only by our imagination.

How will this map out over the next 20 to 30 years? Can we live independently of technology or will we choose to become increasingly augmented, merging man and machine ever more?

Sensors, Wearables, Ingestibles and Feedback Loops

As mentioned in chapter 3, heart disease is one of the single most common causes of death in the developed world. As a result, heart health is one of the biggest disciplines in medicine globally today, second only to cancer and cancer research. It is just one of the areas set to be fundamentally changed by the technology of sensors and the Internet of Things.

A Parisian doctor named René Théophile Hyacinthe Laënnec (1781–1826) invented the first stethoscope in 1816 to "assist with auscultation", or listening to a patient's heartbeat. In 1851, the stethoscope went binaural, and since has had minor adjustments, including even electronic amplification. The next major leap in heart health monitoring, having been used in medicine for more than a century already, was the ECG machine.

In chapter 3, we introduced the Samsung Simband, a wearable with sensors capable of matching the accuracy of a heart rate monitor in an intensive care ward. Heart rate sensors can be placed not just on the wrist but can also be embedded into our everyday environment, including clothing and furniture potentially.

Under Armour and Zephyr Technologies have already developed the E39[7] smart biometric compression shirt for professional athletes with a heart rate band built into the clothing. The sensor-equipped shirt measures an athlete's performance including heart rate, metabolism, body position and lung capacity. The data doesn't just allow coaches and trainers to customise athletes' workouts without risking strain or injury, it could also theoretically be broadcast onto a stadium display to engage spectators in a new way. Could instant recall of a player's breathing rate, time taken to return to resting heart rate or acceleration become the new performance statistics?

At CES 2016, Under Armour released a slew of new smart fitness technologies including the UA Band (a Fitbit competitor, but designed to measure multiple types of workouts), UA Scale (a smart scale that measures not only your weight, but also body fat percentage), SpeedForm Gemini 2 trainers (connected

---

7   Kevin Plank, CEO and founder of Under Armour, has said it was such named because it was based on the 39th prototype that they had produced.

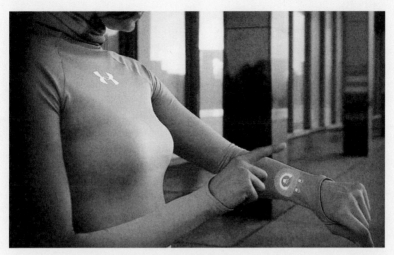

Figure 6.4: Under Armour is very serious about developing smart clothing.
(Credit: Under Armour)

footwear) and new apps. Under Armour already has 160 million users[8] across its various fitness apps, collecting a ton of workout and fitness data daily from a range of sensors.

We've talked a lot about wearables like the Apple Watch throughout the book, but the reality is that we're unlikely to start loading ourselves up with more and more devices in the future. It's far more likely that our existing clothes, glasses, contact lenses and watches will all be simply *augmented* and that such personal technology will become less cumbersome, less invasive over time.

A Canadian TV series called *Continuum* showed a possible future of the augmented man from the year 2077. Inspired by the work of 2015 National Design Award winner and MIT artist/scientist John Underkoffler, the show focuses around the City Protective Services (CPS), a law enforcement agency in the North American Union (a future government and economic construct similar to the European Union). One of the main characters wears a CPS suit, which is made from copper,

8   Lauren Goode, "Under Armour and HTC want to sell you a box full of fitness products," *Verge*, 5 January 2016. *See also* Lorraine Mirabella, "Under Armour raises the Bar on Digital Fitness," *Baltimore Sun*, 9 January 2016.

carbon nanofibres and other metamaterials. The ultimate in smart clothing, it contains displays, advanced sensors including forensic data processing and full biometrics and medical suite to deal with injuries, a magnetic field generator, taser, piezoelectric generation, body armour, some exoskeleton capabilities and even a cloaking capability, all of which work in tandem with the user's neural interface called a cellular memory review/recall, or CMR.

We might be 50 to 60 years away from that envisioned future, but we're already working on the foundations of these technologies. At Google's annual developer conference in 2015, it was announced that Google's Advanced Technology and Projects Group (ATAP) is working on a fabric that can sense touch gestures. Codenamed Project Jacquard, the initiative includes support from Levi's and other manufacturers. To move beyond novelty requires a yarn that can seamlessly work on existing industrial looms. ATAP has been working with textile experts in places like Japan to create a conductive yarn that can withstand the industrial weaving process while also look good enough to make real clothes.

The idea is to make smart clothing that is easy to manufacture and works with existing devices. Google's Ivan Poupyrev demonstrated to developers at Google I/O 2015 a beige jacket made by tailors in London that was able to process gestures and other data. About 15 per cent of the fabric used to make the jacket was ATAP-derived conductive yarn. Poupyrev said at the event that "you would not call it a wearable, you would call it a jacket".[9]

Ten of the typical smart clothing related innovations that are either available or being worked on today include:

- motion detecting pants/trousers
- proximity sensing shirts

- heart sensing bras
- smart running shoes
- networked jacket
- neural transmitting headset/helmet
- bionsensing underwear
- armoured clothing to prevent injury
- nanofibres (various)

As sensors get smarter and smaller, of course, we might not need to "wear" them at all.

Researchers at Stanford University have also developed a new type of wearable sensor that makes heart monitoring very affordable, extremely simple to apply and very low impact to patients. Developed by Zhenan Bao, a professor of chemical engineering, the paper-thin, stamp-sized sensor is made with flexible organic materials and can be worn under an adhesive bandage (or a plaster) on the wrist to monitor the pulse.

Another advancement has taken place in Switzerland where a team of scientists at École polytechnique fédérale de Lausanne

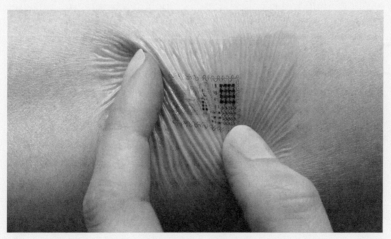

Figure 6.5: Sensors like this will be commonplace in ten years' time.

(EPFL) has developed the world's smallest medical implant to monitor critical chemicals in the blood. The 14-millimetre device measures up to five indicators including proteins like troponin that show if a heart attack will occur or has occurred. Using Bluetooth, the device can then transmit the data to a smartphone for tracking. The device can also track levels of glucose, lactate and adenosine triphosphate (ATP), providing valuable data for physiologic monitoring during various types of activities or monitoring for possible disease conditions like diabetes.

Proteus has already developed an ingestible sensor that is capable of monitoring your internal health. Formerly known as the Proteus Ingestible Event Marker (IEM), the Proteus ingestible sensor can be embedded in a pill and is activated and powered by stomach fluid, which then transmits a signal through the body to a paired skin patch. The sensor, which is the size of a grain of sand, has already been validated for safety and performance in preclinical and human clinical testing for heart failure, hypertension, mental health, transplantation, diabetes and tuberculosis. The skin patch also independently measures patient vitals and physical activity, such as movement, exercise, etc., and wirelessly sends all of the data from the sensor and patch to the Proteus app on your smartphone.

Proteus calls this combination of app, sensor and path the Raisin System. The system collects and aggregates behavioural, physiologic and therapeutic metrics, such as medication adherence, heart rate, sleep patterns, physical activity and stress levels. The data can be shared not only with the patient or user but also with a healthcare professional who has been given the appropriate authority by the patient.

The sensor is constructed from biodegradable materials found in the food chain so it is safe and non-toxic.

"The IEM has two materials which, when they come in contact with stomach fluids, provide power to the IEM. The IEM varies the current flow between the two materials to generate a digital signal which can be detected...The IEM contains no battery, antenna or radio, but rather uses the body to power the device and to pass along the unique, pill-specific signal in a private manner that is far superior to complicated, expensive and privacy-challenged approaches like RFID."

Mark Zdeblick, CTO at Proteus and co-inventor

Applying Moore's Law to implants like this, within five to ten years, this sensor will be reduced to a twentieth of its existing size, injectable and move throughout your bloodstream transmitting health data. Combined with AI, such sensors will be able to anticipate emerging issues and, in tandem with either a wearable device or your personal smartphone, could contact medical authorities to help you in times of distress. Future devices might even administer treatment directly into the bloodstream.

Figure 6.6: Proteus has already developed a pinhead-sized ingestible sensor.

AliveCor, a private heart health technology firm in San Francisco, is working to deskill the process of determining characteristics of arrhythmia, or an irregular heartbeat. Within its app, the company already has an FDA-approved algorithm that can detect the presence of atrial fibrillation. Its app also works to log the context around irregular heart activity, for example, how often it is linked to coffee consumption or stress.

> "In the next few years, I believe that the industry will be able to spot the characteristics of someone who's likely to have a heart attack in the next three days."
>
> Euan Thomson, CEO of AliveCor

While there is an interface on devices like the Samsung Simband device, the ECG data that the sensors collect, married with algorithms that can interpret the ECG data and use that data to predict a heart health event, are the real magic here. You don't manually key this data into these feedback loops, like we used to with keyboards, and you don't need a doctor to collect the data. Instead sensors collect the data automatically, every minute of every day.

If you are experiencing chest pains and visit a doctor, he can only verify what is happening with your heart at that single moment in time, whereas these new technologies enable a longitudinal view of your heart health, constantly compared with your long-established baseline (or even peer group data for your age group, etc.). A doctor just can't compete with that level of data collection capability. Admittedly, the doctor would probably be your first port of call should your smartwatch or sensor-net detect an imminent heart attack, but the critical element here is the data available to the doctor. He'll be better able to treat you not because he's a great doctor or has immense experience in treating heart attacks, but because he can see a gradual change in your heart health over time.

Some have expressed concern that this might just be another reason for an insurer to refuse you insurance, but likely the opposite will be true. Soon there will be a time when an insurer will refuse to insure you *if you don't wear sensors* because you'll simply be too *risky* to insure—there will be no reliable method to assess your ongoing health outside of sensors, but more importantly there will be no way to mitigate health risks in real time.

Given the extremely low costs of such sensors, along with the ubiquity of smartphones, it will be cheaper in the future to issue every person with a sensor and basic healthcare AI cover than any other strategy. Before your political sensitivities get all out of joint, this is not a play for socialism; it is just another example of Moore's Law at play. If it costs pennies for a sensor, linked to an AI, that improves people's health, makes diagnosis more accurate and reduces healthcare costs to the state, it would take some extraordinary political backlash to prevent a future where sensors are part of the healthcare system.

You might be thinking privacy will be what kills this type of technology, but remember that our children already have a very different view from that of our grandparents regarding privacy. The topic of privacy will be tackled in chapter 10.

Enhancing our Senses

Perhaps the earliest augmentation of our human senses was developments in glasses and then telescopes. Glasses date back to 13th-century Italy but were only commonplace by the 1700s. Monks and scholars reportedly wore the earliest glasses, given the detailed nature of their work. The early glasses were held in front of the eyes or balanced on the nose, evolving from magnifying glasses. The invention of the movable-type printing press in 1452, the growing rate of literacy and the availability of books encouraged new designs and the eventual mass production of inexpensive glasses. However, once lens technology appeared, using glass to magnify vision quickly became an application of the technology.

Roger Bacon is said to have invented the magnifying glass around the year 1250. Evidence points to the first compound microscope (combining convex and concave lenses) appearing in the Netherlands in the late 1590s at the height of the Dutch empire. The first person to apply for a patent for a telescope was a Dutch spectacle maker named Hans Lippershey. In 1608, Lippershey laid claim to inventing a device that increased magnification by three times. His telescope had a concave eyepiece aligned with a convex objective lens. One story goes that he got the idea for his design after observing two children in his shop holding up two lenses that made a distant weather vane appear close. Others claimed at the time that he stole the design from another spectacle maker, Zacharias Jansen. A few years later, Galileo Galilei perfected the first device to carry the name "microscope", a phrase reportedly coined by Galileo's associate Giovanni Faber, a German papal doctor, botanist and art collector.

A fundamental law of optics known as the diffraction limit, first described in 1873, states that the resolution of a microscope could never be better than half the wavelength of light being looked at. For visible light, that limit is about 0.2 millionths of a metre, 1/500th the width of a human hair. Thus, it seemed highly unlikely that it would ever be possible to image the details of bacteria and cells, DNA or individual proteins.

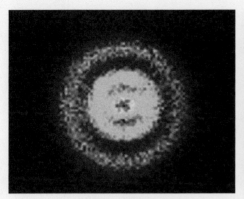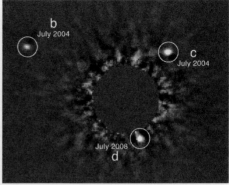

Figure 6.7: The image on the left is the quantum structure of a hydrogen atom as photographed by a photonic-force microscope while the image on the right depicts three exoplanets orbiting a distant star. (Credits: FOMA and Gemini Planetary Imager)

This improbability has now become a reality. In 2014, Eric Betzig, William Moerner and Stefan Hell won the Nobel Prize in Chemistry for their design of a super-resolved fluorescence, electron microscope that broke the 1873 diffraction limit, allowing optical microscopy into the nanodimension range. A year earlier, in 2013, the American Physical Society published the first ever image of the quantum wave functions of a hydrogen atom, showing what is known as "Stark" states (no relation to Tony).[10] Using a quantum microscope developed at the FOM Institute for Atomic and Molecular Physics (AMOLF) in the Netherlands, the research team was able to use photoionisation and an electrostatic magnifying lens to directly observe the electron orbitals of an excited hydrogen atom. Galileo would be proud.

Modern quantum electron microscopes use a technique called squeezed light in which quantum mechanics (and the Heisenberg uncertainty principle) are used to create a beam where the intensity of all the light waves in the beam are reduced, forcing them to all have a similar phase. Researchers believe that they will be able to photograph quantum states down to a nanometre or less using this technique.

10 A. S. Stodalna et al., "Hydrogen Atoms under Magnification: Direct Observation of the Nodal Structure of Stark States," *Physical Review Letters* 110, 213001 (May 2013).

At the other extreme, we're now using exoplanet hunting telescope technology like NASA's Kepler, the Gemini Planet Imager (GPI) or the Transiting Exoplanet Survey Satellite (TESS), which is due for launch in 2017, to not just measure planets orbiting other suns, but even image them. As of December 2015, we've already discovered 1,900 planets orbiting stars outside our own solar system, or exoplanets as they are known, with another 4,700 candidates currently being reviewed.[11]

We've augmented our vision to peer into the structure of the quantum world and to extend light years out into deep space. The next logical field is augmenting our vision on an everyday basis. Whether from *Continuum*, *Iron Man*, *Batman*, *Deus Ex* or the modern-day F22 Raptor fighter jet, the concept of an augmented, head-up display (HUD)[12] vision has been a staple of science fiction and military aircraft for more than 50 years.

When Google Glass launched in 2013, it launched to great media fanfare.[13] Glass was considered the next big leap in both wearable technologies and augmented reality (AR), but as with all such leaps in technology it was met with either unyielding passion or mild derision. In media context, however, Google's first head-up display wearable fit neither the traditional definition of HUD nor immersive AR. It is clearly just a first step in the evolution of enhanced vision overlay.

I know that some of you will be thinking that you'll never wear something like Google Glass, that you'll never be one of those "glassholes", as social media coined the moniker. But if you think of this as part and parcel of the development of humanity's 900-year-long relationship to enhanced vision technology, then it's the next logical step.

---

11 NASA Exoplanet Archive

12 The origin of head-up display stems from a pilot being able to view information with the head positioned "up" and looking forward, instead of angled down looking at lower instruments.

13 Including my pal Robert Scoble (author of *Age of Context*) who was photographed wearing his Glass in the shower—not a pretty sight, I'll warn you, but the photo certainly got widespread media coverage. Augmented reality company Magic Leap, however, thought the image pretty enough to immortalise Robert in a 2015 patent application (*see* http://www.freepatentsonline.com/20150178939.pdf).

One of the most exciting developments in this space is a new intraocular, or "bionic", lens produced by a start-up in British Columbia, Canada, that is led by Dr Garth Webb. The lens, which is undergoing clinical trials, could not only correct sight but give you vision three times better than natural 20/20 vision. The lens is constructed using advanced biosynthetics, customised to each individual, and would replace your eye's existing lens in a simple 8-minute procedure. During the procedure, a small 2-mm incision is made, the existing lens extracted and the bionic lens, folded like a taco in a saline-filled syringe, then placed in the eye where it unravels itself within a few seconds. Lasers are then used to seal the incision, and within days your vision would start to adjust. Given that this procedure could enhance the vision of absolutely anyone, how many people with no vision issues would opt in for this procedure? Super-enhanced vision, why not?

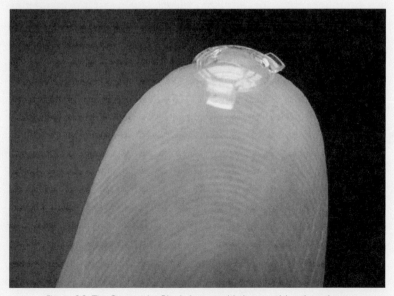

Figure 6.8: The Ocumetrics Bionic Lens could give you vision three times greater than 20/20.

> "This is vision enhancement that the world has never seen before. If you can just barely see the clock at 10 feet [today], when you get the Bionic Lens you can see the clock at 30 feet away."
>
> **Dr Garth Webb, inventor of the Ocumetrics Bionic Lens**

By treating such lenses with technology like Valspar's EnChroma coating, the new lens could even theoretically correct colour blindness. Webb says that the Ocumetrics Bionic Lens could be available to the public within a few years, but we'll just have to wait and see. It is clear, however, that materials science, manufacturing processes and new medical techniques will allow us to make these sort of advancements in the next two decades.

It won't take long before such a lens will have other capabilities embedded in it, too. Google X announced early in 2014 a project with the eye care division of Novartis to develop a contact lens that can monitor glucose levels and automatically adjust focus. For instance, one of the Novartis-Google prototype lenses contains a device about the size of a speck of glitter that measures glucose in tears. A wireless antenna then transmits the measurements to an external device. It's designed to ease the burden of diabetics who otherwise have to prick their fingers to test their blood sugar levels. Google even proposes that the contact lens could be solar-powered.

From biometric sensors and detection through to reality augmentation and night vision, our eyes offer unique opportunities for enhancement. As we augment our vision with data and insights, what are we going to want to see? Are we all going to be walking around with Terminator-style vision enhancement and super-hearing like the Six Million Dollar Man or is this a little more nuanced?

Augmented Reality, Personal HUDs and Vision Enhancement

No doubt, the temptation for many businesses is to think of augmented vision as a new landscape for bridging the gap between digital and the real world, especially in respect to 3D gaming, geolocation-based marketing and contextual commerce. Today, we're already getting a little overwhelmed by the volume of notifications, application feedback and offers. Do we really need this sort of data interrupting our field of vision while we're driving, walking into a shop or working on a document at the office?

Whether delivered by a next-gen Google Glass or a smart contact lens, **context** is going to be the single key driver to the applicability of information augmenting our field of vision. The information that will be delivered via head-up display implementation needs to be super personalised, and highly contextual. Such information will normally be short-lived, and only there to enhance decision-making in the moment, so by nature will have to be backed by some incredibly sophisticated preprocessing algorithms. This is not about simply seeing a pop-up of whoever is calling you or of someone who has liked your Facebook status update.

From 1942 through to 1955, the Telecommunications Research Establishment arm of the UK's Royal Air Force and the US Navy's Office of Naval Research and Development did research on various mock-ups of the early HUD. In 1958, the Royal Navy deployed the *Blackburn Buccaneer*, a subsonic strike aircraft designed for carrier-borne attack, which carried the first operational HUD. An important principle soon emerged with HUD design on such fighter aircraft. If a pilot had to look down at a radar display or instrumentation, particularly in a combat situation, either the flight dynamics could be altered, or the pilot could lose situational awareness rapidly. Thus, HUDs were designed to maximise the ability of the pilot to focus on the immediate operational requirement of flying the aircraft and making decisions, without having to adjust focus. Once it was determined that pilots using this new technology were becoming operationally better pilots, particularly in high stress, dynamic combat situations, the technology became commonplace in fighter aircraft. In the 1970s, commercial aircraft started to deploy similar technologies and, today, it is standard for aircraft like the Boeing 787 to come with HUD.

Taking this one step further, the principle for a personal head-up display (PHUD) is simple—it should augment your vision for decision-making, but not distract you from your core mission. Sorry Larry Page, but more advertisements served directly to your retina is not going to be viable here...

While early attempts at augmented-reality PHUD designs have focused on putting a lot of data in your field of view, the successful implementation of this technology will be about highly filtered, highly personal, tightly correlated context. Part of the success of the personal head-up display will be the right information at the right time. It won't be just another "channel" to push more content to. Your vision can be enhanced, but it should never be obstructed. Your decision-making can be augmented, but distractions must be minimised.

In this instance, the benchmark of HUD design for fighter pilots and commercial pilots is a good baseline. As already mentioned, the early head-up displays were designed to minimise pilot workload. The job of flying was never at risk.

Let's tackle the content first, in order of importance or prioritisation, and then we'll tackle the most promising technology that will give us PHUDs over the next couple of decades.

Figure 6.9: What will your personal head-up display tell you? (Credit: Bern Stock)

Health, Vital Statistics and Biometrics

The most important regular information will most likely be biometric feedback, mainly alerts that you will need to act upon for your overall physical well-being. The sort of alerts we'll see are already starting to make an appearance on Apple Watch and Fitbit notifications, such as you've been sitting too long or your heart rate is elevated. Here are some biometric alerts that will probably evolve in a PHUD:

- elevated glucose levels (diabetes treatment)
- adverse or abnormal levels of iron, haemoglobin, liver enzyme production, etc.

- blood alcohol limit, thus preventing you from driving (image stabilised, of course), or excess consumption of caffeine, sugar, high-fructose corn syrup, etc.
- warnings of potential or impending muscle strain or injury
- abnormal heart, renal or respiratory function
- High stress levels or blood pressure changes
- injury analysis and suggested course of action
- oximetry (oxygen level in the blood stream)
- core temperature or fever warnings
- T-cell or immune system response

This would be part of your integrated health management and would be largely non-configurable in terms of prioritisation of information. In other words, if there were an alert, it would take priority over other issues because the alert would directly affect your health and well-being. Of course, you would have the option of turning off an alert once seen, but I would imagine a critical alert would appear in your vision in some form or another until you dealt with it by enlisting the support of a healthcare professional, taking a specific course of action or taking medication. Ultimately, an ingestible you use might even be able to dispense medication to resolve a short-term issue. For example, a patient with diabetes might have insulin levels maintained through an implant instead of having to have an injection, but this might be a combined action whereby the PHUD alerts you and you then accept the implant's action.

Alerts would be prioritised based on criticality. So you could expect critical alerts to be highlighted by a flashing indicator at the top or bottom of your field of vision (centralised) as opposed to less critical warnings that might appear in one of the corners of your vision. Information that doesn't require an immediate response or recognition would be likely relegated to a personal device, and not necessarily presented in your PHUD at all.

Contextual Decision-making and Optimisation

The next key area is supplemental decision-making capability. This would include situational awareness and navigating day-to-day scenarios in which enhanced information could make a real-time decision easier. Most of these would be configurable and optional. Here are some examples of these types of PHUD scenarios:

- GPS-style directions as you are walking (GPS driving alerts would be contextualised in a vehicle display or relegated to feedback from a self-driving AI)
- Doppler radar alerts to warn you about the danger of falling objects, traffic, etc.
- environmental alerts about weather, toxins, temperature, etc.
- exercise/activity feedback in real time
- reviews of a product you are holding or focusing on while in a retail environment
- spending or money alert to indicate abnormal activity or real-time purchase behaviour
- translation of critical information in a foreign language environment, for example, prohibited areas, danger of electric shock or exposure to a toxic environment, allergens in food, etc.
- image and facial recognition cues

The clear objective here is to give you contextual cues that guide you in real-time decision-making. This would be the type of information that you might typically seek out on a smartphone today before you make a decision or take a course of action.

Instead of being driven by you interacting with your phone in real time, your personal AI would learn your preferences and styles and start presenting the sort of information you most frequently rely on in real time and shifting that to prioritisation in your PHUD.

Vision Optimisation and Enhancement Capabilities (Longer Term)

Advancements in materials science, photoreceptors and image processing integrated into either glasses or contact lenses (longer term) will allow us to enhance our vision in ways that Lippershey and Bacon could have only dreamed of. This will combine image processing and projection. Many of the features listed below are still a few decades down the line but are theoretically possible by combining smart contact lenses with technologies like light field and image manipulation:

- anti-glare polarisation
- digital zoom/magnification
- night vision and low-light enhancement
- colour correction for colour blindness
- infra-red thermal imaging
- video capture

If you recognise some of these features, it is because they are already common in many digital cameras today or in specialised camera equipment. With miniaturisation though, it is feasible that these features could be combined in smart glasses, or even smart contact lenses, in 20 to 30 years.

I can see it now. As you are entering the customs area of the United States, you'll be asked to **please turn off any video capture capable bionic implants, or risk confiscation of your bionic eyes.**

Bionic and Binaural Hearing Enhancements

Development of the cochlear implant started in the early 1950s. Then in 1957, a Parisian professor of medical physics, Dr André Djourno, a Parisian professor of medical physics, and Charles Eyriès, a Parisian otologist, were able to partially restore hearing to a deaf patient with total bilateral cholesteatomas by electrically stimulating acoustic nerve fibres still present in the patient's inner ear, or tympani. In the 1970s, various patents were filed for experimental multichannel implants, but it wasn't until 1997 that the global medical body reached some sort of consensus on the technology. Ultimately, a patent filed by the French company Bertin back in 1977 has heavily influenced the arena ever since.

Cochlear implants have brought hearing to thousands of patients around the world with hearing impairments. The next generation of bionic ears, however, could give us superhuman hearing.

In 2013, scientists at Princeton University 3D printed a human analog bionic ear out of hydrogel, a material commonly used in tissue engineering. The hydrogel was infused with cells

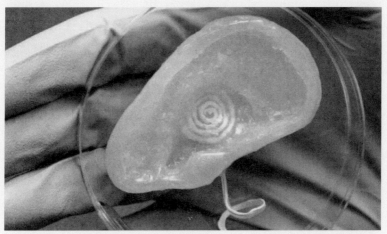

Figure 6.10: A bionic ear that enables you to hear better than your God-given original
(Credit: Princeton)

from a calf and intertwined with a polymer containing silver nanoparticles, which conduct radio frequencies. The calf cells then matured into cartilage and hardened around a coil antenna, as seen in the middle of the ear. When tested, the bionic ear was found to receive signals across an extended frequency spectrum of 1 megahertz (MHz) to 5 gigahertz (GHz), far beyond the normal human range of 20 hertz (Hz) to 20 kilohertz (KHz).

With bionic eyes and lenses that can see three times greater than 20/20 vision, contact lenses that can display a personal head-up display and bionic ears that can hear a thousand times more than the ears you were born with, would you willingly choose to be augmented by such technologies and become post-human?

Living with Augmented and Virtual Reality
The Reality–Virtuality Continuum

Technologies like Magic Leap's digital light field are designed to bring images with real depth into the field of view while Microsoft's HoloLens are first-generation high-definition holographic see-through computing platforms. The most promising field of research being pursued in this area is the use of laser projection, which effectively projects images directly onto the retina from specially equipped glasses. Older AR concepts relied on small screens that were projected via mirrors or reflected into the field of view, Google Glass included. Newer technologies can get higher resolution and clearer images via either see-through displays or organic light-emitting diode (OLED) displays with microlenses in front or via laser or some other projection directly onto the eye's surface. All of these technologies are designed for augmenting reality largely.

In contrast, virtual reality (VR) headsets like the Oculus Rift have a 1080-pixel x 1200-pixel resolution liquid-crystal display (LCD) or OLED panels embedded in a wrap-around viewer/headset. Typical VR headsets feature per-eye displays running at 90 Hz, 360-degree positional tracking, integrated audio, positional tracking volume and a designed focused on wearability and aesthetics.

Unlike AR, which projects into your field of vision and is see-through, VR is designed to be a completely immersive experience that puts you in the virtual world. However, both AR and VR are technology approaches on what is known as the mixed reality (MR) spectrum.

The Mixed Reality Spectrum

To clarify the spectrum:

- The **real world** is what you see today through your natural eyes.
- **Augmented reality** is the sort of technology we're talking about in a PHUD, or more immediately through technologies like Magic Leap and Microsoft HoloLens.
- **Virtual reality** is an immersive experience that puts you in a totally virtual world, and through processing improvements and better screen resolution, VR headsets are rapidly being commercialised in the form of Oculus Rift, HTC Vive, Samsung Gear VR and others.
- **Augmented virtuality** (AV), however, is augmenting a virtual world with real-world artefacts; a merging of the real world into VR.

Augmented virtuality might encompass, for example, projecting your body into a virtual environment so that you can see your hands turn a virtual door handle or look down at your virtual feet as you walk through a virtual environment.

Mixed Reality Spectrum

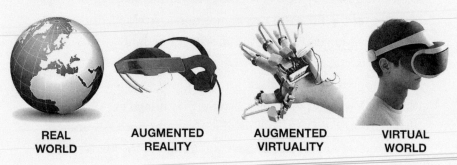

| REAL | AUGMENTED | AUGMENTED | VIRTUAL |
| WORLD | REALITY | VIRTUALITY | WORLD |

Figure 6.11: The mixed reality spectrum

Such actions would be possible via tracking or motion sensors either in the VR headset or in the room where the VR unit is positioned. The tracking system would work by scanning your body in real time, or possibly scanning you in high resolution as part of the environment set-up, and then implementing a virtual body model based on real-time scans.

Early commercial examples of this technology are already being tested using technology like Microsoft Kinect, HTC Vive and VR headsets like Oculus Rift. In the future, however, these tracking sensors will have much higher resolution and discern features like skin pigmentation, the clothes you are wearing, hair colour, etc., and then project your natural features into the virtual world, or precisely track your movements and project those against your avatar in the virtual world.

VR units tend to run through very powerful computers with high-powered graphics cards whereas AR units are designed to be self-contained. Extending from what was discussed in chapter 5 about the quantified self and monitoring, it is likely that as our smartphones, smart clothing and other personal devices gain sufficient computing capability, we'll carry on-body a sort of parallel processing computing platform that will be in constant sync with our own personal processing space in the cloud. In 20 years, this will allow us to have extremely powerful distributed processing capability that will be more powerful than the most capable supercomputers in use today.

Think about it. Currently, the most powerful smartphones and tablets entering the market have 4 GHz multi-core processors that can generate around 180 gigaflops of processing power. Using Moore's Law, we can extrapolate that your typical smart device in 2025 will have approximately *3 to 6 teraflops (tflops) of processing power*! Now combine a smartphone, a smart watch, smart glasses and some other computing power either embedded in smart clothes, other wearables or ingestibles, along with on-tap processing power in the cloud, and you will conservatively wear processing capability that is hundreds of thousands of times greater than the most powerful desktop computer today. You could be wearing on your body and have access to via the cloud over 20 to 30 teraflops of processing power instantly. Processing power definitely won't be an issue, retina display resolutions will be standard, and all of this will be integrated into a personal package that is based on our environment, our personality, our preferences and priorities, our own biometrics and biofeedback, and real-time context and actions.

While still in their infancy, AR applications like Magic Leap and VR applications like Oculus Rift are already generating a lot of buzz. Ted Schilowitz, the resident futurist at 20th Century FOX, has said of Magic Leap:

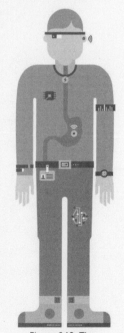

Figure 6.12: The augmented man of 2025

"It's Google's first trillion dollar idea!"

Ted Schilowitz, 20th Century FOX

To back this further, Thomas Tull, the CEO of Legendary Pictures, said of Magic Leap, "It's so badass, you can't believe it!" Legendary, it should be noted, is an investor in Magic Leap. Google led the round of funding that Legendary participated in, putting in more than US$500 million in 2014, and Magic Leap is set to raise another US$800 million in 2016.[14] So just what is Magic Leap doing with all that cash?

Magic Leap's technology centres around a wearable that blends augmented and virtual reality. By placing digital light field generated images in the view of the wearer, this technology has the potential of being more than just a personal HUD, and to be something much more environmentally hinged. It is conceivable that you'll be able to use Magic Leap's technology as an AR headset or PHUD, but also as a full VR unit (probably with the lights down low), or as a mix between virtual and real worlds.

The CEO of Magic Leap has tried to articulate the difference between Magic Leap and other AR/VR applications by calling it "techno-biology".

"You can think of [Magic Leap] as techno-biology," he replied. "We believe it is the future of computing." Techno-biology, he explained, "is the proper application of technology to our biology that leads to the experience of magic."

Rony Abovitz, CEO of Magic Leap, during an "Ask Me Anything" (AMA) interview on *Reddit*, 24th February 2015

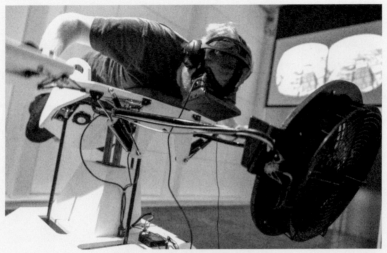

Figure 6.13: The Birdly VR simulation rig

Magic Leap differs from the likes of HoloLens, which is clearly AR, in that the expectation is for a true replication of visual reality or cinematic reality imposed on your vision through digital light field projection.[15] The idea is simple—you won't be able to detect the difference between the real world and objects imposed on your vision.

The timeline for Magic Leap? Two to four years. Bearing this in mind, it would appear that a personal head-up display is going to be something we will live with, if popularised, before 2025.

Virtual reality has some equally as promising applications that could be released commercially well before those designed by Magic Leap. If you want to check out some of the available games already optimised for Oculus Rift, I'd recommend PewDiePie's feed or similar.

Unquestionably, one amazing innovation of VR will be simulated environments that allow you to experience the world in a way an AR headset never could do. For example, Somniacs, a company based in Zurich, Switzerland, has created a flying

---

15 According to an article in *MIT Technology Review*, Magic Leap uses a Lilliputian projector to shine light and images into the user's eyes.

simulator called Birdly. Birdly simulates the experience of flying like a bird by marrying a Oculus Rift VR headset with a rig you lie on that allows you to flap your arms and basically feel like a bird.

> "Ever dreamed of flying like a bird? You're in luck—new flight simulator Birdly lets you do just that, through the power of virtual reality."
>
> *Telegraph* (UK), May 2014

We'll see many more of these applications in the near term, as well as an entirely new form of cinematic development. With the aim of showcasing the technology's potential, Henry, the pixelated star of Oculus VR's virtual reality animated short feature, is an amiable hedgehog that loves to hug. Being a prickly fellow, this creates an obvious pickle that leaves Henry sad and friendless, and as the 10-minute virtual reality short film *Henry* opens—with narration by Elijah Wood—Henry is celebrating his birthday. Strapping on a VR headset puts you in the 360-degree virtual world of Henry where you not only watch the movie, but participate in it. You are actually in the world of Henry, and not just watching it.

Imagine recreating movies of old like *Star Wars, Titanic, Avatar, Casablanca, Top Gun* or others where you are in the environment, playing an extra or even a main character. Perhaps the *Star Trek* holodeck is not such a far-fetched experience after all!

Wherever you stand on the possibilities of mixed reality, the future has some incredible things planned for our vision and senses. We will not be limited by our God-given senses and the physical world around us.

Augmented Intelligence

In what year was Napoleon born? What was the date of the first moon landing? What element on the periodic table has the symbol Ba? How many base pairs are there in the average human genome? How far is Pluto from earth right now? What animal is a thylacine and when did it become extinct?

Very few people could answer all of these questions off the cuff, but there is virtually no question that we couldn't answer if we have access to Google or the Internet in general. In fact, many people's instinct nowadays is to not bother remembering such facts because they can simply google the answers.

In 2011, a group of psychologists published a study entitled "Google Effects on Memory: Cognitive Consequences of Having Information at Our Fingertips" that showed the effect of Google on the way we process information and store memories.[16] The results suggest that when faced with difficult questions, people are primed to think about computers and that when people expect to have future access to information, they have lower rates of recall of the information itself and enhanced recall instead for where to access it. The Internet has become a primary form of external or transactive memory, where information is stored collectively outside of our brains.

Henry Roediger, a psychologist at Washington University in St. Louis, said in a commentary of the study, "...there is no doubt that our strategies are shifting in learning. Why remember something if I know I can look it up again? In some sense, with Google and other search engines, we can offload some of our memory demands onto machines."

In a broader sense, the overall IQ of humans has been climbing over the last century or so. The Flynn Effect is a well-known long-term study on IQ studies and examinations. It

---

16 B. Sparrow, J. Liu and D. Wegner, "Google Effects on Memory: Cognitive Consequences of Having Information at Our Fingertips," *Science* 333, no. 6043 (2011): 776–778.

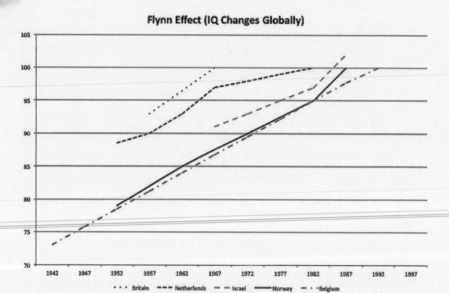

Figure 6.14: The Flynn Effect, or the world's increasing IQ

looks at the substantial and long-sustained increase in both fluid and crystallised intelligence test scores measured in many parts of the world from roughly 1930 to the present day. While rates vary, the improvements in IQ globally have been remarkably consistent. The Flynn Effect is attributed to a range of possible influences including better schooling, familiarity with testing, more stimulating environments, better nutrition, reduction in infectious diseases and more genetic diversity as populations have migrated due to better transportation systems, etc. Having said that, recent testing may be showing that the Flynn Effect is flattening. Is Google dumbing us down?

The pursuit of intelligence is clearly an overall human mission. The very knowledge base we have today means that we are clearly more intelligent, are better at problem solving and abstract reasoning and have access to better information than the average populace 100 years ago, and most certainly 1,000 years ago.

Going back even further, when men 3,000 years ago looked up and saw patterns in the constellations of stars and named planets after gods moving through the night sky, they were trying to give context and meaning to the unknowable. Today, we're photographing those constellations in incredible detail and learning that stars within a constellation are sometimes hundreds of light years apart. That, for instance, Mars is not a god, but our closest neighbour, with two moons, water ice and finger-like markings that indicate it was once a warm planet with flowing rivers. We've gone from the Wright Brothers' first powered flight in 1904 to sending a spacecraft to photograph Pluto in just over a century.

We've tried to improve our intelligence for millennia. Looking to overcome our cognitive limitations, humans have employed everything from writing, language and meditative techniques straight through to today's nootropics. But none of these compares to what's in store.

While one part of humanity is pursuing artificial intelligence, there is another sector of society seeking to leverage off the pre-existing intelligence platform we were born with. This field of research is commonly referred to as intelligence amplification, or IA. The goal of this research is simple—we're trying to create a world of super-Einsteins, or persons who are qualitatively smarter than any human being that has ever lived.

Neural implants offer the ability to repair damaged brain function, but also in the future to gain access to direct neural stimulation and external information processing as well as enhance our visual cortex. The path to IA is typically articulated in three distinct phases:

1. **Neural Data Integration:** Think of this as "telepathic google", the ability to recall information through a neural link to the cloud or similar.

2. **Comprehensive Brain–Computer Interfaces:** Augmenting the visual, sensory, tactile and auditory cortex. Boosting spatial visualisation techniques and the ability to "download" visualisations or information. We are not talking about a PHUD overlay for the eye, but rather an internal display manufactured from the wetware of the brain itself. That totality, i.e. normal vision, plus any virtual reality overlay, plus internally generated visual perceptions

3. **Augmented Pre-Frontal Cortex:** The holy grail of IA research, in other words, enhancing the way we combine perceptual data to form concepts. The end result would be cognitive super-MacGyvers, people who perform apparently impossible intellectual feats.

Unlike the depictions of enhanced intelligence in movies like *Limitless*, the reality is that the brain is not particularly fungible. The reality is that normally, when we try to manipulate brain chemistry or "overclock" the brain in respect to processing, we tend to break it. Chemicals are simply not targeted enough to produce big gains in human cognitive performance. For that, we need to rewire the brain. The best brain–computer interfaces today have around 1,000 connections. To get anywhere near the IA goals we're talking about, we'll need brain implants with connections to millions of neurons. This is going to take another 15 to 20 years but it is viable nonetheless.

The real improvements in IA will come with nano-manufacturing, which allows for implants with neuron level integration. Given that there is yet very little development in atomically precise manufacturing technologies, nanoscale self-assembly seems like the most probable route to million-electrode brain–computer interfaces. I would recommend reading Ramez Naam's *Nexus* trilogy for one possible path or outcome for this type of nano-technology brain interface. When I interviewed Naam, he had this to say about nano-tech:

> "I'm very much an optimist, but an optimist that believes the future is messy. I think things will move slowly in this area, probably more like 2040 time frame, because we're always very hesitant to experiment on humans. Do no harm is the first rule. But certainly DARPA have a big program on brain–machine interfaces because they want to put things in the brains of fighter pilots, or soldiers who have lost their sight or been paralysed in war, both healing and enhancing performance.
>
> They showed off a vision they had at an event in San Francisco recently called a cortical modem. They envision this device, it's the size of two nickels, they can build it for $15, implant it in the brain of someone and give them the ability to beam vision into that person's brain."
>
> Ramez Naam, author of *Nexus*, on VoiceAmerica
> (Breaking Banks), 12th March 2015

The problem with enhanced intelligence or IA is that you are dealing with human beings having greater processing power, and human beings are flawed. People with enhanced intelligence could still have human-level morality, leveraging their vast intellects for hedonistic or even genocidal purposes. Artificial general intelligence, on the other hand, can be built from the ground up to simply follow a set of intrinsic motivations that are benevolent, stable and self-reinforcing. We can build constraints into AIs that we may not have with IA.

Indeed, you could argue that the warnings of Stephen Hawking and Elon Musk about the development of full AI not benefitting humanity in the longer term are because they are inputting typical human motivations like greed, selfishness and ambivalence onto AI.

Chapter 7

Life Stream, Agents, Avatars and Advisers

"My personal challenge for 2016 is to build a simple AI to run my home and help me with my work. You can think of it kind of like Jarvis in *Iron Man*.

I'm going to start by exploring what technology is already out there. Then I'll start teaching it to understand my voice to control everything in our home—music, lights, temperature and so on. I'll teach it to let friends in by looking at their faces when they ring the doorbell. I'll teach it to let me know if anything is going on in Max's room that I need to check on when I'm not with her. On the work side, it'll help me visualize data in VR to help me build better services and lead my organizations more effectively."

Mark Zuckerberg, 3rd January 2016, via Facebook

Living with your Personal Life Stream®[1]

Think about all of this computing power at our fingertips, all of this data and an increasingly smart collection of algorithms anticipating our needs and running interference for us. What would it be called? Until I come up with something better, I'm going with Life Stream, or maybe Life Cloud.

Life Stream is not a personal control panel similar to the one you have in Windows or the system preferences of OSX because it could be distributed across multiple devices and spaces. It's not an interface as there could be dozens of individual interfaces across devices and embedded computer platforms. It might have a primary AI or agent in a decade or so that knows you and talks to other computers or even other humans on your behalf. It includes sensors and other programs that will monitor you, but you'll willingly trade off that loss of privacy for the benefits it gives you, after all, it will be your private data. It won't be one cloud account, it will be a collection of data subsets that only make sense to you, but are often essential for you personally. It could be considered your personal operating system although, as you'll see later, I don't think an OS analogy quite cuts it.

Here is the broad collection of elements that might make up your Life Stream:

| Interfaces | Sensors and Monitors | Embedded Computers | Data Repositories | AIs and Agents |

In the movie *Her*, the intelligent operating system that Theodore Twombly (played by Joaquin Phoenix) uploads onto

---

1   Just kidding! I haven't registered the trademark—yet!

his computers and smartphone is called Samantha. Twombly ends up falling in love with the intelligence before the collection of OSs like Samantha merges into a hyperintelligence that goes off to another dimension. In the popular video game Halo, the hero's personal AI is called Cortana, also the name of the AI assistant embedded in Microsoft Windows 10. In the video game, Cortana is an AI that helps fill in gaps of knowledge and hack into systems, etc. It is fairly specific in its goal of helping Master Chief complete his mission parameters but, at the same time, could easily fit the premise of an AI like Spike Jonze's Samantha who fits into your daily life if the user in this instance wasn't in a war against the Covenant!

There are two basic directions that this intelligence can go over the next ten years. We either centralise our lives around an Apple, Google or Microsoft cloud with some AI/agent built in (an enhanced Siri if you like) or we diverge from this considerably and have a separate collective agent/ intelligence that is both device and platform independent. Supersets of data and analytics are, in my opinion, likely to diverge from an OS-owned model because they have to be more disparate. You can't guarantee that your smart, autonomous vehicle is going to be running iOS with Siri. Thus, my guess is that it will work much like apps or social networks do today, sitting on top of devices or the various operating systems

Figure 7.1: Facebook M is aiming to be the first personal AI assistant.
(Credit: Facebook)

rather than being embedded. We'll have to wait and see but there is value in an agent that works through any interface.

Regardless, the forces driving us to a Personal Stream and Interface are becoming increasingly clear. We have lots of devices, lots of screens and soon more data than we will logically be able to process personally or collectively as humans, so it will need to be curated by algorithms. Whatever curates all that data and allows us to interact will be the personal interface to these systems. Whoever cracks this problem will have a business bigger than Facebook by the middle of next decade. In fact, Facebook is hoping to be this business with its work on Facebook M, billed as a digital personal assistant.

This software intelligence will have two broad capabilities: first, direct input, visualisation and feedback; second, collection, synthesis and agency.

Direct input is requesting an input or configuring software in a particular way, either via settings or training the software over time. Visualisation and feedback is whenever the software delivers feedback via a screen, an interface, haptic touch (vibration, force feedback, Force Touch, etc.) or through voice.

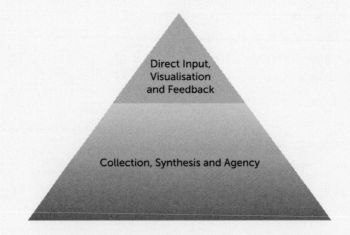

Collection of core data will occur every day through cameras, accelerometers, geolocation data points, iBeacons, payments ecosystems, apps and a broad range of sensors, both personalised and external. This data will go into pools of data both in your own cloud or personal repositories and external data stores where algorithms will look for certain behaviours, and will synthesize data for feedback.

Agent Avatars at your Command

The most interesting developments in personalisation will not just be in respect to visualisation and feedback but also in respect to these AI-based agents that will learn your behaviour, needs and typical responses and, over time, begin to act on your behalf. These agents and avatars will eventually morph into a personal AI that is akin to a super tech-savvy personal assistant. How will this evolve?

The first use of agency, which is already emerging, will be to carry out simple tasks as an extension of Siri or Cortana, such as the following:

- Siri, book me an Uber car home.
- Cortana, transfer $1,000 from my savings account onto my credit card.
- Siri, buy me $200 worth of bitcoin for my wallet.
- Jibo, order me the usual from my favourite Chinese restaurant (via Seamless).
- Siri, wake me up at 8 a.m. tomorrow.
- Cortana, start my engine and warm the car up to 70 degrees (linked to OnStar or the BMW app).
- Jibo, vacuum the floor downstairs (linked to my Roomba).
- Cortana, make sure my heater is on at home for my arrival.

The next phase, within the next five to ten years, would be an agent that can call and make an appointment with your hairdresser, book your car in for a service and so on. You might even start to personify your agent. Tasks like the following will be common:

- <Lucy> book me a flight next Wednesday afternoon to Florida in first class. Pay using the corporate account.
- <Bob> call my hairdresser and see if they can fit me in on Friday.
- <iThing> can you find out if there are any good matinee shows available in the West End this Saturday?
- <Alfred> find me a Mexican restaurant near the theatre and book me a table for three.

This next level of agency requires the ability for negotiation and interaction with either other agents or with humans. Thus, you need some basic neural networks or learning algorithms that can work to determine the correct response for these types of interactions. These learning algorithms will be shared and publicly available so that collectively these machine intelligences get better at anticipating and reacting appropriately to various response states.

In this level of agency, there is also the ability for your agent avatar to learn your preferences. In the examples above, for instance, <Lucy> would know you prefer a forward window or an aisle seat, <Bob> would know that you need to allow 45 minutes plus waiting time at the hairdresser's and <iThing> would know you don't like musicals. As such interactions become more common, we'll build service layers that allow these agents to negotiate in real time without any human involvement. In other words, computer agents talking to other computer agents or machine-to-machine dedicated interactions.

At this stage, some of you may be thinking about privacy and how to ensure that your agent wouldn't divulge information without your permission. Keep in mind that the volume of these interactions will quickly mean that it will become impossible for humans to operate as effective intermediaries for very long. There will simply be too much data and too many interactions. Humans will just slow things down and degrade the experience so they'll be rapidly removed from the role of agents. Sure, you'll still have your elite concierge service that will enable you to speak to a human, but guess what? Those humans will use agents to do the heavy lifting and repetitive tasks. So, in the end, everyone will be using agents. We'll even have our agent listening in on our meetings and conversations so it can respond in real time as required.

Imagine sitting in a business meeting or participating in a conference call and agreeing to meet your client or boss in another city next Wednesday afternoon. Then seeing that your agent and theirs have already communicated, put a meeting on the calendar and your agent has already booked you a flight out Tuesday night so that you are there in plenty of time.

None of the above requires full artificial intelligence. A digital personal assistant or agent avatar that could carry out all of those tasks might appear to be quite intelligent, but there is a defined set of experiences it might be able to handle, just like the librarian portrayed in Neal Stephenson's classic novel *Snow Crash* (1992). At some point, the capability of these agents will become so good that it will cease being Siri-like (where we laugh at her canned responses) to something we rely upon every day and solves quite complex problems. It simply doesn't matter that it isn't full AI.

This capability is most likely to sit on top of multiple operating systems, rather than being dedicated to a specific device. For example, when you are in your self-driving car and you give <Lucy> instructions, is the car using your iPhone 12 embedded agent or is your agent present in your car and home as well as in your smartphone/device? It's highly likely that this will be a distributed capability and will be tied into the cloud, rather than just an app or service layer in a specific single device. The capability of these algorithms to learn across a wide range of inputs will be the core success factor in anticipating your needs and applying them to context. These algorithms can also learn in different ways depending on the particular device. For example, a smart car may learn your preference for driving routes or preference for the types of restaurants you frequent, perhaps better than your smartphone. Your smart watch with its sensor array might learn which music is optimal for your workout based on how that music changes your physical response to your exercise regimen, or it might learn what time of the day is best for you to have a coffee so as to maximise your alertness.

You'll recall in chapter 3 our proposition that user interfaces have got increasingly powerful and more capable, but also less complex to operate. At the same time, the platforms that carry those user interfaces are now becoming distributed so that experiences are not limited to one screen. For example, Facebook has a fairly consistent experience across devices, from your smartphone and tablet through to your PC, and Twitter is integrated into your phone as an app, within websites you use and as a stream of notifications. Banking is already spread across an ATM device, your browser for Internet banking, a mobile app for day-to-day banking or monitoring your financial health, Venmo, PayPal or Dwolla for sending money to a friend instantly and your near field communication (NFC)-equipped iPhone with Apple Pay or Android phone with Android Pay for paying at a store.

For your AI agent, however, this will be even more pervasive. So an interesting question to pursue is like Samantha in *Her*, could you develop a relationship with your agent avatar, your personal AI?

What Hatsune Miku Teaches Us about Avatars

The first appearance of artificial intelligence in popular literature was through a series of articles and subsequent novel published by Samuel Butler in the late 1800s. *Erewhon*,[2] published in 1897, contained three chapters grouped into a story entitled "The Book of the Machines". In these chapters, Butler postulated that machines might develop consciousness through a sort of Darwinian selection process.

> There is no security against the ultimate
> development of mechanical consciousness,
> in the fact of machines possessing little
> consciousness now. A jellyfish has not much
> consciousness. Reflect upon the extraordinary
> advance which machines have made during the
> last few hundred years, and note how slowly the
> animal and vegetable kingdoms are advancing.
> The more highly organized machines are
> creatures not so much of yesterday, as of the
> last five minutes, so to speak, in comparison with
> past time.
>
> Samuel Butler on machine consciousness in *Erewhon*

There are various repetitive themes in science fiction when it comes to AI. There is the concept of AI dominance, human dominance and control over AI, plus the emerging sentience

---

2   Available at http://www.gutenberg.org/ebooks/1906.

of AIs along with the ethical struggles it results in. There are also AIs like the Librarian in Stephenson's *Snow Crash* that, for whatever reason, have been prevented from reaching sentience.

The thing is though, if you are going to talk to an AI, you are going to bestow upon it certain human characteristics. Which is why the representation of AIs has also been a consistent theme in literature, cinema and on TV.

The first avatar, or avatar-like character, to hit the mainstream was Max Headroom. This fictional AI first appeared on British television in 1985 in a cyberpunk TV movie entitled *20 Minutes into the Future*. Channel 4 then gave Max his own music-video show, *The Max Headroom Show*, which led to a brief stint doing advertisements for Coca-Cola's "New Coke" formula. Though he was billed as "The world's first computer-generated TV host", technically Max Headroom wasn't an avatar or computer-generated at all. Portrayed by actor Matt Frewer, the computer-generated appearance of Max Headroom was achieved with prosthetic make-up and hand-drawn backgrounds as the technology of the time was not sufficiently advanced to achieve the desired effect. Preparing the look for filming involved 4.5 hours of make-up preparation. Frewer described the preparation as "gruelling" and "not fun", likening it to "being on the inside of a giant tennis ball".

Figure 7.2: Max Headroom, the first computer-generated TV host ... or so we thought
(Credit: *The Max Headroom Show*, UK's Channel 4)

The classic look for the character was a shiny dark or white suit (actually made out of fibreglass) often paired with Ray-Ban Wayfarer sunglasses. Only his head and shoulders were depicted, usually against a "computer-generated" backdrop of a slowly rotating wire-frame cube interior, which was also initially generated using traditional cel animation, though actual computer graphics were later employed for the backdrop. Another trademark of Max was his speech; his voice would seemingly pitch up or down randomly, or occasionally get stuck in a loop, achieved with a pitch-shifter harmoniser.

It was only a few years before Max Headroom that computer avatars made their appearance in popular literature. The word *avatar* is actually from Hinduism and stands for the "descent" of a deity in a terrestrial form. In Norman Spinrad's novel *Songs from the Stars* (1980), the term "avatar" was used to describe a computer-generated virtual experience, but it was Neal Stephenson's *Snow Crash* that cemented the use of the term in respect to computing. In Stephenson's novel, the main character, Hiro Protagonist, discovers a pseudo-narcotic called Snow Crash, a computer virus that infects avatars in a virtual world known as the Metaverse, but in doing so carries over its effects to the human operators who are plugged into the Metaverse through VR goggles that project images onto the users' retinas via lasers. Interestingly, Stephenson also described an entire industry built around the business of avatars and the Metaverse, including designers who can fashion a body, clothes and even facial expressions for your virtual persona.

Today, the term "avatar" describes any virtual representation of a user in the digital realm. From Steve and his buddies in Minecraft to characters in Halo, the Guardians in Destiny and avatars in virtual worlds like Second Life. However, the development in computer animation to depict virtual characters in parallel can also be seen as contributing to the possible futures of interaction.

Figure 7.3: Aki Ross, a computer-generated human analog actor in *Final Fantasy*
(Credit: Square Pictures)

From Woody in *Toy Story* through to James Cameron's *Avatar*, the development of computer character animation has evolved into a multi-billion dollar segment of the software industry. The first attempt to depict a photorealistic actor on the big screen was in the 2001 movie *Final Fantasy: The Spirits Within*. The groundbreaking graphics made some moviegoers uncomfortable, and the film flopped, losing Columbia Pictures US$50 million. For some, the faces were just too human, too close to real life.

> "So when you see the curvaceous Dr. Aki Ross (voiced by Ming-Na) trying to save our decimated planet from invading phantoms, you're seeing the handiwork of a computer, not of Mother Nature. Ever since Sony Pictures previewed *Final Fantasy*, online critics have been predicting doom. But the film exerts a hold... At first it's fun to watch

...But then you notice a coldness in the eyes, a mechanical quality in the movements."

Peter Travers, *Final Fantasy, Rolling Stone*, 6th July 2001

As discussed in chapter 4, the roboticist Masahiro Mori postulated this problem in an obscure journal called *Energy* in 1970, calling the effect of watching human-like robots *Bukimi no Tani Genshō* (不気味の谷現象), or what has been translated as the "uncanny valley".

So it would appear to be a choice between either super realism or some form of representation that is human-like, but clearly distinguishable from human. Enter Hatsune Miku, the Japanese anime, Vocaloid pop star.

"She's rather more like a goddess: She has human parts, but she transcends human limitations. She's the great posthuman pop star."

Hatsune Miku fan site

Miku had her start as a piece of software designed as a voice synthesiser by the Japanese company Crypton Future Media. In 2007, Crypton's CEO, Hiroyuki Itoh, was looking for a way to market a virtual voice program he'd developed using Yamaha's Vocaloid 2 technology. What he felt the software needed was an *aidoru*, or "idol". He engaged Kei, a Japanese illustrator of graphic novels, to come up with something. Kei came back with a rendering of a 16-year-old girl who was 5 foot 2 inches and weighed 92 pounds. She had long, thin legs, coquettish bug-eyes, pigtailed blue locks that reached almost to the ground and a computer module on her forearm. Her first name, Miku, meant "future"; her surname, Hatsune, "first sound".

Figure 7.4: Hatsune Miku, the Japanese Vocaloid, avatar, anime pop star worth billions
(Credit: Crypton Future Media)

Facts about Hatsune Miku

- She has over 100,000 released songs, 1.5 million uploaded YouTube videos and more than 1 million pieces of fan art.
- She has her own Dance craze called the MikuMikuDance, MMD.
- Nomura Research Institute has estimated that since her release in 2007 up until March 2012, she had already generated more than ¥10 trillion (approx. US$130 billion) in revenue.
- She has more endorsements than Tiger Woods and Michael Jordan combined.
- She has over 2.5 million fans on Facebook.
- She has performed more than 30 sold-out concerts worldwide, with performances in Los Angeles, New York, Taipei, Hong Kong, Singapore, Tokyo, Vancouver, Washington and, more recently, in the United States with Lady Gaga.

Miku today has millions of adoring fans all over the world, both online and in the real world. So how has a piece of voice synthesis software become such a huge hit as an avatar or Vocaloid pop star?

For digital natives who have grown up with technology in every aspect of their lives, seeing an avatar perform at a concert is no different experientially to seeing a human performer. For future generations, growing up with an AI or agent in their lives will seem like the most natural thing ever. Of course, there will be a transition from today's world where such things are novelties, to where they are just a natural part of life. For those of you concerned about privacy, the uncanny valley or how you'll never have an AI book a restaurant for you, think about it. In 20 years' time, all of this will be the norm.

Miku has taught us that you don't need to be human to be a pop star. It is the first time in history that a computer construct has reached this level of real-world popularity. Sure, there have been cartoon characters, fictional characters and comic book superheroes that weren't real that have been popularised. However, this is the first time an avatar that is absolutely virtual (and not a human analog) has crossed into the real world so completely to compete side by side with humans.

Whether in the form of an avatar or a photorealistic representation of a human being, having a day-to-day working relationship with a computer agent or AI is not even a slight stretch of the imagination. In all likelihood, we won't need much visual representation of our agent. As in the movie *Her* and today's implementation of voice recognition in smartphones and vehicles, the use of agents initially will be via voice. Research so far does not indicate that we have an "uncanny valley" issue with voice interactions, only in physical robotics. The reality is

Family & Relationships > Singles & Dating   Next >

 Help! I'm in love with Hatsune Miku?

Asked this question a bit ago, but didn't get a answer that really solved my problem.. So I'll ask again

I can't seem to get her off my mind, every waking minute I'm not studying I'm playing project diva or listening to her music. I've already turned down a girl because of this problem and I think I am becoming over obsessed, she's just perfect in every way. Is there anything I can do about this?
P.S. Kaito sucks

☆ Follow   ⊡ 2 answers

that agents will be rarely personified in a robot. For most of us in the future, we'll live our lives with an agent that is entirely virtual, and never physical. But we will personify it.

When human fans start adoring and mimicking a virtual pop star, then you can't argue about acceptance. Miku has taught us that we can adore or, yes, even fall in love with a virtual computer-generated character. For many of us today, this seems difficult to believe but, in 20 years' time, will it really be that unusual or strange?

Think about it. These agents will be designed to cater for a large part of our daily needs but will be heavily personalised around our individual likes and dislikes, our patterns of behaviour, our biases and reactions. Over time, these agents will get better and better at determining our needs and tailoring responses to us personally. When it comes to human relationships, we often need to change our approach or compromise our own beliefs and feelings to have an effective relationship. In fact, it is very difficult to have a relationship without some form of compromise. When it comes to AI or agency relationships though, you may not have to compromise your behaviour, beliefs or responses at all. In that way, I think it is not hard to see why some might come to feel closer to their agent than other humans.

While some such as Elon Musk and Stephen Hawking raise the spectre of robot overlord AIs that will take over the world with their hyperintelligence, we should also raise the spectre of AIs and avatars that we could very well fall in love with— that capture not only our minds, but also our hearts. This is something we're only just beginning to explore culturally, but it is a distinct possibility.

Death of a Salesman

For the last 50 to 100 years, we've developed service businesses that require a high degree of technical competency and knowledge such as medicine, consulting, financial services and advisory, software, etc. For the 1 per cent, the ultimate expression of wealth might well be having a full-time dedicated concierge or personal assistant that organises your appointments, travel and other activities. The ultimate expression of banking is to have a private banker, your personal one-to-one adviser for all things investment and banking. Having a dedicated nanny and tutors for your children, and having your own personal trainer or dietary/nutritional adviser, rank up there, too.

In each previous age, the core technologies have mainly disrupted infrastructure and processes. In the Augmented Age, however, it is experiences and advice that are being disrupted and scaled today, not processes and distribution.

Age	Core Technology	Core Disruption
Machine or Industrial Age	Steam Engine Combustion Engine Electricity	**All about Mass + Infrastructure** Individual trades to produce goods in favour of factory processes
Atomic, Jet or Space Age (Tronics)	Jet Aircraft and Spacecraft Atomic and Solar Energy Telephone	**All about Speed** Slow, inefficient production processes and generation Transport and communication systems

Digital or Information Age	Computers Internet	All about the Data Manual Record Keeping Physical Distribution and Products
Augmented or Intelligence Age	Artificial Intelligence, Smart Infrastructure, Distributed UX and embedded computing	All about the Experience Experience and Advice

Experiences that will be most easily disrupted over the next 30 years are service experiences. Experiences where humans and our inefficiencies, inaccuracies and idiosyncrasies are replaced by intelligence, of the machine kind. Experiences designed from the ground up that fit into our lives in a much more seamless and intelligent way than those human advisers we've needed up until now.

Imagine having a dedicated concierge, a personal trainer, a tutor for your children and such, not as a dedicated human resource, but built into technology around us. The fact is that human advisers are going to have significant disadvantages competing with their so-called robo-adviser challengers. Here are the most significant disadvantages:

The Big Data Theory: AIs Will Analyse much more Data

The example used earlier in chapter 3 is that of IBM Watson either competing against humans in the game show *Jeopardy!* or providing advice to doctors and nurses in the field of cancer research and treatment. Watson has been provided with millions of documents including medical journals, case studies, dictionaries, encyclopedias, literary works, newswire articles and other databases. Watson is composed of 90 IBM Power 750 servers, each of which uses a 3.5 GHz POWER7 8-core processor, with four threads per core. In all, the Watson system has almost 3,000 POWER7 processor threads and 16 terabytes of RAM.

This means that Watson can process the equivalent of more than 10 million books per second, much like having a photographic memory that can recall anything from those books and sources instantly. Rumour has it that Watson finished med school in just two years. When the cancer research fellows at MD Anderson's Leukemia Cancer Treatment Center were asked to summarise patients' records for the senior faculty in the mornings, Watson always had the best answers.

> "I was surprised," said Vitale, a 31-year-old who received her medical degree in Italy. "Even if you work all night, it would be impossible to be able to put this much information together like that."
>
> "IBM's Watson computer turns its artificial intelligence to cancer research," *Herald Tribune Health*, 14th July 2015

Rob Merkel, who leads IBM Watson Health, said the company estimates that a single person will generate 1 million gigabytes of health-related data throughout a lifetime. That's as much data as in 300 million books. Multiply that by the billions of people on the planet and it is clear that no human will ever be able to analyse that data efficiently, and definitely not in real time.

We are now well beyond the realms of a human adviser being able to have his "finger on the pulse" of the right information to give you accurate advice. More importantly, human advisers in the field of financial services, for example, have been notoriously bad at synthesizing individual investment styles, risk appetite and other personal parameters and introducing those into investment advice. This is where AIs will have a huge advantage—they'll be able to synthesize all of this type of data into "advice".

Whether it is the latest industry data, the latest research or just information about the last stocks or symptoms you looked up on the web, machines will have more data, more immediate access and the ability to have instant recall at anytime day or night. Simply put, for the last 200 years, advisers have worked on the principle of information asymmetry, where they have had better information than their clients. Today, we are at the point where machine intelligence has information asymmetry over advisers, and that's only going to get more acute and more asymmetrical as time goes on. The only possible hope for human advisers is that they co-opt machine intelligence into their process.

The Best Advice Is Real Time

At best, an adviser is "just a phone call away", but at worst is only available by appointment, dependent on availability. Advice, however, no longer needs to be hinged on access to the adviser as a precursor to whether you can get access to certain information.

The first concept we need to challenge is simply that you need to "go to an adviser" to get advice. Advisers have used their information asymmetry previously to insist that unless you come to them, you won't get the right advice, or they have used asymmetry to price in a premium into the service or product. So if you wanted the right advice, not only did you have to jump through their hoops, go to their branch, office or clinic, but you also had to pay a premium for the best advice, maybe waiting days or even weeks to get to see the best advisers. Your ability to pay, or your access to a specific network, no longer needs to be a factor as to whether you can get good advice on things like your money, health care, fitness, etc.

Whether it is an Apple Watch or a Samsung Simband tracking your heart health in real time and asking an AI to analyse that for anomalies, your electric vehicle telling you the optimal time of the day to recharge or to travel (even automatically scheduling it), your bank account telling you if you are spending too much money, your smart contact lenses telling you to eat a piece of fresh fruit to improve your blood sugar levels or your smartphone telling you to reduce your caffeine intake for the next three hours, advice is going to increasingly become embedded in our lives through technological feedback loops.

Let me try putting it another way.

What is better? A personal network of smartphone, smartwatch, smart clothing or ingested sensors that monitors your heart health over time, finding that your heart health is deteriorating due to increasing incidence of cardiac arrhythmia OR waiting until you have chest pains to see a doctor and hoping that when he hooks up the ECG in the clinic it shows the sporadic arrhythmia that is causing the issue?

What is better? A financial adviser you meet once a year who gives you guidance on your portfolio and investment strategy, and basically tries to pitch you the hot investment fund of the month OR a bank account that is smart enough to monitor your daily spending as you tap your phone to pay and then coach you on how to change your behaviour so you save more money, as well as looking out for the best deals on the things you really want to splurge on, and a robo-adviser that is constantly optimising your investment portfolio to maximise your returns, with lower tolerances and better information than the best financial adviser in the world has access to?

Whether it is advice on how to optimise your day's activities from your bathroom mirror, an interactive chef that helps you cook your next meal or a travel advisory algorithm that optimises which flights you should book to increase your chance of an upgrade, there will increasingly be advice embedded into the world around us where it matters the most. There will be very few instances where a human who can give you advice at a future time with inferior data will compete with technologically embedded, contextual advice in real time.

Machines Will Be Better at Learning about You

Machine learning has been limited in the past by pattern recognition, natural speech and other deficiencies, but machines are beginning to catch up quickly. The advantage that machines connected to the Internet of Things and sensors will have is that they will be able to learn about your behaviour much more efficiently than service organisations today.

How do service organisations today learn about your preferences? There are really only four ways:
- demographic-based assumptions
- surveys, marketing databases and user panels
- data you've previously entered into the system or on a form
- preferences you might input into an app, online portal or other configurator

All of these are imprecise ways of measuring your preferences and behaviour, and at a very minimum depend on both your diligence and honesty in answering, and the effectiveness of the organisation in collecting and synthesizing that data.

In the banking arena, there is a classic example of this type of data conflict. If you survey customers about whether or not they "prefer" to do banking at a bank branch, most customers will say yes, particularly for an activity like account opening or applying for a mortgage. However, if you actually monitor the behaviour of customers, you'll find that more than half of new customers sign up online today, and in most developed economies we're approaching a third of customers who no longer visit the branch. Asking people questions in a survey is just not as accurate as observing their behaviour in the real world.

Observation field studies are a study method that works great in actually seeing someone in an environment where they are using a physical space, or a device, as long as you can get enough clarity on what they are doing, and have their permission to use that data. It is, however, very labour intensive and expensive. You just can't do it frequently.

Sensors have the ability to change all of that. The sensors we are embedding in the world around us such as cameras, accelerometers, GPS geolocation tracking and so forth in our smartphones, heart rate and biometric sensors in our watches, plus WiFi hotspots, app plug-ins, web cookies and so forth are collecting data about our behaviour constantly. This data could even assess our emotional state, but most certainly will have a much more comprehensive view of our behaviour over time.

Ultimately, the future of service interaction is clear. Massive data processing capability is at the core of what will make AIs better advisers than humans, even if humans have access to the same data. Synthesis of data is where humans can no longer compete. It is where services provided by AI agents in the future will differentiate. Get used to telling people your smartphone AI knows you better than you know yourself.

If you are an adviser of some sort today, this is undoubtedly daunting, just as it must have been for the textile artisans of the early 1800s when steam machines were emerging. Nevertheless, it doesn't change the likely future heading our way.

Part 3

The Augmented Age

Chapter 8

Trains, Planes, Automobiles and Houses

"I think it will be quite unusual to see cars that don't have full autonomy... Any cars that are being made that don't have full autonomy will have negative value. It will be like owning a horse. You will only be owning it for sentimental reasons."

Elon Musk, CEO of Tesla, Tesla Earnings call, November 2015

Living with Self-driving Cars

At the CES in Las Vegas in 2015, Mercedes launched a self-driving car called the Mercedes F015. In fact, it reportedly drove itself to the venue. Where it differed from the likes of Google's self-driving car, or those from Volvo, Audi or Tesla, is that it was specifically designed as a "third place" for consumers, as Dieter Zetsch, head of the German company, put it at the time. If our home is our first place and our office or school our second place, then where is the next place we spend a large portion of our time? Our car is the next logical place or space to personalise as a living space, especially once autonomous.

Zetsch described the redesign of the space in the Mercedes F015 as a return to the days of the "carriage". In the days of the horse and cart, you would sit in the back in comfort while the driver did all the work up front. The same will be true for autonomous vehicles. In the past, driving in a car required focus and attention on driving. The vehicle's utility was all about safety, navigation and the ability to get from point A to point B. However, as self-driving cars evolve, the requirement for the car to be driven or for the driver to focus on driving will disappear or become minimalised. As a result, the need to have a car designed around the act of driving will probably be trumped by the need to design the "carriage" space and how you utilise it when you are being driven.

Despite the suggestion of self-driving cars being considered fantastical by some, we may actually be much closer to that reality than many anticipate. Elon Musk, the CEO of Tesla, believes we are much closer to that future.

> "We're going to end up with complete autonomy, and I think [Tesla] will have complete autonomy in approximately two years."
>
> **Elon Musk, from an interview with *Fortune* magazine, 21st December 2015**

Google's self-driving cars have now accumulated close to 2 million driving miles (autonomous and manual driving combined) without causing a single incident, accident or fatality.[1] A Google self-driving car has been pulled over by

---

1 There have been multiple incidents of other cars running into the back of Google's self-driving cars at intersections, and other incidents when human drivers have been driving the cars. However, the cars have yet to have an accident while in autonomous mode.

police, although it somehow avoided getting a ticket.[2] An average American driver is likely to have an accident every ten years or so, or about once in every 165,000 miles.[3] So Google is already more than ten times safer than the average human driver on a purely statistical basis. Data gleaned from the Google self-driving car project has yielded other critical observations, too.

When comparing autonomous driving patterns with those of drivers in control of Google's vehicles, Google found that when a human was behind the wheel, Google's cars accelerated, cornered and braked more sharply than when the car was piloting itself. Other data showed that the autonomous software was much better and more consistent at maintaining a safe distance from the vehicle ahead.

"We're spending less time in near-collision states," said Chris Urmson, the leader of Google's autonomous car project at a robotics conference in 2013. "Our car is driving more smoothly and more safely than our trained professional drivers."

Google's self-driving car has the most data publicly available about this incredible autonomous capability, but other car manufacturers like Tesla, Audi, BMW, Mercedes and Volvo all say similar things about the future of driving. Autonomous vehicles will most likely be significantly safer than those driven by humans within a decade or so.

Giving further insight into this technology, Google has disclosed that the sensors on the Google self-driving car capture nearly 1 gigabyte (GB) of sensor data every second, and subsequently process that information to identify risks or anticipate issues that it may need to react to. It reads traffic all around the vehicle, including any moving hazards on the road that could obstruct its path, it tracks the lanes and shape of the

2 The car was reportedly pulled over for driving too slowly. *See* Marco della Cavva, "Google self-driving car pulled over, avoids fine," *USA Today*, 13 November 2015.
3 US Federal Highway Administration, AllState Insurance

Figure 8.1: What the Google self-driving car "sees" (Source: Google Self-Driving Car Project)

road, referring to GPS data and available map information, as well as any signage or other information that determines the speed the car can travel or where it has to respond to road conditions. It can even isolate a cigarette butt thrown on the side of the road, or a child running in front of the vehicle while chasing a ball onto the street.

The current generation of Google's self-driving car has a Velodyne 64-beam laser embedded in the nose of the vehicle, which generates a 3D map of everything it sees around it. The on-board computers combine this with high-resolution maps of the world, historical driving data and camera and radar images. The vehicle carries four radars (two at the front, two at the rear), a camera that detects traffic lights, a GPS, a wheel encoder and an inertial guidance and measurement unit.

The computers powering these autonomous vehicles are not particularly large either. About the size of an old laptop, they typically fit in the boot of a regular vehicle. In 2014, Audi released a computer called zentrales Fahrer Assistenz Steuergerät (zFAS), or central driver assistance control unit, that is small enough to be mounted in the rear quarter of the vehicle, accessible from within the boot. The zFAS computer powers the Audi autonomous race vehicles Ajay and Bobby that we discussed in chapter 3.

The reaction of many diehard drivers, of course, is to say that they'll "never trust a self-driving car to drive them". Given the facts though, that argument is just as illogical as the one used by people who refuse to fly in aircraft and prefer to drive. Statistically, flying is significantly safer than driving a car. It has often been said that you have a greater risk of being killed on the way to the airport than in flight. Put another way, the odds of dying in a motor vehicle accident are 1 in 98 spread over your lifetime, but 1 in 7,178 for commercial air transport.[4] Those are pretty good odds, odds that show that autonomous piloting is statistically very safe.

For 90 per cent of the time that you spend in a modern commercial aircraft, an autopilot computer is flying it.[5] Many of the newer aircraft flying today have auto landing systems (ALS) that even allow them to land at designated airports unaided by a pilot. While ALS systems are rarely used, redundant systems, better training and simulators, autopilots and modern navigation aids have all made flying the safest form of mass transportation known to man. So it may be argued that the same autopilot capabilities when applied to driving might have similar results.

We've managed to improve car safety systems considerably with seatbelts, rigid passenger shells, airbag deployment, safety glass, anti-lock braking systems (ABSs), collision avoidance systems and other such capabilities. Yet in the United States, Australia, Canada, Germany and the United Kingdom, there are still an average of around five to ten deaths for every

4   2009 figures released by the National Safety Council
5   John Cox, "Ask the Captain: How often is autopilot engaged?" *USA Today*, 11 August 2014.

100,000 vehicles, or about one death for every 100 million miles driven. We can combat drink driving and put more controls on speeds and road conditions, but the reality is that we can't significantly reduce the number of vehicle deaths further because of the remaining human factor. While fatalities have been declining, they've been doing so at a slower and slower rate. Indeed, the biggest risk we have when it comes to driving these days is simply human error. To emphasise the fragility of these statistical gains previously made, it is estimated that nearly 25 per cent of all accidents in the United States in the last four years were caused by people texting while driving. As a result of such factors, since 2011, fatalities have started to increase slightly again, bucking decade-long declines.

Technology is distracting us, and the only way to combat that is to either raise awareness and ban the use of phones while driving (which has had limited success) or introduce autonomous vehicles so that our use of technology is no longer a factor.

Taking all of this into account, it turns out that machine intelligence is going to be able to demonstrate fairly quickly that it is better and safer at driving than us humans. In fact, based on Google's beta testing of its self-driving cars, the existing units are about ten times safer than human drivers. For every 1 million miles that the existing fleet of self-driving cars undertakes, without *causing* an accident, we will see that number effectively double. Probability means that at some point a self-driving car will cause an accident, and that at some point it will probably be involved in a fatality, but these self-driving cars will still be demonstrably safer than human drivers.

As Brad Templeton, a Singularity University professor who worked with Google on the self-driving car, articulated to me during a recent interview:

"Self-driving cars don't get tired, don't get drunk, don't get distracted, don't get road rage and don't need a rest, unless it might be to charge."

Brad Templeton, Singularity University,
author interview in May 2015

Within ten, or even five, years in developed economies, semi-autonomous or self-driving cars will probably be commonplace. Think about that for a moment. In about the same time that it has taken for the iPhone and smartphones to dominate every corner of society, we will see smart, autonomous cars exploding onto the scene. *Business Insider* has estimated that we'll have 10 million cars with self-driving features on the road by 2020. The exponential curve of this technology means that there will be close to 100 million self-driving cars on the road just ten years after that.

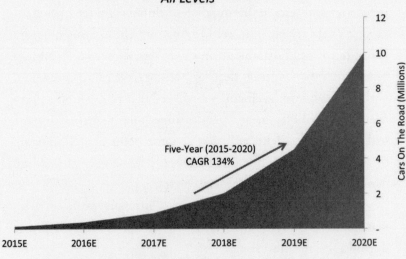

Figure 8.2: Business Intelligence projections on self-driving vehicles (Credit: BI)

Within 15 years, we can expect that major cities and local authorities will be giving strong preferences to self-driving cars. Within 20 years, cities like London and New York won't just have congestion charges, there will also be charges for traditional, human piloted vehicles to enter the city centres, or more probably even banning them from city streets. While there will be some protests against banning "human drivers", remember that the generations making these governance decisions will be Gen Y and Gen Z, not the likes of the baby boomers who grew up with gas guzzlers, V8 engines and the oil boom. Our kids expect this to happen and will be quite happy to trade in the art of driving for more screen time in an autonomous vehicle.

Elon Musk said on a call before the 2016 Detroit Motor Show that within 24 to 36 months, you'll even be able to summon a car to drive itself across the country to meet you:

> "If you're in New York and the car's in Los Angeles, you can summon your car to you from your phone and tell the car to find you, and it'll automatically charge itself along the journey."

Although the current barrier of entry to autonomous vehicles is cost, that cost is rapidly shrinking. In 2010, the cost of Google's self-driving technology was around US$150,000, of which US$70,000 was just for the highly accurate laser-based radar, or light detection and radar sensor (lidar). German supplier Ibeo, which manufactures vehicular lidar systems, claims that it will be able to mass-produce them by 2017 for as little as US$250 per vehicle. Computational processing is probably another large component of the overall price, and it has a long history of exponential cost reduction. In addition, we can expect battery technology to improve dramatically and allow self-driving vehicles to eventually get through an entire day without the need for a charge.

The sharing economy for vehicles will thrive. Electric, self-driving vehicles will be significantly cheaper to run, but the average city dweller won't even need to own a car, or they may choose to own a share in a vehicle. The user will simply rent a vehicle by the hour, and each vehicle will shuffle between owners or renters themselves, stopping to charge at the required charging station in quiet periods.

The trend of young adults moving away from vehicle ownership is already becoming evident. Instead of asking for their own car when they reach driving age, teens are now asking their parents for an Uber account.[6] So this is not just a factor of electric, self-driving cars; the sharing economy is already starting to shift behaviour towards dramatically different vehicle ownership models. Children who have grown up with parents who use Uber or ride-sharing services will do the maths and find that it is cheaper to not own their own vehicle in an average city with good public transportation and an autonomous vehicle network.

For those with a commute, this is where the Mercedes vision of the self-driving car gives us a glimpse of the near future. Realising that a self-driving car does not need to be optimised for driving, the interior space could instead be used for entertainment, eating your breakfast on the way to the office, as an office itself or just as an extension of your personal space. How will users of self-driving cars personalise their vehicles? The future customisation of a self-driving car may be along the lines of how you personalise your home today, instead of how you may have personalised a car in the past. The choice of

---

6 Including my 15-year-old daughter. In fact, she said instead of buying her a car I should get her an Uber account.

entertainment system, seating, display tech, even a 3D-printer food processing unit could be all the rage in this new personal space. Maybe living in your self-driving car might be fashionable for entrepreneurs, making it a sort of mobile home/office.

The only thing that might hold all of this back, conceivably, is legislation. However, once manufacturers demonstrate the safety of self-driving car systems, it is far more likely that both passengers and legislators will start to opt in voluntarily. Some legislators will insist that autonomous vehicles must have the option for a human to "take over", and there will no doubt be purists who try to hack around autonomous routines in some way. Moreover, we can expect lobby groups of manufacturers who fall behind in autonomous technology to attempt to muddy the waters with figures around safety. The first death of a passenger or a pedestrian by an autonomous vehicle will be a watershed moment. It is unlikely, however, to stop autonomous cars from dominating our future. Interestingly, the CEO of Volvo, Håkan Samuelsson, has already said that Volvo will accept liability when a self-driving car is involved in an accident.[7] That is a big deal!

Early applications of self-driving technology will likely be commercial. Self-driving delivery trucks combined with either drones or delivery robots (to drop a package at your door) will be much cheaper to run than the human-operated FedEx and postal service trucks that we see on the roads today. The delivery of shipping containers to ports, and other such transportation, will also quickly become autonomous.

While Uber is investing heavily in this area, there may still be some humans in the driving services business for some time. Initially, the wealthy will express their wealth by owning a self-driving car, but there will most likely be a U-turn at some point in the future, where having a human driver becomes an expression

---

7 Volvo Press Release, https://www.media.volvocars.com/global/en-gb/media/pressreleases/167975/us-urged-to-establish-nationwide-federal-guidelines-for-autonomous-driving

of wealth, and not the other way around. For transportation of goods, however, no such humanity is required or beneficial in the medium term. Self-driving cars will lower cost, injuries and fatalities as well as increase the utility of transportation networks considerably. Particularly if those autonomous vehicles are electric vehicles.

For those of us who regularly commute today, with self-driving cars we'll suddenly have a great deal more time on our hands, and that will change the way we think of driving in fundamental ways. The family road trip might take on a whole new meaning. So the logical next question is: how long will it be before we have flying cars like the one Doc drove/flew in *Back to the Future?*

Beyond the A380, Flying Cars and Robot Drones

Flying car enthusiasts may recognise the name Paul Moller. In 1974, Paul Moller touted a flying saucer type car he called the Discojet, raising funds for the project. In 2003, Moller was fined by the Securities Exchange Commission (SEC) for making false and misleading statements to investors. As the SEC put it: "As of late 2002, Moller International's approximately 40 years of development has resulted in a prototype Skycar capable of hovering about fifteen feet above the ground." In 2013, Moller launched a crowdfunding campaign on Indiegogo[8] to raise a further US$958,000 for the project. It closed in January 2014, having raised just US$29,429.

We have been dreaming of flying cars since the 1950s.

> When the U.S. civil aeronautics administration
> certified the Aerocar for operation in 1956,
> it seemed inevitable, at least to aerospace

8 https://www.indiegogo.com/projects/actually-fly-the-m400x-skycar-into-history

engineers, that before long the flying car would take its place as a fixture in the garage of the typical suburban ranch home. Yet that was not to be. The Aerocar, which looked like a car but had wings and could take off on a short runway, was too expensive to justify mass production. Aerocar International built only six of these vehicles, leaving the promise of the flying car unfulfilled—except in episodes of *The Jetsons*.

> "The Flying Car Will Finally Fly—and Drive,"
> *Scientific American*, January 2013

Today, however, at least two companies have made flying cars a reality. The Terrafugia Transition and the Aeromobil flying car have both successfully made the transition from car to flight and carry actual passengers.

The Aeromobil is the more futuristic looking of the two vehicles. This flying car is capable of 125 mph (200 km/h) powered flight and has a range of 435 miles (700 km). Built in Slovakia, an unlikely destination for the future of flying cars, the Aeromobil is the result of 25 years of development. With the advance of composites and engine design, the promise of this technology has finally caught up with reality.

But don't expect to walk down to your local Aeromobil dealership and start flying anytime soon. At best, the Aeromobil will be classified as a sports aircraft, requiring a sport pilot licence or a minimum of at least 20 hours of flight training. The Aeromobil can indeed fly, but it still needs a runway like a conventional aircraft and is subject to all the same rules as a Cessna, Cirrus or Piper aircraft. Want to fly a car? You'll still need pilot's wings.

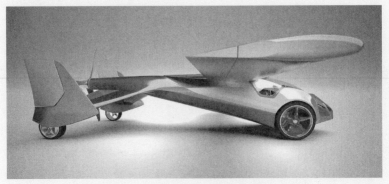

Figure 8.3: The Terrafugia Transition (Credit: Terrafugia)

Figure 8.4: Slovakian-built Aeromobil (Credit: Aeromobil)

That may change in the future, however. Increased computing capability has a role to play here but airspace governance is the key. Currently, separation[9] of aircraft flying in either controlled or uncontrolled airspace is a function of pilot awareness, collision avoidance systems and radar vectoring by air traffic control (ATC). The Next Generation Air Transportation System (NextGen), which is emerging in the United States, could possibly set the basis for autonomous flying cars.

Between 2012 and 2025, the implementation of NextGen is expected to cost US taxpayers between US$20–25 billion but

---

9 Separation refers to the distance maintained between aircraft while flying. The opposite of separation is, of course, an in-air collision, which is generally not positive.

will result in travel delays in the United States being cut by more than 30 per cent, with savings well in excess of the investment. At the heart of NextGen is a technology called automatic dependent surveillance–broadcast (ADS–B). ADS–B enables an aircraft to determine its position via GPS satellite, and to broadcast that to ATC and other aircraft that can maintain separation. ATC systems currently use radar and transponders to identify aircraft. While sophisticated, these are still prone to both technical and human errors. ADS–B works like an asynchronous communications network in which aircraft are nodes, and allows aircraft movements to be coordinated in real time much more accurately than current systems. ADS–B allows aircraft to maintain separation independently in the absence of radar coverage or access to the ATC radio network. It is entirely conceivable that ADS–B could evolve into part of an autonomous network with aircraft that can fly themselves in the not too distant future.

The ADS–B network would conceivably allow the deployment of vehicles like the EHang 184, an autonomous helicopter drone that has seating for a single passenger. The drone was launched at CES in Las Vegas in 2016, and represents the first possible deployment of an autonomous flying vehicle.

Unlike self-driving cars, which are focused primarily on the comfort of passengers, it is more likely that the first self-flying vehicles won't be passenger aircraft at all, but drones. On 1st December 2013, Amazon CEO Jeff Bezos appeared on *60 Minutes* to launch an audacious plan to ship purchases to Amazon Prime customers via drone. If this had been aired on 1st April, most of the US population would have assumed it was an April fool's joke, but Bezos was serious. He pointed out that 86 per cent of Amazon's orders were less than 5 pounds in total weight and that orders in this category could be fulfilled in

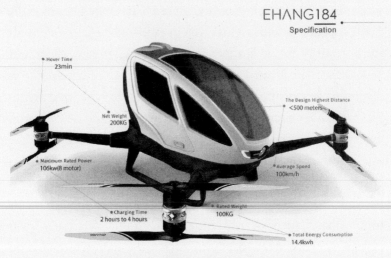

EH∧NG184
Specification

Hover Time
23min

The Design Highest Distance
<500 meters

Net Weight
200KG

Maximum Rated Power
106kw(8 motor)

Average Speed
100km/h

Charging Time
2 hours to 4 hours

Rated Weight
100KG

Total Energy Consumption
14.4kwh

Figure 8.5: EHang 184 flying transport (Credit: EHang Inc)

30 minutes or less using a drone-based delivery system. Sounds like science fiction? Bezos doesn't think so.

In a letter dated 9th June 2014 to the Federal Aviation Association (FAA), Bezos made a number of very interesting points in respect to Amazon's development of its Amazon Prime drone fleet. He pointed out that Amazon is already deploying its ninth generation of aerial vehicle, has ex-NASA engineers (including an astronaut) on staff working on the project and that "one day, seeing Amazon Prime Air will be as normal as seeing mail trucks on the road".

The use of drones has been toyed with in battlefields since World War II. The United States started working in earnest on drones as early as the Vietnam War, but it wasn't until the 1982 Israeli conflict with Syria when unmanned aerial vehicles (UAVs) were used with significant success. Since then, the drones being deployed in the theatre of war have become incredibly sophisticated. On 16th April 2015, the US Navy

Figure 8.6: A prototype Amazon Prime delivery drone (Credit: Amazon)

demonstrated the ability of its X-47B unmanned carrier air vehicle demonstrator (UCAS-D) to conduct mid-air refuelling with a KC-707 tanker. The same X-47B has already demonstrated the ability to consistently land on US carriers at sea. However, this ability has not come without controversy.

Since 2004, the US government has conducted hundreds of attacks on targets in Northwestern Pakistan using UAV drones. The debate regarding civilian versus military casualties in this so-called "drone war" is significant, with recent estimates ranging from 286 to 890 civilian casualties (168 to 197 of those being children).[10] The Peshawar High Court has ruled that these ongoing attacks are illegal, inhumane and violate the UN charter on human rights and constitute a "war crime".[11]

The use of drone aircraft is set to explode, but in this respect while armed drones will probably remain the purview of the armed forces and perhaps police, aerial surveillance capability is now widely available to the public at large.

10 Bureau of Investigative Journalism Report. October 2014 Update: US Covert Actions in Pakistan, Yemen and Somalia.
11 A. Buncombe, "Pakistani court declares US drone strikes in the country's tribal belt illegal," *Independent*, 9 May 2013.

This afternoon, a stranger set an aerial drone
into flight over my yard and beside my house
near Miller Playfield. I initially mistook its noisy
buzzing for a weed-whacker on this warm spring
day. After several minutes, I looked out my third-
story window to see a drone hovering a few feet
away. My husband went to talk to the man on the
sidewalk outside our home who was operating
the drone with a remote control, to ask him to not
fly his drone near our home. The man insisted that
it is legal for him to fly an aerial drone over our
yard and adjacent to our windows. He noted that
the drone has a camera, which transmits images
he viewed through a set of glasses.

Capitol Hill Seattle Blog, 8th May 2013

It may be that the novelty for drones wears off in the future, relegated to history like the Segway. However, given the application of drones for professional photography, recreational use and so on, it is unlikely. The FAA certainly doesn't believe that this problem is going to go away. Consequently, it has been putting increasing effort into regulating the use of unmanned aircraft systems (UAS). In February 2015, it listed the following restrictions for people flying UAS for personal use, essentially classifying these UAS as model aircraft:

- Fly below 400 feet and remain clear of surrounding obstacles.
- Keep the aircraft within visual line of sight at all times.
- Remain well clear of and do not interfere with manned aircraft operations.
- Don't fly within 5 miles of an airport unless you contact the airport and control tower before flying.

- Don't fly near people or stadiums.
- Don't fly an aircraft that weighs more than 55 lbs.
- Don't be careless or reckless with your unmanned aircraft—you could be fined for endangering people or other aircraft.

Specifically in respect to photography or video, these FAA rules suggest that taking photos for personal use is recreational. However, for the same reason why you can't climb a tree and photograph what your neighbours are doing in their backyard, using a drone to photograph someone on their own property is illegal, and will at some point in the near future result in a significant lawsuit being brought against a pilot of a "hobby" drone.

On 24th December 2015, the FAA announced further controls over privately owned drones, requiring all aircraft weighing more than 0.55 pounds (250 grammes) and less than 55 pounds (approximately 25 kg), including payloads such as on-board cameras, to be registered.

Criminals are using drones consistently too. In prisons across the United States, drones are now regularly being used by operators to drop contraband into prison yards. The US authorities have detected half a dozen similar attempts at corrections facilities in the past two years. In the same period, there were also reported attempts in Ireland, Britain, Australia and Canada.

Drone drops are the high-tech equivalent of smuggling a file into a prison in a birthday cake, and it underscores the headache that drones are now creating for law enforcement, who have very few ways of stopping them for now. Smartphones, drugs and smartphone chargers are the hot property for drone drops. For instance, the warden of the Lee Correctional Institute, Cecilia Reynolds, said that her officers had found 17 phones in one inmate's cell. These prison officers suspected that the phones were delivered via drone. Prison phone calls and emails are monitored today so smartphones circumvent that monitoring. Will prisons be forced to install anti-drone-aircraft defence systems in the near future? Maybe a net over the recreation area might have to do...

As mentioned earlier in chapter 3, Facebook is developing a network of solar-powered drones codenamed Aquila (the Latin word for "eagle") that will stay aloft for months and continuously beam Internet access via laser to millions of users on the ground. This is designed to give coverage to users in remote communities, such as in Africa where mobile coverage is scant or bandwidth non-existent. Facebook's Aquila drone has the wingspan of a 767 aircraft but weighs less than a car. The company commenced test flights in the summer of 2015.

The use of new composites, solar power and even the resurgence of zeppelin technology could power a real renaissance in the use of the skies. Of course, it could get pretty crowded up there as a result, which is why systems like ADS–B are critical, but is also why AI in aircraft is a given in the future, if just for collision avoidance alone.

Within 50 years, the case for self-flying cars will be much stronger than it is today. The real question that remains is not whether we could have self-flying cars, because the technology for automation seems mainly achievable, but what will fuel these self-flying cars?

Maglev and the Hyperloop

On 21st April 2015, a new maglev train near Mount Fuji in Japan clocked speeds of 375 mph (603 km/h). Maglev is short for "magnetic levitation" and is a technology that allows a train (or object) to be suspended above a rail with no other support than the use of magnetic fields. In this instance, the Japanese maglev train is suspended about 10 cm from the electrically charged magnets that are effectively the "track" or rail. Such a design produces a much quieter, smoother and faster ride than conventional high-speed rail.

Three years earlier in July 2012, at a PandoDaily event in Santa Monica, California, Elon Musk mentioned to an assembled group that he was thinking about a "fifth mode of transport", calling it the Hyperloop. On 12th August 2013, Tesla and SpaceX (both companies founded by Musk) released preliminary designs for a Hyperloop Transportation system on their blog sites. Musk called this open-source design, asking others with interest to contribute to the design.

The initial proposed route for a US$6 billion passenger version of the Hyperloop ran from the Los Angeles region to the San Francisco Bay Area with an expected transit time of 35 minutes. The Hyperloop would thus traverse the 354-mile (570-km) route at an average speed of around 598 mph (962 km/h), with a top speed of 760 mph (1,220 km/h). In January 2015, Musk announced that he was building a privately funded Hyperloop test track in Texas, about 5 miles (8 km) in length, for university and private teams to test and refine transport "pod" designs. Two additional start-ups, Hyperloop Technologies and Hyperloop Transportation Technologies, are both building their own two-mile and five-mile test tracks, respectively.

The Hyperloop is a form of vactrain, or near-vacuum train. The biggest challenge traditionally in creating high-speed rail that is able to compete with air transportation systems has been the ability to circumvent friction and air resistance as speeds climb. Magnetic levitation transportation systems such as the Japanese train mentioned above use a number of very large magnets to propel the train. In fact, the JR-Maglev trains have superconducting magnetic coils. The amount of horsepower required to push a car or a train significantly above the 311 mph (500 km/h) barrier starts to climb steeply and means that if you want to get to aircraft-type speeds, say 500 mph (800 km/h), the mathematics don't work. There's just too much friction and air resistance.

As early as the 1960s, a proposal was put forward to build a transatlantic tunnel between New York City and London using a 3,100-mile (5,000-km) long near-vacuum tube with vactrains, or maglev trains operating in near vacuum. The system, which resembled earlier patents issued to Robert Goddard (the father of modern rocketry), was theoretically capable of allowing speeds of up to 5,000 miles (8,000 km) per hour. Meaning the transit time from New York to London would be less than an hour.

The "Musk" Hyperloop resembles these vactrain proposals but would operate at approximately one millibar of pressure, qualifying as a "partially evacuated tunnel". Because of the low-pressure, warm air proposed for the Hyperloop steel tubes, the pods projected to travel at around 760 mph (1,220 km/h) through these steel tubes would not actually break the sound barrier. Therefore, the pods would not need to be designed for passing through the transonic phase or coping with the shock of a sonic boom.

In any respect, Elon Musk thinks that he can get you from New York to Los Angeles in around 45 minutes with this technology, so I for one would be keen to try it out!

Home Is Where the *Smarts* Are

When Nest introduced its smart thermostat, many people probably thought "so what". However, the company quickly went on to be acquired by Google for US$3.2 billion following huge early success. In a 2014 article in *Forbes*, it was revealed that Nest's digital, smart thermostat was in 1 per cent of US homes, or about 1.3 million households, that the company was selling more than 100,000 new units every month and that sales were accelerating.

It's simple how the product works. Nest connects with the existing heating, ventilating and air-conditioning (HVAC) system in a home or office in the form of a smart thermostat that more or less anyone who can use a screwdriver can install in a few minutes. The thermostat then interfaces with the web and optimises your home heating and cooling system based on whether you are at home, what the temperature outside your home is and on peer group analysis. The average Nest user reported savings of 10 to 12 per cent on their heating bills and 15 per cent on their cooling bills,[12] or an estimated average savings of between US$131 and US$145 a year. Smart thermostats are just the start, however.

In *Iron Man*, Tony Stark's lab and home are interfaced with an AI called J.A.R.V.I.S. (Just A Rather Very Intelligent System) that controls all of the smart elements of Stark's lab including security systems, power, telecommunications and even the manufacturing of Stark's latest suits. As we'll see in our chapter on Smart Cities, there is a definite move towards smart infrastructure as part of the Augmented Age, but smart buildings and smart homes are all part of the mix.

We talked a bit about Jibo and Amazon Echo in chapter 3, but out of the two, Amazon Echo is about the closest we have to a *Star Trek*-style computer (that we can talk to) in our home today (if you have one, of course).

12 http://www.nest.com

Amazon Echo's capability is fairly typical of the core smart house capabilities that we'll see emerge over the next decade or two. As devices like our TVs, lights, thermostats, garages, cooking appliances, coffee machines, robot vacuum cleaners and so on will all connect to the Internet (the Internet of Things), we'll need some basic household management capability that looks after them. These devices will be smart enough to talk

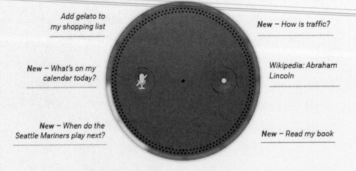

New – Play 'Today's Hits' station on Pandora

Set an alarm for eight a.m.

Add gelato to my shopping list

New – How is traffic?

New – What's on my calendar today?

Wikipedia: Abraham Lincoln

New – When do the Seattle Mariners play next?

New – Read my book

What's the weather in Los Angeles this weekend?

New – Turn off the lights

Figure 8.7: Amazon Echo is a Siri-like smart home entertainment/interface. (Credit: Amazon)

to each other, but we'll have both a management layer and an interaction layer in the home (or in the cloud).

Apple has also been working on a core capability for household management called HomeKit. Through its system, the management of your home will become largely automated. We're not talking about just home automation technology here, as we've traditionally labelled this, but more an integrated home ecosystem that helps you set up and manage the smarter elements of your home.

As technology like HomeKit, Echo and individual devices become more intelligent, such resource management will have some primary goals and objectives:

1. manage the home efficiently
2. personalise your home environment around your tastes, likes, etc.
3. respond to real-time events and requests as required
4. learn
5. inform

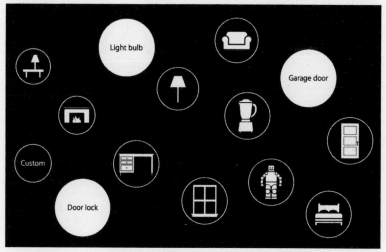

Figure 8.8: Apple HomeKit sample functions or node controllers (Credit: Apple)

Two key areas of the smart home that will undergo augmentation are the kitchen and the bathroom.

Despite years of talking about smart fridges that order your groceries via the Internet, the closest we've got is Amazon Dash Button. However, by 2030 with robotics, drone delivery and the like, you will have the ability to have your groceries and shopping delivered automatically from a smart kitchen initiated order. It's also likely that we'll continue to automate cooking in the kitchen. While a *Star Trek*-style replicator is decades away, a 3D printer that prints a burger or a pizza will be viable by 2030, if not earlier. Natural Machines launched a kickstarter campaign in 2014 for its 3D "Foodini" printer, which will be capable of printing various foods like pasta, cookies, crackers, bread, snacks, etc. A robotic chef (shown below) like the one Morley Robotics is working on is also a distinct possibility within the next 10 to 15 years.

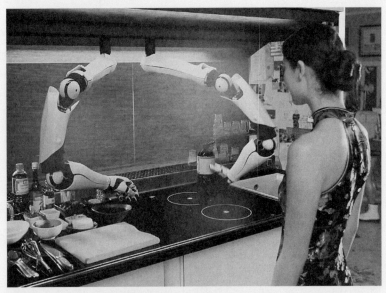

Figure 8.9: A robotic chef (Credit: Morley Robotics)

The smart bathroom is sure to incorporate not only smarts into the bathroom mirror, but smarts into other appliances. It is quite possible that your smart toilet will be analysing your waste and looking for imbalances or evidence of emerging health conditions.

Ultimately, this technology around your home will just integrate with your personal AI. It's one of the reasons why personalised AI assistants, what I refer to as Life Stream in chapter 7, are going to be such huge business. Google, Facebook, Apple and Amazon are all investing in this technology, but the big business will be integrating this across our homes, offices, cars and smartphones.

Chapter 9

Smart Banking, Payments and Money

> "The root problem with conventional currency is all the trust that's required to make it work. The central bank must be trusted not to debase the currency, but the history of fiat currencies is full of breaches of that trust."
>
> Satoshi Nakamoto, pseudonym of the anonymous creator of Bitcoin

The evolution of banking and payments has often been correlated with technological advancement. Today, the primary method of transferring money between banks globally is a transaction called a wire transfer or telegraphic transfer, so named because the instructions for these transfers were sent via telegraph or "wire" initially, then later by Telex and now via interbank electronic networks like SWIFT.[1] The first mainframe computer ever built was for a bank, too.

---

1 Society for the Worldwide Interbank Financial Telecommunication

Today, we talk about using distributed ledger systems like the blockchain to send money from wallet to wallet, or account to account, instantly between devices or value stores across the globe. The future of money, payments and elements of the banking system is going to be materially and fundamentally changed by a range of technologies being deployed today. The biggest change will likely be in respect to what we call our "bank account", and how people get access to banking around the world, but the way banks and payments operate is also being transformed fundamentally. Within 20 years, we'll probably see the elimination of around 40 to 50 per cent of the household names in banking today. In fact, we're already seeing the creation of new alternative banking and financial service providers that will soon be bigger, in terms of customers and influence, than financial powerhouses like JPMorgan Chase, HSBC and Citibank. We're already seeing this shift quantified in the daily activity of bank customers.

The United Kingdom, the United States, Spain and a host of other countries are seeing the lowest number of bank branches in decades. In the United Kingdom, you'd have to go back 60 years[2] to find lower numbers of bank branches than there are today. In the United States, banks like BofA, Chase and Wells Fargo have cut more than 15 per cent of their branches in the last four years alone, bringing their branch levels back to those of the early 1980s. While the United States has seen declines of around 1 to 2 per cent per year in branch numbers, branch space or square footage may be a much better indicator of the waning support for branches:

> Aramanda: So branch banking is, in your view, a
> channel that is here to stay?

---

2   Graham Hiscott, "Number of bank branches at lowest level for over 60 years," *Mirror*, 5 July 2013.

Stumpf: Yes. For right now, it surely is. We don't
know how to grow without [branches]. We
can't grow without [them]. But, we have taken
the total square footage of the bank from 117
million square feet at the time of the merger with
Wachovia in January of '09, to about 92 million
square feet today, and we're continuing to go
down from there...

**John Stumpf, CEO of Wells Fargo, during an interview with
ClearingHouse.org in December 2015**

Wells Fargo has reduced its branch square footage, or total
real estate, by 22 per cent in just six years. The reason why all of
these banks are reducing branch numbers and branch space is
simple—customers simply aren't using branches as much as they
used to. They don't need to. It's not a branch design problem; it's
a customer behaviour problem. So what has changed customer
behaviour? We can largely thank Steve Jobs for the shift as the
iPhone started it all.

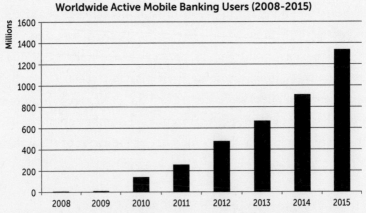

Figure 9.1: Worldwide mobile banking adoption, monthly active users (Source: Various)

As banking becomes augmented, much of what we value today in banking will be eliminated, and we're not just talking about branch locations. The big shift for banking will be in the very nature of how banking works, what we call a bank account and the products we get from banks, or their near-term replacements. In respect to automation and AI, there is hardly a single job in banking that won't be affected. In fact, in 100 years when we look back at all of these changes, we'll probably identify the **bank teller** or **cashier** as the equivalent of the telegraph operator of the early 20th century, the one job most impacted by changing technology. When it comes to the Augmented Age, the greatest challenges for banking are about to hit, and hit hard.

Always Banking, Never at a Bank

As of 2010, half of the world's population didn't have a bank account, which accounts for more than two billion adults worldwide. Traditionally, we have called these people "unbanked" because they don't have access to traditional banking services. Being unbanked may not be an issue much longer though.

Access to financial services is seen as one of the core ways that individuals can step out of extreme poverty. Various studies by the World Bank and a recent 2012 study in Africa have shown that "promoting access to formal financial services increases the level of income of the rural dwellers and thus a retarding effect on the level of poverty in the rural areas."[3] In places like Africa, these mechanics fundamentally matter. Standard Bank and Accenture conducted a survey in 2014 that concluded that of the 1 billion unbanked on the African continent, more than 70 per cent would need to spend their entire savings, or the equivalent of an entire month's salary, just to get transportation

---

3 H. M. Aliero and S. S. Ibrahim, "Does Access to Finance Reduce Poverty," *Mediterranean Journal of Social Sciences* 3, no. 2 (May 2012): 575–581.

to visit an available bank branch. The simple fact is that we won't get people access to banking fast enough through branches. Thankfully, we don't have to.

If you look at Kenya with less than 50 branches per 1 million people and financial inclusion[4] of 20 per cent through the traditional bank system, the obvious conclusion would be that this country needs more branches. That is, until you learn that since 2006 Kenya's financial inclusion has grown to a whopping 85 per cent thanks to the M-Pesa mobile phone or mobile money account.

It's pretty simple. If you allow someone who has no banking services access to basic banking via a mobile money account on a smartphone or feature phone, this will change his or her life dramatically. In the case of M-Pesa, it means that mobile money users are likely to save 25 per cent more annually[5] than their unbanked contemporaries. If you insist that someone has to have a driving licence or identity document and then needs to get to a physical branch to fill out an application form in order to open a bank account, you are actually increasing the likelihood of financial *exclusion*. You will actively prevent the poor from having access to financial services. This is a key problem in markets like the United States, India and Italy. In these countries, it is not access to branches that excludes people from banking services, it is the rules that bank regulators have created around opening bank accounts. For Italy and the United States, their high branch density (two of the top five countries in the world for branch availability) has not stopped them from seeing a decline in the number of people with bank accounts over the last few years.

For the first few years after M-Pesa's creation, the big banks in Africa tried to get it shut down, but that horse had long ago

4 The percentage of the population who own a bank account
5 Alliance for Financial Inclusion (AFI)

bolted, with more than 75 per cent of Kenya's adult population being users of the service. It was then that the Commercial Bank of Africa (CBA) realised that "if you can't beat them, join them".

In 2012, CBA launched a simple savings account linked to M-Pesa called M-Shwari.[6] The uptake was incredible. In the three years that followed, M-Shwari added 12 million new accounts, for 4.5 million customers (that's one in five Kenyans). It took in US$2.2 billion in deposits in that same period. That makes M-Shwari the biggest "bank" by number of customers, or by deposits, in Kenya. It is the single most successful banking product on the African continent today. It takes just 10 seconds to sign up for an M-Shwari savings account—10 seconds! But a more interesting statistic is that 80 per cent of M-Shwari customers have never visited a bank branch,[7] and it is unlikely that they ever will.

Yu'e Bao (pronounced "yu-eh bow") is the largest money market fund in China today, but what makes this fund unique is that it is offered not by a bank but by Jack Ma's Alibaba payments division called Alipay. In fact, Yu'e Bao is the most successful mobile banking product in the world. In just eight months, 81 million investors throughout China deposited an astonishing 554 billion yuan, or US$92.3 billion. Within three years of its launch, Yu'e Bao is projected to make up around 8 per cent of the total Chinese deposit market,[8] an incredible feat. These two very successful examples show that you no longer need a bank branch to be able to take deposits.

Mobile Is the Bank Account
The top five banks in the world are Industrial and Commercial Bank of China (ICBC), Wells Fargo, China Construction

6 *Shwari* is the Kiswahili word for "calm".
7 "Banking on FinTech," Breaking Banks podcast interview with Mohammed Jama Dalal of CBA, 19 October 2015.
8 Chinese International Capital Corporation (CICC) estimates

Bank, JPMorgan Chase and Bank of China. Together, they have **550 million bank accounts**, with 250 million mobile users. Combined, these banks have a market cap exceeding US$1.2 trillion and employ close to 2 million people. Big numbers, right?

By 2025, the world's bank account will be a mobile phone—not a chequebook, not a passbook, not a plastic card, but a mobile smartphone that keeps your money safely locked away behind a biometric security layer.

What exactly is a bank account? It is essentially a **value store**; a safe place where you can store money or monetary value for the purpose of savings or for the future potential of purchase and money movement. If we count a bank account as a value store that you can use to pay for goods and services, it might provide a better definition. You can use a Starbucks app or Starbucks card to buy a coffee, for example, but no bank is required. Is the Starbucks mobile app actually a banking app? No, because technically we classify the "bank account" underpinning the Starbucks app as a "gift card". And yet the Starbucks app accounts for 21 per cent of all purchases made at Starbucks, or roughly $4 billion in purchases annually.[9]

There are actually a whole host of other mobile value stores that are widely adopted and accepted globally today. These include the likes of your iTunes account, PayPal, Bitcoin or Alibaba's Alipay. How do these compare in terms of reach and number of users or accounts? If you take just iTunes, PayPal and Alipay, they currently account for **1.2 billion account holders**. That is more than double what the top five banks have in terms of the number of individual customers with bank accounts. If you include M-Pesa, MTN Mobile Money, bKash, GCash and other mobile money services, you can easily add another 300 million account holders.

9 Starbucks Fourth Quarter Results, 29 October 2015

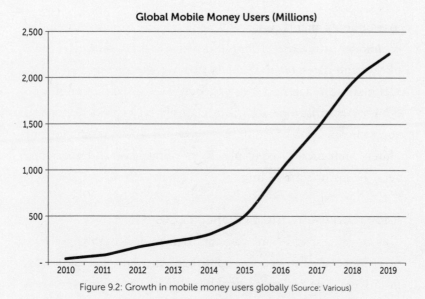

Figure 9.2: Growth in mobile money users globally (Source: Various)

That means quite simply that *mobile bank accounts, mobile value stores or mobile wallets already outnumber traditional bank accounts two to one.* Yes, you read that correctly. Yet the growth in mobile money accounts is set to surge further in the next few years, and most of this growth will be fuelled by people using their phone as their primary or sole means of payment.

Within ten years, most of the world will be using their phone to pay for things every day. More critically, 2 billion people will have been "banked", or first able to save money to an account or value store, via their phone. More than 75 per cent of these people will have never owned a debit card or passbook, will have never written a cheque and will never visit a bank branch in their life. By 2025, well over half of the planet will be using their mobile device—or their personal AI—to do banking more than any other means or method of banking.

This will surely change the way we think about banking itself. Clearly, a merchant will be penalised if he doesn't offer access to mobile payments. Cash will be in decline in most developed economies as the use of mobile payments skyrockets. The most likely candidates to go cashless first are Nordic countries like Denmark, Sweden and Norway, but the United Kingdom and other parts of Europe are not necessarily far behind. What will you call your bank account? Whatever it is, it will reside on your phone—not on a piece of plastic, not in a book and you won't get it by visiting a building.

Impact on the World's Financial Ecosystem

This modality shift of bank accounts to smart devices and the ability of artificial intelligence to supplement the financial ecosystem means that the utility of banking will be measured not via a "network" of branches or the products and services we get from a bank today, but via the way money, payments and credit works in your life every day. Financial education and financial literacy will be embedded in tools on the smartphone, not prerequisites that prevent someone from getting access to the system.

In that way, the mobile wallet platforms embedded in phones such as Apple Pay, Android Pay (Google Wallet 2.0) and Venmo have much greater utility than banks. The utility of retail banks has been largely driven off three pillars:

1. access to branch banking (often as mandated in the United States, India and Italy)
2. access to advice (read: product advisory for investment, mortgages, etc.)
3. access to proprietary, regulator-backed value stores and payments rails

All of these pillars are being challenged by technology shift but the core of banking will be pretty simple.

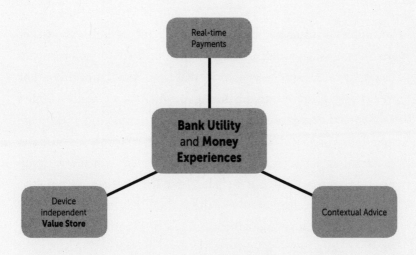

As algorithms get better at predicting behaviour and offering options, the best advice in banking will work like emerging systems like Apple's HealthKit or Fitbit, not only providing you the right product or service at the right time, but also wrapping these decisions in context or awareness of your own financial health so that you can make a smart decision. Thus, we eliminate the need for financial literacy, financial education, complex product constructs and budgeting in favour of tools that monitor, advise and solve financial problems as they occur, in real time.

By 2020, we're going to see 50 billion devices connected to the Internet, and by 2030 potentially 100 trillion sensors. Everything around us will be smart. Smart fridges that order your groceries;[10] kitchens that can tell you what you can cook using what you have in your fridge and cupboard; sensors you wear on your wrist or in your clothes that monitor your health and activity; cars that talk to each other and drive themselves; smart mirrors that show you how you would look in that new shirt or with that new hairstyle; robot drones and pods that deliver your groceries or Amazon orders.

---

10 For those sceptical of the "Internet Fridge" example, keep in mind that you can already order groceries from Amazon Echo or Amazon Dash, essentially in the same way a smart fridge could.

Our smartphone will soon be able to book us flights or a ticket for a train journey simply because we ask it to do so, or just by listening to our conversations in real time. Underpinning all of this is an expectation that banking, payments and credit will just work, in real time, solving our problems and helping us manage our money every day. Smart devices and smart stuff will need to do money "stuff" all the time; these devices will increasingly need to transact on our behalf. That means that within just ten years, more transactions will be done machine-to-machine (M2M) than those involving a human or a traditional banking product like a credit card.

No More Credit Cards

As we start using Apple Pay and Android Pay increasingly, we're pretty quickly going to eliminate the need for plastic altogether. We'll just download a token or a payment app to our phone, linked to our bank. We won't use a card number anymore, simply because it will no longer be securable. We'll tap our phone, authenticate via our fingerprint and receive a notification that the payment has been successful, or we'll just walk in and out of a store where payments are automatically made without a traditional checkout experience.

If we download an app or a token to our phone, then it won't be a credit card, but does it still need to have the same properties? Not really. Think about how we generally use a credit card today and how we might redesign that in a real-time, augmented world.

The two primary use cases for a credit card today could be illustrated thus:

- I'm at the grocery store and have swiped my debit card but the transaction is declined because, unexpectedly, my salary hasn't hit my account yet. As I really need to buy these groceries, I'll use my credit card and worry about why my salary hasn't hit my account later.

- I really want this new VR headset but I can't afford it based on my savings. If I use a credit card, I can buy it today and then pay it off over the next few months.

If we are redesigning this for a mobile world, banks won't need to sell us a physical credit card for these types of transactions.

The grocery store scenario becomes a sort of "emergency cash" credit facility, a real-time overdraft or line of credit that we deliver in one of two ways. We either preempt the cash shortage because we know the customer regularly shops at Tesco and spends £300, but only has £100 in his account, or we offer it in real time when the tap of the phone to pay fails due to insufficient funds. We can eliminate rejection of a typical credit card application because we will only offer the emergency cash to someone who qualifies. I'm actually working on this at my start-up Moven right now; we hope to deliver this sometime in 2016 (so stay tuned).

For the in-store financing, there's an array of new product approaches. We can allow people to put a *wish list* on their phone of things they want to save for, and when they walk into a store where a wish list item is available, we can offer a discount combined with contextualised credit offering. We can use a preferential low- or zero-interest 12-month financing deal, getting them to switch payment vehicles at the point of sale, or we can trigger an offer based on geolocation. We can use iBeacons and geolocation technology to match a very specific offer with a unique customer that includes a preferential credit deal (more on iBeacons in chapter 12). We can message you online that your Amazon Prime membership gives you access to instant credit, even when you are not on Amazon.com.

Basically, we can redesign the way we message credit facilities, the way we determine risk (based on behaviour). We can better match risk and behaviour to the type of credit line and we can eliminate the need for a physical product or any conventional application process at all.

> "We'll probably be the last generation to use the term "credit card" and "debit card"... It will probably be "debit access" or "credit access", and it will likely be loaded on to a mobile device."
>
> John Stumpf, CEO of Wells Fargo, at the Goldman Sachs US Financial Conference, 8th December 2015

Ultimately, a piece of plastic won't be necessary to get credit at a time of payment, and you won't need to pre-apply for a set credit limit. It will all happen in the moment. This requires us to rethink "bank" product design for the augmented world. We may even have to reengineer the way our money itself works.

The Role of Money in Augmented Commerce

It's hard for many to conceive a world without little bits of paper that we today denote as currency. In fact, money is so ingrained in society that we've come up with hundreds of slang terms around the world to describe the stuff. In the United States, you might hear the term "Benjamins", "dead Presidents" or "greenbacks". Can you guess which countries gave birth to "bucks", "clams", "loonies", "dough", "shtuka", "two bob" and "moola" when it comes to describing money?

Money is vitally important, if not central, to commerce in society, but when presented with the concept that cash might disappear or that the use of physical currency is in decline, you

Figure 9.3: During the Great Depression in the 1930s, clams were issued by local merchants in Pismo Beach, California, to cope with the collapse of the economy.

will get passionate responses from large swathes of the population diametrically opposed to even the thought of such a shift. When a new cryptocurrency like Bitcoin emerges, you'll likewise have those who are passionate in their belief that Bitcoin will replace all existing currencies on the planet and eliminate the need for a conventional banking system, as opposed to those who think Bitcoin is purely an instrument for geeks and/or criminals who want total cross-border anonymity for their transactions. The fact is that "hard" cash is actually a relatively new concept in the modern world.

It wasn't until 1861 that the US government started to print its own banknotes, preceded by the First Bank of the United States, which issued private currency starting in 1791. Prior to this, in 1696, the Bank of Scotland issued the first banknotes for Great Britain. Today, Queen Elizabeth II, the second longest reigning head of state (behind Thailand's King Bhumibol Adulyadej), holds the record for the most countries that issue currency carrying her image or likeness. Back in those early

Figure 9.4: The note with the most zeros in the world is the Zimbabwean 100 trillion (100,000,000,000,000) dollar banknote (issued in 2009). The note has 14 zeros printed on both the front and the back.

days, it was actually common for small communities to start their own banks and for those banks to issue their own currency. Over time, centralisation of currencies became more efficient for trade and commerce, and thus you also had the emergence of "central banks" that could issue a currency respected across the community.

Prior to the use of banknotes, there were, of course, coins. Before coins, you might imagine that barter was the primary mechanism to enable trade, but there were other forms of currency that existed thousands of years ago that were a good proxy for the notes we carry around in our wallets today. The earliest recorded such currency from 3000 BC was called a "shekel", which carried the distinction of being both a measure of weight and an early form of currency. Shells were used by many nations in the Americas, Asia and Pacific. The ancient Greeks, however, were the first to mint actual coins back around 600 to 650 BC, and by the 1st century such coins were increasingly the most standard form of monetary value exchange around the world.

Making Money More Efficient

Today, cryptocurrencies like Bitcoin are emerging as a type of next generation currency. While classifying Bitcoin as a currency is the most logical characterisation for most of the public at large, it is by design something that is more efficient than traditional currency, resembling more closely something like the digital equivalent of the shekel in terms of mechanics or valuation. The problem money faces today is that it is not particularly efficient for the various types of commerce that are rapidly emerging.

As a result of the increased use of plastic debit cards, mobile payments and the like, cash use peaked in most of the developed world last decade. Cash today accounts for just 34 per cent of the total value of consumer spending globally.[11] While non-cash payments are highest in the developed world, as mobile payments and mobile bank accounts emerge, the use of physical currency will enter a steeper decline.

Most commodities traded on global markets like oil, gold, diamonds, titanium and so forth are priced in US dollars because it is easier to measure relative market performance. However, the more significant shift is in the fact that whether I'm on Amazon, Alibaba or Airbnb, I can pretty much buy anything from anywhere in the world today, in real time. This is putting incredible strain on market mechanisms that assume you'll be transacting in one currency, and you have to be a local resident to purchase goods locally. How does sales tax work? What about exchange rate mechanisms? What about identity and privacy concerns—can I trust you? If you live in Nigeria and are buying something in China using a USD denominated account, to get the product shipped to Lagos, should the seller wait for payment before shipping or should you pay only when the goods are shipped or when you receive them?

---

11 *See* "MasterCard's Cashless Journey" at http://www.mastercardadvisors.com/cashlessjourney/.

As we go real time, as infrastructure becomes smart and as global barriers to commerce drop, physical currency is essentially a hurdle to commerce. It's too slow and too difficult to handle safely. Specific currencies that today are geographically bound appear largely arbitrary, except that they remain accepted by large groups of people willing to recognise the value of that currency in local commerce.

Just as paper money was created to standardise value exchange within a community, and to make trade more efficient, those same forces have created the need for more efficient forms of payment and more relevant currencies today. If not for those needs, my guess is that Bitcoin would never have emerged, just as paper money would not have emerged without clear drivers back in the 17th century. Paper money can still compete today, but in an increasingly digital world, it might very well find itself outclassed by new, more efficient methods of payments in the form of mobile phones, lower friction transmission mediums and more relevant global community value exchanges like Bitcoin. Will Bitcoin become the new global form of currency? It's extremely unlikely given its recent volatility; however, our eyes have been opened to new possibilities in terms of commerce and we can be sure that Bitcoin won't be the last attempt that we'll see at developing Money 2.0.

The more interesting development emerging out of the Bitcoin movement is actually the technology that underpins the way Bitcoin is transacted and recorded. We call this the blockchain, and this could quite possibly be the answer to a world full of smart, transacting devices.

Why We Need a Blockchain
Traditional banking asserts that a bank account is owned by an

individual and that individual must be identified so that he can safely and legally transact over the networks, pipes and wires maintained by the chartered banks of the world. This is why the creation of Bitcoin was somewhat of a headache for bank regulators around the world. Essentially, Bitcoin wallets are anonymous at the time of a transaction. If the user identifies himself, then you can link an account to a person, but it's not required in order for a transaction to take place.

Fearing an explosion of anonymous illegal transactions across the blockchain, such as those that made the dark web e-commerce trading site Silk Road possible, regulators around the world attempted to rein in Bitcoin's explosive growth. Bitcoin, however, is decentralised so it is impossible to block it or stop it without effectively pulling the plug on the entire Internet, which would seem like overkill. The only way to regulate Bitcoin's activity was to control how people bought, sold and traded BTC,[12] or how they converted other currencies into bitcoin through exchanges.

The way regulators eventually cracked down on this in places like the United States, China and Russia was to make unlicensed bitcoin exchanges illegal. You could not buy, sell or trade in bitcoins unless the exchange was a licensed money transmitter or financial services business. This enabled the regulator to ensure that each user or owner of a Bitcoin wallet had his identity verified as per the traditional banking system. The motivation was twofold: identify users of the Bitcoin system/currency and prevent criminal money laundering systems from circumventing existing controls.

At the core of Bitcoin is a decentralised ledger system that means that no one person, organisation or government controls the way Bitcoin works. There are only a few thousand Bitcoin nodes,[13] but the distributed ledger system that allocates the

---

12 BTC and XBT are the commonly used abbreviations for bitcoin as a cryptocurrency.
13 As of 1st January 2016, bitnodes.21.co recorded an average of 6,400 nodes on the Bitcoin network, but it has been as high as 10,000 nodes in the past.

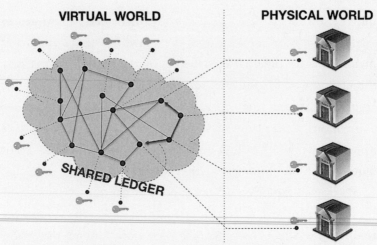

Figure 9.5: At the heart of Bitcoin is a distributed ledger system that is far more efficient for digital transactions than the existing banking system.

millions of bitcoins around the world is constantly syncing and updating the records of digital currency moving from one wallet to another. For the same reason that regulators generally don't like the Bitcoin system, i.e. a wallet functioning independent of the wallet holder's identity, it makes the blockchain or something similar, much better suited to the future of money. It has much higher redundancy than exiting banking systems, and works to reinforce itself constantly. There is no such thing as a bitcoin, of course, at least not in the physical sense. The blockchain simply keeps track of an ever-expanding list of addresses, and how many units of bitcoin are at each of those addresses.

If you own bitcoin, what you actually own is the private cryptographic key to unlock a specific address with a value stored in it—it just so happens that value corresponds to the number of bitcoins you hold. The private key looks like a long string of numbers and letters. You may choose to store your key, or keys if you have multiple addresses, in a number of places including a paper printout, a metal coin, a hard drive or via an online service. Some have even tattooed their Bitcoin wallet address on their person.

The banking system of 2025 will need to work more like an IP, or peer-to-peer, network than the current centralised banking networks that we have today; and the blockchain is a better, future-proof example of that.

We are moving to a world where smart devices can have a value store or multiple value stores and can act as agents transacting on our behalf or on behalf of a group of people. We're also moving to a world where identity won't be tied to your driving licence, signature or social security number, but instead managed as a construct based on biometrics, unique identity markers, behavioural data and heuristics. Identity could itself be managed on a blockchain, as could contracts, assets and other information that need to be secured in a distributed, redundant system of record.

Today, the banking system says that only banks (and licensed money transmitters) can send money from one trusted party to another, and only through those proprietary, restricted networks. You only get to use those networks (opening a bank account) if you have provided your identity to a bank, generally by physically going to a branch. This means that in most countries if you don't have a driver's licence or passport, it's almost impossible for you to open a bank account. The augmented world will need a much more flexible ecosystem to be able to respond to the needs of smart transactions.

State regulation of bank charters today require a bank to capture customer information in a way that is known as "know your customer" (KYC) before you are allowed to open a bank account. This sort of system will quickly become redundant and outdated in the Augmented Age. Why? It would be like insisting that before you use a computer or a new smartphone, or connect to a new ISP or WiFi hotspot in a café, you need to submit your identity documents, confirm the name of your employer and establish proof of your address. In fact, it will quickly become impossible to conduct commerce with this constraint in place.

In a real-time banking and payments world, the idea of a vault that secures your money in a building, and thus requires an identity to be verified in that building, is anachronistic. The current licensing system for bank charters, payments and remittances is trying to regulate a 19th-century problem in a 21st-century digital ecosystem. Let me give you a simple example of why the banking system that today requires a person's identity to be tied to a bank account cannot survive this shift.

When Your Self-driving Car Has a Bank Account

While owning a car will definitely be an option in the future, many Millennials and their descendants will opt to participate in a sharing economy where ownership is distributed, or where self-driving car time is rented. So let's take a scenario in 2025 to 2030 when a Millennial subscribes to a personalised car service guaranteeing access to an autonomous, self-driving car for a certain number of hours each day, or where they buy a "share" in a self-driving car.

The car picks up the Millennial and takes them to work. During the journey, the car is alerted that it will be required again in approximately 6 hours. After dropping off the individual at their shared workspace, the car goes off and collects two more of the collective owners of the vehicle and delivers them each to their required locations. At this point, the car makes a decision to find a charging station and recharge for an hour. It drives to a local car park where supercharging stations are located and hooks in. As the car was making its last drop-off for the morning, it had already worked out that it would need to recharge so it had communicated with the car park's machine interface, negotiating a price for both the parking facility and energy it would need.

A company owns the actual car park, but it has allowed individual investors to each own or lease a supercharging station connected to a solar grid on the roof of the car park to offset the costs of retooling the car park with charging stations. Each supercharger has its own wallet linked back to its owner(s), and the energy used by the self-driving car as it recharges is paid for in kilowatt-hour (KwH) directly between the car and the supercharging station. Likewise, the car parking fee is paid to the garage owner.

The self-driving car, then calculating it has approximately 3.5 hours before it will be required by one of its owners again, logs in to Uber and makes itself available for a 3-hour block as a self-driving resource. It is immediately called out to a pick-up, and after 3 hours has earned $180 in fees, which it puts away in its own wallet.

The wallet in the self-driving car is not linked to a single individual owner. It is a collective account. Any earnings it makes are used to offset ownership costs, energy costs, parking and registration fees, etc. The owners just top up the self-driving car's own wallet on a monthly or weekly basis as required, but the self-driving car's ability to pay for energy, or earn income for rental time, is independent of a typical identity structure or bank account. It is an IoT wallet or value store.

The wallet in the self-driving car is analogous to the debit card you carry around in your wallet today, but there is one big difference. A person does not own this wallet; it is linked to the car and may or may not have multiple human owners and the identity of those owners could change frequently. In today's banking world this might be marginally possible, but only through a torturous series of contracts, declarations and identity verification (IDV) processes that would essentially require all of the owners of the vehicle, and the self-driving car itself, to personally front up at a bank branch. That's clearly ludicrous.

Whether a self-driving car, a smart fridge that orders your groceries, a smart house that both consumes and generates data and energy, a solar array or any AI that negotiates specific transactions, all of these will need independent access to the banking system, along with their own bank account. This obviously raises some very interesting questions.

You can't ask a self-driving car or a fridge to identify itself at a bank branch with a signature, so will it have its own identity? Will the self-driving car have to pay tax on the money it earns as part of a sharing economy, or will this be passed on to the collective owners? If a self-driving car is involved in an accident, who would ultimately be liable in the case of injury: the car, the joint owners or the manufacturers of the self-driving car itself?

Initially, regulators will try to enforce a structure whereby a "person" owns a smart asset and the bank account of that asset is linked back to the owner. However, within five to ten years, we'll see start-ups built specifically for the purpose of enabling joint or shared ownership of assets like self-driving cars. Uber will be in this game for sure. This is all going to shift in about the same time it took Apple to launch its first iPhone in 2007 through to the launch of the Apple Watch in 2015. Disruptive indeed!

Why the Augmented Age Is really Bad for Banks

Day-to-day banking and payments are set for some pretty radical changes. The most immediate of these will be how you pay for goods and services in your daily life. The most efficient form of payment is simply to walk into a store, restaurant or service business and when you are done, walk out. At best, you'll simply need to authorise a payment by tapping on your phone to accept the charges or responding with an "air" gesture that your smart glasses recognise. There will be no checkout, no swipe, no tap, no need to fish in your pockets, wallet or purse for change—the payment will have effectively become invisible. We might very well augment payments with data that gives you better deals, encourages you to use a particular payment vehicle or shop at a specific merchant or provides context to your spending decisions that simply helps you manage your money more effectively.

This will radically alter store design and stores that digitally engage customers will enable better in-store moments and improved sales. Over the next couple of decades, one of the most important decisions that you'll make as a consumer will be pairing a specific wallet to a specific retailer or agreeing to use a specific payment method based on a specific behaviour set. For example, if I'm in Starbucks buying a coffee, use my Starbucks app. If my app has a low balance, top it up using my Simple or Atom bank account, and if that hasn't got enough cash, use my Bitcoin wallet. If my personal AI is booking a flight for me while I'm in a business meeting, use my corporate travel account. If my self-driving car is off driving for Uber, use those credits for future travel on Uber instead of recording it as income. If I walk into a store where I regularly purchase merchandise and my spending account has less than $1,000 in it, give me a warning that I'm low on funds on my PHUD or smartwatch.

Apple Pay, Android Pay, Samsung Pay, PayPal, MasterCard, Visa, Amex and Alipay are currently in a race to dominate your in-store (or via e-commerce) payment choices. Each of them wants to be the primary wallet or app that you use to pay, and they are all starting to recognise that it isn't about being able to offer you more airline miles but having *more* data about *your* payments behaviour—where you like to shop, when you shop and what you buy—that they will then be more likely able to influence your purchase decisions in the future. They might be able to influence what store you walk into, when you choose to purchase something you've been thinking about buying or whether you use your savings or an in-store finance offer to be able to afford that new thingamabob.

You might notice that I didn't mention any "banks" when I talked about payment choices in this new world. Well, the banks are increasingly being pushed out of the payments space. The main reason why is that they were just way too late to the game; most banks in the United States, for example, don't offer anything near to real-time payments or link to wallets on a mobile phone. They're still stuck in an era where cheques are considered one of the most efficient forms of payment. On top of this, they're still trying to sell Millennials checking accounts[14] when they walk in the door, and Millennials don't even write cheques (or checks as they are known in the US)!

It is very unlikely that anything but the very biggest banks will have any real role in this future payments ecosystem medium term. Yes, these banks will be forced to link to the apps and wallets that enable payments, because otherwise the bank accounts they try to sell you will be largely useless, and you certainly won't be swiping their plastic card. You'll be using a mobile or device-based payment capability that pulls money from an account or value store, and you'll have plenty of choice where to "store" your money, including with numerous non-banks that underpin these wallets.

---

14 While the rest of the world calls these current accounts, perhaps we should just now call them digital or mobile spending accounts?

An example of this is an iTunes account. Half a billion people have linked their credit and debit cards to iTunes today, and many are buying coupons or prepaid cards and vouchers to top up their iTunes accounts. The balance you carry on your iTunes or PayPal account is not a bank account, it is a non-bank payment account or value store. Your balance on your Starbucks app or card is the same. In 2015, Starbucks took in more than US$3 billion in deposits on its app, meaning that the company took more deposits than about 70 per cent of the banks in the United States. But as I said before, Starbucks isn't a bank, despite the fact that it takes more deposits than most.

We will see a lot of these value stores in our augmented future, and as we move to decentralised ledgers and payments systems like blockchain, it will become less important day-to-day that these value stores are government guaranteed or nationally insured deposits. Your big deposits and savings will still sit in a bank, but a lot of your day-to-day operational money will be distributed in a non-bank ecosystem backed by technology. But will it be safe?

For over ten years, people have been using PayPal without requiring that their deposits be guaranteed. PayPal isn't going out of business anytime soon, and the number of people who have issues with their PayPal accounts is very small compared with the daily transactional activity, and certainly less than the average bank deals with today as a result of fraud. Ultimately, the safest systems will be the most used systems because they will build trust within their community of users, and these become even safer and more robust as the more people use those networks.

What this means, however, is that the so-called Universal Banking Model will start to fail and break apart over the next two decades. The concept of *universal banking* is that you open your first bank account at school, transition that account when you get your first job or go to university and then build your credit through that bank by taking your first car loan and eventually a mortgage, all with the same bank. You probably choose that bank because of its location in the community or based on your parents' recommendation. In the new augmented world, however, we'll choose payment options, value store options and credit lines based on utility and experiences, driven much more by immediacy and core value proposition than by the location of a branch.

We won't apply for a mortgage, we'll just buy a home and the application for credit to buy that home will be a part of the home-buying process. At first, this shift will be in the presentation of a fairly typical mortgage offer, but in real time as you are out and about looking at homes. In the future, however, it will be an experience-based financing decision as you are buying the home, with various service partners offering you different ways of assessing their capabilities to finance your home.

For example, the estate agent might send you the contract for the home electronically and then you'll link your identity to that contract. By doing so, you will expose specific information about your salary, credit history and so forth that can be used to underwrite a credit decision. In real time, your device or cloud-based Life Stream Agent will then negotiate with a number of credit providers to present you with a financing option for the home. You might be presented with a visualisation of how long you want to take to pay off your home, and as you interact with the visualisation in your field of view in your smart glasses, you might attempt to reduce the length of time it will take for you to own the home fully down from 25 years to 15 years. As you do this, the visualisation will start to warn you as you go below 18 years that your current salary and living expenses won't allow you to own the home sooner. However, as you go about your daily life, you'd be able to occasionally put some money into your "home" credit line, thus reducing that time frame to full ownership, or you might draw down on the credit line in real time to underwrite a new car purchase instead of taking a car loan.

The key difference from today's banking world is that we won't apply for these products, wait and then fear rejection by the bank for the loan. We may be asked to provide our information for access to various facilities, but it will be the bank or lender's ability to assess our "risk" that will materially change from today's system. This data-driven approach will allow a lender to assess your viability so that you don't have to fill out an application form; you'll just be offered a credit facility in real time. If you don't qualify, you just won't get an offer. That still beats being rejected, right?

The products we currently get from a bank, namely a debit card or current account, a mortgage, an overdraft, a certificate of deposit, a car loan or lease, etc., will disappear. Payments, value stores, investments and credit lines will all be available but they won't be packaged as distinct products that banks offer today. They'll simply be utility featured in distributed, embedded, day-to-day experiences built around your money and your life. Most banks will be too slow and too fixed in their ways to adapt to this era. Consequently, we're likely to see 50 per cent of the household bank names we know today give up their existence to a range of new FinTech providers and technology companies that will own or enable those day-to-day money moments and experiences we'll have each day.

FinTech, HealthTech, Everything Tech

The term "FinTech", like HealthTech, is an amalgam of "finance" and "technology" and has come to represent a group of disruptive technologies, start-ups and innovations that are challenging the traditional financial system. In 2008, US$930 million was invested in FinTech initiatives like Dwolla, StockTwits and other start-ups. By 2013, that figure had ballooned to investments of US$4 billion, and was expected to double in 2014. However, it actually trebled to $12 billion,[15] and then hit a whopping US$21 billion in 2015.[16] The figure for 2016 could be as high as US$100 billion.

This supports the underlying thesis that every industry is becoming a technology-based industry as a result of the infusion of capital and technology into transformation and automation. The fact is that industries like financial services have products and constructs that are hundreds of years old, and it doesn't take a lot of technology to be disruptive when that state exists.

> "BBVA will be a software company in the future."
>
> Francisco González, chairman of BBVA,
> speaking at Mobile World Congress in 2015

The future is about putting the bank in the lives of customers with zero friction (ok, well, minimal friction) every day. That means banks have to come to terms with the fact that *anytime they stick a piece of paper in front of a customer, it is just **pure friction***, and it certainly won't allow them to build revenue or relationships on a mobile phone, iPad or in a self-driving car *in the moment*. Let me state that again to be crystal clear:

Paper and signatures have no future in the banking world—at all.

---

15 "The Fintech Revolution," *Economist*, 9 May 2015.
16 Some estimates put this number as high as US$30 billion in 2015.

Am I sure? Yes. Not least of all because with facial recognition, image recognition on driver's licences/passports and other identity verification technology (geolocation, social media, heuristics, etc.), *a physical identity verification is now fifteen to twenty times riskier than a digitally automated identification process.* Why do you think every customs department in the world is turning to the biometric verification of passports at borders? The answer is simple. Humans are the single weakest link in the security process—the most prone to errors, the least likely to recognise a false ID document. An algorithm never gets tired, or makes mistakes, and they can now see better than we can.

Think about that. *The single riskiest thing banks do today is have a face-to-face account opening based on a piece of paper with a signature. Put it another way, the single riskiest thing you can do today, the easiest way to be a victim of fraud, is to sign a piece of paper in a financial transaction!*

Keep in mind that every FinTech company that was founded in the last few years doesn't use paper or signatures—each of these companies is way ahead of the curve on this. They have got no legacy process to circumvent; they're just figuring out how to use technology to make it easier for customers.

Most physical artefacts of banking will have disappeared for the majority of customers within ten years, not least because 2 billion people who get their first "bank account" on their phone in the next decade will never use a plastic card or chequebook.

The component utility of banking, namely a **value store, a payment, a line of credit,** a **savings rate**, etc., will be integrated into experiences defined by context. The future of product design actually isn't products at all, it's experiences—money experiences, payment experiences and credit solutions.

Along with fossil fuel generation facilities and energy retailers, banks, accountants and financial advisers will be amongst the hardest hit industries over the next 20 to 30 years. Some banks will survive, but it's very unlikely that they'll look anything like the banks your parents grew up with.

Chapter 10

Trust and Privacy in an Augmented World

Contributed by JP Rangaswami

"The best way to find out if you can trust somebody is to trust them."

Ernest Hemingway

Trust Is Connected

There was a time when I knew everyone who lived near me. The Calcutta (these days it's called Kolkata) I grew up in was like that; residential areas had very little turnover, people lived (and died) in houses where their family had lived for decades, sometimes centuries. Very rarely, someone moved, because of rites of passage, and someone new would enter that fragment of society. Long before that happened, everyone else would know everything there was to know about the neighbours-to-be. How many of them there were. Where they were coming from. Why here and why now.

Ours was a high-trust society. Everyone knew everyone and

everything. Crime was low. People didn't lock their doors. They didn't have to. A stranger would be spotted long before he or she could get anywhere close.

In those days we had a lot of home delivery. The milk came, still in the cow, served fresh at the door. Papers were delivered at dawn. The pot-and-pan man would exchange old saris for shiny new cooking vessels. The comic-wala would do his mobile lending library bit, walking miles while carrying his wares in voluminous satchels. Hawkers would walk past with fruit and the sugarcane man would wend his way. In summer, the ice-cream man would show up occasionally, it all depended on whether he had any ice left by the time he got to our street. Ice that was covered in wood shavings and hessian in order to try and extend its life.

Entertainment also came to the door. Monkey grinders, snake charmers, flautists, even the odd bear tamer. We didn't have television in those days, the transistor radio hadn't made its way to our shores as yet, and the valve version needed something that was scarce at the time—electricity. So we played in the street: cricket, football, hockey, skipping, hopscotch, cowboys and Indians, tag, whatever. And we were safe.

Everybody knew everybody. Even the itinerant vendors were often regulars, generation upon generation. A high-trust environment. Essential for society, for business, for pleasure. The Calcutta I describe was where I grew up nearly 60 years ago; by the time I left there 35 years ago, it had already begun to change. A diaspora was coming.

This wasn't just about Calcutta. There was a time when it was common everywhere for most people to live and die within a few miles of where they were born. Migrations happened, but usually in bulk, and usually because there was some irresistible force. Invaders wanting to kill you. Drought. Famine. Earthquake.

That sort of thing. Migration was expensive, too. So you didn't do it unless you had to or unless you wanted particularly to be an explorer, in which case you had to find yourself a patron, preferably royal and well-heeled. Yes, migration was expensive.

With the advent of the Industrial Revolution, all of this began to change. We learnt earlier in the book about the machine age's effect on employment, but the side effect of inventions like the bicycle, trains, steamships, cars and planes was that each in turn began to gradually decimate the cost of migration. It was only a matter of time before individuals began to exercise their new-found right to migrate. And so they did. The diaspora had arrived. A cursory look at the patterns and volume of human migration over the last two hundred years will tell you all you need to know about that phenomenon.

As the cost of individual migration dropped, and as public policy removed some of the other frictions, the pace of the diaspora became unrelenting. Soon it became normal for city dwellers not to know their neighbours, so much so that people actually began to revel in their new-found anonymity. After all, they didn't have to deal with the social brake of gossip any more, and they could enter a hitherto forbidden world of anything goes. Trust died. Nobody knew anybody anymore.

Fast-forward to the late 20th century, and something new started to happen. The cost of person-to-person communication began to drop. When I left India in 1980, it cost me over £1 per minute to phone my mother from the United Kingdom, at a time when my take-home pay after tax and bills was around £100 per month. That was when you used to have to wait at least three years to get a landline in India. Today, I can Skype my mother for nothing, and get a mobile phone while waiting for my luggage at the airport on arrival. Times change.

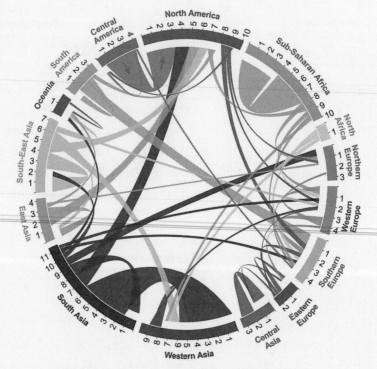

Figure 10.1: Global migration between 2005 and 2010 across the world
(Source: Circos/Krzywinski, M. et al.)

As the costs dropped, more and more people began to get connected with each other; and so to today, where families and friends may be physically disparate yet otherwise connected. And through these connections, trust begins to emerge again.

Closed immobile societies were torn apart as humans could afford to migrate at whim, and we learnt to live in low-trust environments. Then, as humans could afford to reconnect at whim, we began to rebuild the closeness of erstwhile societies, physically separate yet logically close. We began to learn how to scale trust, in fact we had to.

The Internet, the web and smart mobile devices have all had roles to play in this, and it's exciting to explore the possibilities afforded by the explosion in wearables, implantables, ingestibles and other forms of augmentation that Brett and Alex mentioned in chapters 5 and 6. Connectivity helps solve some of the problems of trust in a distributed world, and augmentation of trust has the power to extend this capability in ways we don't yet fully understand.

To understand what that might be, it's worth taking a leaf out of the book of a very old and long-established industry— banking. Let's take the term "bankrupt". Where did it come from? Centuries ago, bankers used to conduct their business sitting on benches, derived from the Italian word *bancos*. In fact, that's how they got the name "bankers", from those very benches.

When the bankers met, they worked on the basis that a gentleman's word was his bond. All was hunky-dory as long as each person kept his word; the community was at peace. Trust levels were high. But if a banker's word turned unreliable, trust was broken, and this was not a good thing. Consequently, the others would pick up the banker's bench and break it in half, in effect ejecting them from the circle of trust. The *banco* was *rottura*, or ruptured. *Banco-rottura* became banko-rupt. You see, bankruptcy was never just about money; it has always been about trust. The trust that was central to the 14th-century economy of Sienna and Verona was a trust that let you do something, be part of something, usually a trading community. And this trust could be taken away if you didn't act in keeping with the values of that community.

Bankers too had to deal with the challenges of diaspora and distance. There was a time when everyone knew everyone. Then along came shipping and trade routes and suddenly people wanted to do business with each other across great distances, and without really knowing each other to begin with. Nature abhors a vacuum; so does business. An opportunity was smelt, and the merchant bank of the trading empires was born. These banks worked closely with the trading houses as well as the burgeoning London Money Market. They formed an Acceptance Houses Committee that had an agreement with the discount houses in the London Money Market. If a bill had to be discounted in some far-flung place (far-flung from London, that is), then as long as a member of the Acceptance Houses Committee could be found to vouch for the bill payer, all was good. That member "accepted" the bill by signing it, and upon seeing the signature of an accepting member, the discount house would provide the funds. So the discount house no longer had to know the organisation upon whom the bill was drawn, it only had to recognise the acceptance house.

Friend of a friend, or FOAF, has long been a traditional route to solving problems of trust over distance. Come to think of it, that's probably how passports came into use. The person who bears this document is a friend of mine. You're a friend of mine as well. Please look after them while they are in your territory, as a favour to me.

When I was growing up in India, there was no centralised way to clear cheques there. If you had a cheque drawn on some bank far away, it was classed as an "outstation" cheque; it had to be posted by your bank to the other bank, the funds had to be remitted to your bank (also by post) and weeks, sometimes months, later, you would be able to get to those funds.

If your bank knew the person who had drawn the cheque, it may have offered to "purchase" the cheque. This meant giving you the funds in advance of them clearing, but for a fee. If you were a very important customer, the bank may even have waived the fee. Sometimes, even if the bank didn't know the drawer of the cheque, but it knew the drawee (you) very well, it may have done the same thing as a favour, on the basis that you were good for the money in the event the cheque went bouncy bouncy. Friend of a friend, in different dimensions.

When I moved to the United Kingdom, there were some other notable developments in this space. You could "special" a cheque. What this meant was that your bank would do something very simple. It would call the other bank, the bank the cheque was drawn on, and say, "Hey we have this cheque drawn on one of your accounts, is it any good?" And if the answer was in the affirmative, you'd have your money. This was the trust network between banks.

Credit and debit cards were also instruments of trust in different ways. If you were travelling in a foreign land, the signs for Amex or Diners or Visa meant a number of things. You could pay without having to use up the limited amount of cash you carried. (After all, who wants to carry loads of cash in a place you've never been to before, a place you barely know?) More importantly, if something went wrong with your purchase, there was some sort of guarantee in place. Most of the time, your card provider would stand for the transaction, refunding you in the event of fraud or malfeasance.

Those trust dimensions have now permeated into the world of e-commerce. I can still remember the first time I entrusted the web with my credit card details. Yes, I cannot tell a lie, it was Amazon. Its "one-click" was what finally got me. As a voracious book reader and collector, I was there to be got. And got I was. I entrusted it with my credit card details, and spent happily in the knowledge that Amazon would refund me if anything went wrong. This is how I went seamlessly into ZShops, its original marketplace, which I guess has been merged into the main site now. The freedom to buy goods for value from people I don't know in places I had never heard of. A freedom made possible because I only had to trust Amazon, I didn't need to know much about the entity I was buying from.

Banks were platforms, initially isolated, later networked, much later interconnected. Credit and debit cards went through the same evolution: isolated platforms that grew exponentially as they interconnected and became interoperable. The Internet and the web made each of us participants in a much greater platform, and the same network effects were afforded to us as well.

And then the smart mobile device came along and made all this possible on the move, allowing us to discover trust "independent of time and distance". Context became discoverable: we could identify where we were, who and what we were near, what was approaching us, the whole nine yards.

That's the context into which the Augmented Age fits today. Augmentation will allow us to do many things we could not do any earlier. How so? There are four distinct avenues that progressively build upon each other in respect to the development of augmentation and how it effects our perception of ourselves, our community and the trust that links us.

Notifications and Status Alerts

We have to imagine wearables and personal AI as the extension of our desktops and mobile devices, with the ability to connect to those devices, the ability to receive notifications and alerts from them. So now your watch or your wristband, or your glasses or your belt, or your shirt or even your bionic ear is able to receive messages from others, or a synthesis of data from your personal AI. In the days of the PC, you could only see those messages if you were by your device. As you moved to laptops and portables, you could receive them where you were, but only in places where it was socially acceptable for you to look. You can't take your laptop out of your case in the middle of a film or concert, or at dinner, just to check for messages. Tablets have the same problem of social unacceptability. Phones are borderline. However, discreetly checking your watch is usually okay. "Your bank balance is close to your overdraft level." "Please buy milk on the way home."

Contextual Warnings and Alerts

"Four of your Facebook friends are in this lounge." "The following open WiFi networks have been detected in range of where you stand." "There's trouble ahead on the road." Brett described many of these types of contextual developments or alerts that could take place in the emergence of personal head-up displays, too.

Access Tokens

One of the ways in which trust is maintained in physical and logical networks is that you need multifactor authentication to get in. Wearables extend the possibilities in this respect, using near field communications or geolocation tagging to signal your presence and acceptability, a permission that you add to with some other form of identification or signalling. Wearables will even allow certain behavioural heuristics or biometrics like your individual heartbeat to be a unique access token or trust indicator.

Presence Signalling

It's not hard to imagine a world where each of us represents some peculiar scarcity, that we keep the knowledge of the scarcity to ourselves, but when it comes to an emergency, the scarcity is discoverable and able to be encoded or signalled. What kind of scarcity? A person who has a rare blood type may want to have that fact suppressed but make it available in an emergency, just by hitting a switch, or in the instance that the wearable or ingestible detects an emergency.

All of this, of course, is in addition to "traditional" modes of augmentation, those that existed before the current wave of the Internet of Things and the wearables revolution.

In those traditional modes, your vision and your hearing could be "augmented" by information that was pulled down from the cloud; the original Shazam service was a classic example, where the service would display the details of the song being played. Over the last decade or so, a number of such services have emerged, with the same construct and principle. View or listen to something. Send a snapshot of that view or sound segment to an external service, get a reply that adds to the information you have about that view or sound. That's basic augmentation.

What's been happening recently is of a different order, as context truly enters the zone of augmentation. So now it's not just what you're viewing or hearing that gets augmented, you also receive information about the context. In its simplest form, it's like being told "people who did A also did B", as a comment on what you just did or intended to do. Instructive, simple collaborative filtering. People who bought this book also bought this one. People who liked this song also liked this group.

Trust Is Always Social

The era of "social logins" like Facebook Connect is one of the most powerful moves made in this regard. It does this by bringing together the power of the social graph into play, augmenting the information we have access to in order to make a decision. I'm a child of the late 1950s, which means I like listening to music made between 1964 and 1977, give or take a few years. Maybe I should just say, "I like music made in the Sixties and Seventies." Strangely enough, when I go to concerts nowadays, that statement can be interpreted differently: I now spend time listening to musicians who are *in* their sixties and seventies (and a few in their eighties as well, though I never was a fan of that decade).

I therefore land up booking tickets to go to these concerts: with human longevity increasing, there are more and more people my age wanting to do our not-quite-geriatric-yet thing, so demand for these concerts is high. Leonard Cohen and John Mayall are probably the first two musicians over 80 that I have seen perform live; Bob Dylan, Donovan, Jethro Tull/Ian Anderson, The Moody Blues, Paul Simon, the Grateful Dead, Steve Winwood, Eric Clapton, John Martyn, Pentangle, Don McLean, Cat Stevens, the Rolling Stones, Joan Baez, Bruce Springsteen, James Taylor, Crosby, Stills & Nash, you get my drift. When I book tickets, another form of augmentation kicks in, because I use a social login. Would I like to go on Saturday or on Sunday? Here are the friends going on Saturday, here are the ones going on Sunday. Would you like to sit near your friends or as far away from them as possible so they don't see you dancing like a mad man? Choices.

Human beings engage with each other in relationships of trust. That trust was easy to build and retain in the closed system of historical small towns and villages, when human migration was low. All that changed when we began to migrate at will a couple of hundred years ago, and the rate of migration continues to grow. That migration, that continuing diaspora, creates a challenge in terms of trust. The "connected world" we live in seeks to overcome that challenge in a number of ways, teaching us how to "scale" trust.

That scaling of trust is to some extent enabled and accelerated by our devices, our wearables and our ability to augment the information we're presented with. Augmentation of this sort helps us with identity (who is this? what is this?), context (where is this? when is this?) and relationship (who else knows this person or thing? who amongst my friends has seen this? who amongst my friends has experienced this?). Reputation and rating schemes are ways to standardise some of this feedback: my children tend to check Rotten Tomatoes before they even consider going to see a film.

It's not just about trust: there are many other ways in which the connected world, the social graph, wearables and augmentation improve our lives. Alex described how the quantified self is improved by measuring your own performance against your peers, or even working out with your peers. Peer group data, however, is being used in even simpler ways to form sort of trust "contracts".

All of these social platforms are leading us to make better decisions. One category of those decisions—whom to trust—is more important than any other, when it comes to living our lives.

Today, we can choose a restaurant or coffee shop based on a rating from our peers. In real time, we can ask the crowd for a recommendation. We can look at a peer-group or influence score like Klout and assess an individual's suitability for a certain task or whether we should trust their advice. We can review their employment history and whether anyone has recommended them on a forum like LinkedIn, or even ask a shared connection for their opinion on their suitability for a job. An Uber driver is rated based on their smile, service approach and vehicle cleanliness. Given that, some might only opt to take an Uber vehicle if the driver has a 4.5 score or higher or if someone in your network has vouched for the driver. Uber customers are rated as well. Customers with a score of 4.8 or higher get the option to choose Uber's VIP drivers when they book a car.

Trust, like everything else in this world, is becoming real time. We went from those days in Calcutta where everyone knew everyone else and trust was a very tangible element of that close-knit society to a society where everyone was essentially anonymous. Anonymity created the potential for "fear"—I don't know who you are, you look different, you don't speak my language, etc. But the augmented world will allow you to establish trust in real time.

In the old world, everyone was connected: I knew your parents and they knew me. There are probably still people living in that old part of Calcutta who can tell you a story of the mischief I got up to as a lad. But we lost some of that connection as the world became more mobile, as migration occurred as societies became more complex and less homogeneous.

As we once again become connected, this time via sensors, data, social and context, we'll have to think about trust and privacy in different ways.

Trust and Privacy at Odds

I have a thesis here that trust and privacy could actually be at odds in a community that requires trust to operate efficiently. The more private you make your world, then the less trust is implied or implicit. If I don't know you, how can I possibly trust you? This is really where the pendulum of trust is swinging back towards more transparency and openness in the

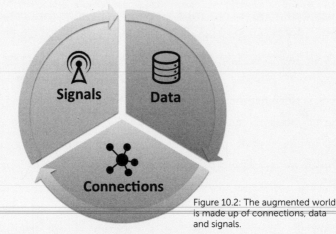

Figure 10.2: The augmented world is made up of connections, data and signals.

Augmented Age, largely spurred on by social media, data and collective awareness.

There is obviously data we hold sacred. Our heart rate, our fingerprint, our home address and other such data are things that we may very strongly feel need to be protected today. At the same time, however, we likely share our Waze app data, our pictures taken around the home and other such artefacts that have our home address encoded within the data.[1] If we're going to get advanced medical care in the future, we'll need to share bio data. All of this is somewhat fungible in the traditional sense. There's black, white and grey.

Today, if we want to travel on a commercial airline, we need to share our personal information with an airline and security staff at the airport. If we don't, they just won't let us fly. Why do we trust an airline employee to deal with our date of birth and home address more than someone in our place of work, for example? It's somewhat arbitrary, but those signals are encoded in interactions. Some interactions require more transparency, less privacy.

---

1   Exchangeable Image File (EXIF) data in image files often contain GPS or location tags.

Signals of trust will become implicit components of the world we live in, but what data needs to be shared for you to be trusted? If you walk into a retail store, I don't need to know if you have a criminal record, where your children go to school or whether you are in good physical health. However, I do need to know that you have enough money in your account to make a transaction, enough information to verify that you haven't stolen someone's digital wallet.

Whether data, our network of friends or just messages that come from our network or sphere of influence, the augmented world will be about trade-offs, exchanges in value and trust built in real time.

Ironically, the more you seek to hide your data from the world, the more private you seek to become, the less trusted you could be. While there is data that must be secured, must be held as private for the majority of interactions that will take place in the augmented world, other data must be more open. You won't be able to drive a self-driving car and tell it not to share any of its data with other vehicles or the satellite network that helps its navigation—it would be a disaster for you and those around you. If you refuse to wear a heart rate monitor or use ingestibles for biofeedback, then you'll be penalised by having to pay higher health and insurance premiums. If you don't have a digital employment profile, then it will be assumed you are either a Luddite or you have something to hide.

If you insist on being absolutely, truly private, the augmented world will treat you with suspicion. Just like those days in Calcutta. If you moved into our old neighbourhood and didn't make yourself known quickly, then everyone would start making up stories about who you were and what skeletons you had in your closet. The easiest way to tackle that mistrust was to be open, and move to quickly establish some credibility. The augmented world is once again just like that.

We warn our kids not to put their personal information on Facebook, Instagram or Snapchat but, 20 years ago, we were very comfortable having a telephone book distributed across the city that contained our name, address and phone number for all to see.

The Augmented Age will allow you to be more secure and have more control over what data you share than ever before, but be prepared that there will be a minimum required level of transparency in order for you to credibly function in this society. Trust in the Augmented Age is correlated absolutely with your adoption of technology, and leveraging that technology in a digitally enabled community. You won't be able to establish trust without sharing, without the tech or the profile. Sure, don't overshare, but don't be a stranger either.

Figure 10.3: Yes, we used to publish our addresses and phone numbers for all to see.

11

Augmented Cities with Smart Citizens

By Alex Lightman and Brett King

"We form the cities—then the cities form us."

Jan Gehl

It is estimated that about 110 billion humans[1] have lived throughout the entire history of mankind on our planet. Most of those humans did not live in cities, and none of us have really lived in smart cities. Historically, the single biggest social change until recent decades was arguably the massive movements of populations from the rural countryside to cities, which influenced human politics, conflicts, religions, cultural development and myriad other factors.

The first city was arguably Ur, in modern-day Iraq, with a population of around 60,000 in the year 2000 BC. The first metropolis was Rome, founded in 753 BC, which eventually grew to over a million by the 2nd century AD. Rome provided benefits such as clean water from aqueducts, large-scale public

---

1 Population Reference Bureau

entertainment in open forums and shopping malls (one was four storeys tall and had 150 shops). The largest pre-industrial city is actually thought to have been Angkor, Cambodia,[2] with an elaborate system of infrastructure connecting an urban sprawl of at least 1,000 square kilometres (390 square miles) to the well-known temples at its core. Angkor served as the seat of the Khmer Empire, which flourished from the 9th to 15th centuries, but even at the height of its popularity the city is thought to have only supported around 0.1 per cent of the globe's population.

If you want to find the oldest, continuously inhabited city in the world, you have to go to Syria. Damascus is the capital of Syria, and it is thought to have been continuously inhabited since as early as 9000 BC (via use of carbon dating methods), but no large-scale settlement was established within the city walls of Damascus probably until around 1700 BC, when the city was part of the Amurru province of early Egypt.

Large cities like Rome were a rarity; its size, economy and population were not equalled in the Western world for another 16 centuries. It's only been recently, after some 2,000 centuries of human existence, that a majority of humans on the planet can reap the potential benefits of living in such a large-scale city or metropolitan area.

As a citizen of the Augmented Age, you (or your children) will likely have the ability to chose the best city for yourself, your family or your company. We will assess cities based on whether they are smart (that is, include data-driven feedback loops that let you know where things are like open parking spaces or snarl-free traffic routes), green (getting the majority of energy from renewable sources) and augmented.

For purposes of this chapter, which introduces the concept

---

2 Evans et al., "A comprehensive archaeological map of the world's largest pre-industrial settlement complex at Angkor, Cambodia," *Proceedings of the National Academy of Sciences* 104, no. 36 (23 August 2007).

of the Augmented City, it is one in which the citizens, residents and visitors can make use of state-of-the-art augmented reality, robots, AI and drones to connect, amplify, accelerate, protect and monetise their activities and relationships to an extent beyond what could be done with humans alone.

Why Do We Live in Cities?

> "The 19th century was a century of empires; the 20th century was a century of nation states. The 21st century will be a century of cities."
>
> Wellington E. Web, former mayor of Denver, Colorado

Before the Industrial Revolution, most people lived in the countryside. In 1800, only 3 per cent of the world's population lived in cities. By 1900, 12 cities had more than 1 million people, but still the vast majority of people lived outside of urban centres. In developed countries today, 70 per cent of the population lives in cities, meaning that more than 50 per cent of the planet today lives in an urban location. By 2050, 70 per cent of the world will live in urban centres.[3]

During the 19th and the beginning of the 20th centuries, cities grew rapidly, especially in Europe and North America, primarily because new industries were created and people were finding jobs. Later on, city growth slowed as they became overcrowded and diseases spread faster. Today, mortality rates in cities are lower than in rural areas, mainly because we have immediate access to better doctors and more hospitals.

Today, cities like London and New York have stopped growing, but cities like Lagos, Mumbai (formerly Bombay) and Kolkata (formerly Calcutta) are growing rapidly. About

---

3 UNICEF/Periscope Study

40 cities around the world have a population of over 5 million. Five million is what you need today to reach "megacity" status. About 80 per cent of these megacities are in poorer or developing countries, primarily due to influx associated with people seeking employment.

The list of benefits for "city-augmented" people living in the largest cities of the world is extensive and includes:

1. Public security in the form of police, fire and emergency medical technicians who will show up within minutes of an emergency services call, and often already know your location by tracking the phone that originated the call.

2. A rate of innovation 17 times greater than that of non-city dwellers.[4]

3. The ability to purchase billions of different products and services, including movies that cost up to hundreds of millions of dollars each to make for only US$5 to US$20, and high-tech products like the Apple Watch on the same day that they enter the global market.

4. Access to better education, free classes and training in a wide variety of applications/fields.

5. Networking with many thousands of people, for business, pleasure and education.

6. Cuisine prepared by expert cooks, bakers and chefs from hundreds of nations with authentic ingredients and flavours, permitting a city dweller to go for decades without having to have the same meal twice (unless you want to).

7. Many thousands of different jobs, entrepreneurial start-ups or self-employment opportunities, with hundreds of different options of profession. A citizen can choose from dozens of jobs, and change careers or professions.

4 J. D. Johnson, "Success in innovation implementation," *Journal of Communication Management* 5, 2011, 341–359.

8. The ability to walk, bike, taxi or take public transportation to work or play, without having to own a vehicle or needing to have a driver's licence. People in most cities are now able to call an Uber or Lyft via a smartphone.

9. The ability for quick access to an airport that enables travel to anywhere on earth within a day, and to many destinations within a few hours.

10. The ability to take advantage of the economies of scale that a city offers, to reduce the total costs of energy, transportation, fresh food, equipment and services, with options such as buying in bulk, taking advantage of competition in the same market and making use of shared-economy apps that allow joint ownership or shared use.

11. Access to parks, gardens, museums, art galleries, theatres and other public spaces.

So what makes a smart city?

Building truly Smart Cities

> Until the Rio Operations Center opened in 2010, it took an impossible dose of patience for a citizen to report a darkened streetlight, a clogged sewer or a missing trash receptacle. One agency passed a caller on to the next, then the next, and then the next. Now you can do this on an Internet site or by calling a central phone number. The Center has at last put the entire city on the map.
>
> Julia Michaels, author and resident of Rio de Janeiro

Many guidelines have been offered for deciding whether a city is "smart" or not, including elements such as employment factors, how green the city is, access to public transportation and support for bike lanes, etc., that limit traffic, energy efficient and smart buildings, the presence of high-tech businesses and entrepreneurial start-ups, and open and effective governments.

A more nuanced definition should include elements such as:

- An urban area that uses information and communications technologies (ICT) to improve the performance of urban services, to reduce the costs and consumption of resources, and that engages with its citizens as stakeholders.[5]

- Specific sectors that have been transformed with such technology include government services, traffic management, energy, health care and reduced air and water pollution.[6]

Smart cities are smart not only because of the services they offer their citizens, but also because of their responsiveness to critical issues such as natural disasters and their day-to-day utilisation of resources. As the effects of climate change impact more and more cities, the ability of a city to respond will be a key differentiator. However, the temptation will be for governments to focus on areas like support for start-ups with technology hubs or a few smart, green buildings and to then proclaim they are now a smart city. A real smart city will have to be re-engineered from the ground up around an urban environment that uses technology to make life better for its citizens, offers smart employment, transportation and living and enables a positive environmental impact (reversing pollution, etc.) including independence from fossil fuel generation. New York, for example, is already planning ways to reinforce Manhattan Island against rising sea levels and more storms like Superstorm Sandy, which

5 M. Deakin. *Smart Cities: Governing, Modelling and Analysing the Transition* (London, UK: Taylor and Francis, 2013).
6 N. Komninos. *The Age of Intelligent Cities: Smart Environments and Innovation-for-all Strategies (Regions and Cities)* (London, UK: Routledge, 2015).

rendered the southern subway systems inoperable for months.[7] Smart cities will need to respond dynamically to changes in the environment as needed.

Smart Collaboration: Governments and Citizens Working Together

Judicious use of ICT in a city can increase the visibility of government actions and the achievement (or lack thereof) of stated goals toward becoming "smart". On the other hand, lack of visibility can frustrate such goals. Many government leaders around the globe are perversely motivated to fight visibility for reasons that include corruption and fear of job loss.

Figure 11.1: @BeijingAir is the real-time Twitter feed of the US Embassy's air quality monitoring station.

In 2008, everyone knew that Beijing was badly polluted, but it wasn't possible to quantify how bad the pollution was as the official government monitoring data was unreliable or unavailable. That year, the US Embassy in Beijing installed a rooftop air-quality monitoring station and the device began automatically tweeting out data every hour on the pollution's severity (@BeijingAir). It became clear that the Beijing city government's lack of reporting (or restriction of reporting for reasons of "national security") was simply a failure of government to act on a growing problem.[8]

---

7 After Superstorm Sandy, the then New York City mayor, Michael Bloomberg, launched a US$19.5 billion Climate Resiliency Plan to protect New York from similar future events and the effects of climate change in general. *See* http://www.climatecentral.org/news/new-york-launches-20-billion-climate-resiliency-plan-16106.

8 A study by researchers at Berkeley Earth found that outdoor air pollution contributes to the deaths of an estimated 1.6 million people in China every year, or 4,400 people each day. *See* Dan Levin, "Study Links Polluted Air in China to 1.6 Million Deaths a Year," *New York Times*, 13 August 2015.

> At first, the Chinese government pushed back and pressured the [US] Embassy to stop releasing the data, saying that "such readings were illegal"... Eventually, the Chinese government relented and began implementing an effective monitoring system of its own. By the beginning of 2013, it had succeeded in setting up around 500 PM2.5 stations in over 70 cities. Later that year, completing its about-face, China pledged hundreds of billions of dollars for cleaning the air and began to implement pollution reduction targets for major cities.
>
> "Opinion: How the US Embassy Tweeted to Clear Beijing's Air," *Wired Science*, 6th March 2015

Government and corporate bureaucracy can also intentionally hamper progress towards smart city status by demanding excessive red tape and obscuring data on progress. Citizen action groups and social media can help this situation by reporting government abuses. Such reporting revealed that government offices in Odessa in Ukraine routinely charged bribes of US$7,000 for foreign businesses to get residency permits, and delayed imports of high-tech equipment with similar demands. The resultant delays interfered with the smart city plans of Mikheil Saakashvili, the governor of the region. Consequently, he fired almost the entire staff that was involved and replaced it with a more streamlined organisation.

Citizen engagement via social media and through personal smart devices is critical to smart cities; in fact, prominent smart city experts such as Mark Deakin consider that a smart city is not possible without it. An increasing number of mobile apps have enabled citizens to report crimes, racist abuses, needed street repairs and corruption, as well as mudslides, fires and other dangers during emergencies or disasters.[9] Whereas the volume of social media inputs such as Twitter feeds can be overwhelming, the Red Cross and others have developed smart AI tools that can filter and interpret such masses of citizen data.[10] Twitter has been working with the United States Geological Survey (USGS) and researchers at Stanford University to measure earthquake impact in real time via Twitter activity and it appears to closely correlate with USGS monitoring data.[11]

New AI-based tools for smart cities will soon enhance the visibility and effectiveness of city management, as well as dramatically improve city planning and design processes. Tools like decision infrastructure for collaborative operational planning (DICOP), developed by DARPA, use causal models and influence diagram graphics to graphically show how various assumptions and resources affect planning. Visualisations and simulations utilising 3D models allow city managers and planners to understand complex relationships and conduct "what if" explorations such as, "What if we deleted new parking structures and put in public transit instead?"

Smart Transportation Systems

One of the most dramatic paybacks from investment in smart city technologies can be the reduction of time spent in cars, with resultant frustration, costs and CO_2 emissions. Intelligent traffic management systems can manage signal lights, detours and traffic flows. Holland has implemented such a system, called TrafficLink, for its Amsterdam Smart City (ASC). TrafficLink enables staff to monitor traffic flows and report conditions to roadside and in-

---

9   Adam Crowe. *Disasters 2.0: The Application of Social Media Systems for Modern Emergency Management* (Boca Raton, FL: CRC Press, 2012).
10 P. Meier, "New information technologies and their impact on the humanitarian sector," *International Review of the Red Cross* 93, no. 884 (2011).
11 *See* https://blog.twitter.com/2014/using-twitter-to-measure-earthquake-impact-in-almost-real-time.

Figure 11.2: Amsterdam's TrafficLink system (Credit: Rijkswaterstaat Verkeerscentrale)

vehicle displays. Since its implementation, the system has reduced vehicle loss hours in Amsterdam by 10 per cent.

In Melbourne, Australia, the use of boom gates at railway crossings is an example of existing infrastructure that dramatically limits the ability of a city to implement smart transportation. At some crossings in the city, boom gates obstruct primary arterial feeder roads 70 to 80 per cent of the time during peak hours, adding a collective 16 to 20 hours of driving time each day to commuters. It has been estimated that removing such obstructions would return AUD$6 for every AUD$1 of investment in improvements in road infrastructure. You can't have a smart city without redesigning transportation systems, traffic flow and utilisation of city roads, rail and transit infrastructure.

Systems like Mobypark use sensors at car parks, parking garages and on-street parking to report parking spot availability in real time via its website and app throughout Holland and other countries. The average time spent looking for a parking spot is

20 minutes; Mobypark has reduced that time by over 50 per cent.

Another new technology being embraced by many smart cities is real-time ridesharing, a service that enables one-time shared rides at very short notice. Companies such as Uber are able to accomplish this as a result of GPS navigation devices to determine the driver's route and ride demands, smartphones for users to request rides from anywhere and social networks to establish trust and accountability between passengers and drivers. Ridesharing cuts down on the time spent finding and getting out of parking spaces, and saves the time traditionally spent kerbside in a city while waiting for a taxi to come along.

Ultimately, redesigning cities for autonomous, smart vehicles will be required. Fewer parking spaces will be required as people opt-in for shared ownership of vehicles. More charging spaces will lead to solar-powered charging installations being commonplace. As we discussed in chapter 8, some cities will restrict access to human-driven vehicles in the future (or charge significant fees) purely due to the fact that humans aren't as safe as their AI-driven counterparts, and the city often carries liability, especially for transport-related injuries. On college campuses and industrial estates, cars will give way to self-driving "pods" that feed people to public transportation systems. Autonomous public transportation systems will increasingly become solar-powered, reducing carbon emissions in-city too.

Road ecosystems will need to change in favour of the self-driving autonomous, electric vehicle (EV). Assuming EV is the dominant form of transportation in the future, we can expect to see either wireless charging roads or even smart road surfaces. One company in Idaho, USA, is working on solar-powered roadways that include dynamic intelligent and adaptive capabilities, such

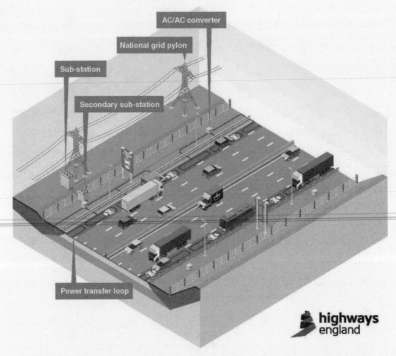

Figure 11.3: Smart, wireless charging roads are being trialled in the United Kingdom.
(Credit: Highways England)

as signage and dynamic lane management. Highways England (UK) has announced trials of a road surface that allows EVs to charge wirelessly as they drive.

Buses and trains will become automated through the increasing use of AI, dynamic scheduling and routing. As buses and trains will be driven by AIs, they will be able to work longer hours without fatigue and overtime consideration. Autonomous, electric transportation systems and vehicles will also be much cheaper to maintain and operate. The costs of the driver will have been eliminated, and electric motors will require far less maintenance than typical combustion engines and the associated drivetrain.

Smart transportation networks in large urban centres will work like a living organism. Small autonomous carts and pods

Figure 11.4: Autonomous modular transportation systems like the Next pod will replace conventional public transport and vehicles. (Credit: NEXT Future Transportation)

will drive around campuses and shopping areas feeding people to ridesharing locations or public transport stations. Public transportation will be optimised around demand, events, weather and other considerations, all reactive in real time and dispatched by AI controllers. Car parks and parking garages will start to dwindle as it becomes unfashionable and increasingly costly to have your own combustion engine vehicle around town.

Does this sound like science fiction? In 20 years, we believe that this type of smart transportation network will be the expectation of citizens living in a smart city. Not just because it will provide better transport for citizens, but because it will cost a fraction of what public transportation systems cost today to maintain and run.

Smart Grids and Energy Systems

Smart energy encompasses a wide range of technologies and initiatives, including the improved distribution and monitoring of electric power as well as better insulation of homes and offices. Renewable energy (RE) is important to the citizens of a smart city for a number of critical reasons:

- reduced air and water pollution for better health and productivity

- decreased costs (as solar energy and other RE costs come down)
- resilience, with power availability even in case of network disturbances due to overloads, natural disasters or terrorist acts

The benefits of using renewable energy to population health can be dramatic, with thousands saved from illness or death. As we pointed out in early chapters, RE generation has become much more efficient in the past decade, with costs that now compete with fossil fuel generation. Germany has been at the forefront of solar and wind power generation, which initially resulted in significant reductions in pollution. However, after the earthquake and subsequent tsunami in Japan in 2011, the German government opted to close most of its nuclear-powered generation facilities, creating a surge in CO_2 emissions from coal-fired plants and thereby negating much of the reductions it had already achieved.

A remaining major challenge for widespread use of renewable energy is storage, the ability to store excess power generated for times when the sun does not shine or the wind does not blow. A number of technical solutions are being worked on to solve this issue, including electrochemical storage (using electric power to generate and store NH_3, or ammonia, which can later be burned as fuel, with no CO_2 emissions), battery storage, etc. Tesla is heavily investing in this effort in the United States with its Gigafactory in Nevada, but it is also tracking multiple battery developments globally.

"Right now, we track about 60 different efforts around the world to develop improved batteries

and some of them hold some long-term
promise. We rate all of them from one to five,
where five is we should be doing business with
them and one is complete BS."

Elon Musk, CEO of Tesla, *Tech Insider*, 10th November 2015

Perhaps unsurprisingly, Japan has been pressing hard for effective RE storage in recent years. Since the shutdown of its nuclear plants after the Fukushima nuclear accident has reduced its electrical output by around 20 per cent, the country has developed extensive solar power capabilities but must find a way to store this energy for times when it is cloudy or dark. Mitsubishi Electric is assembling 50 and 30 megawatt (MW) battery systems for this purpose, at a government-sponsored cost of US$257 million for both projects. Ahmad Chatila, SunEdison's CEO, says that improvements in RE storage are critical for smart energy management based on solar generation.

"The most important technology we can develop
right now is storage."

Ahmad Chatila, CEO of SunEdison

Alternative smart energy systems might include:
- distributed generation networks (resilient against terrorist attack and natural disasters)
- fuel cell generation/storage systems
- small module thorium reactors (shipping container-sized reactors that generate 300 megawatt hours (MWh), or enough for 45,000 homes on demand)
- retooling skyscrapers and government buildings with transparent solar cells (otherwise known as PV window panes)

- coastal cities with surge walls that also generate energy from tidal forces

Smart Health Care

As discussed in chapter 5, recent technology developments in mobile health monitoring systems, also called mHealth, incorporate wearable sensors and algorithms that will track a patient's vital signs and condition. We also reviewed the consumer angles behind this in chapter 5, but cities that leverage off this data will have huge advantages over cities that don't, especially in reducing the cost of health care.

Supporting the development and implementation of mHealth is expected to be increasingly important for cities, especially in light of the pandemic of obesity in wealthy countries such as the United States and the United Arab Emirates, resulting in an explosion of type 2 diabetes with concomitant healthcare cost increases and work absenteeism.

Potentially, the biggest problem here is the politics of health care. In the United States, health care is restricted to big pharma and medical providers who are licensed and come up through the rigorous testing environment of the Federal Drug Administration (FDA). mHealth and smart cities, however, will need to break away from those paradigms to be effective. Rather than promote treatment of diseases and the symptoms of various maladies, the new emerging HealthTech industry is focused on the use of technology like genotyping, biometric tracking, microfluidics and chip-based lab testing, along with personalised risk assessment to assist in disease prevention or stimulate behavioural change. These technologies have the potential to reduce the likelihood of an expensive, critical health event. The HealthTech systems emerging are potentially in conflict with an industry that is geared towards treatment of disease, over one that emphasises pathology and diagnosis in the prevention of emerging problems.

City governments will have to tackle privacy concerns and data sharing provisions to enable HealthTech to thrive and provide intelligent healthcare systems to support its citizens. Resistance in favour of the status quo supporting centralised drug regimes and institutionalised medical care will, by nature, prevent cities from being smart when it comes to health care.

The smartest cities of the future will build healthcare systems in tandem with device and sensor manufacturers and private AI-based health databases to reduce the long-term healthcare burden. Technologies like gene therapy, personalised medicine and smart drugs will no doubt be part of treatment regimens, but the real art for cities will be changing citizen behaviour so that overall healthcare issues are reduced or minimised. Costs will be a fraction of those of the healthcare systems today.

In this future, Obamacare won't be an issue because the cost of care will have been dramatically reduced. Call it socialism 2.0—social care that doesn't require the massive budgets we've come to expect.

Smart Pollution Reduction

Pollution of water and air is a major challenge for modern metropolises. Large cities such as Jakarta, Beijing and Mexico City have tens of thousands who fall ill because of such pollution. As an example, tests in Jakarta in 2004 showed that 46 per cent of all illnesses were respiratory related, and illnesses related to air pollution increased the average workdays lost per capita by about four days per year. In addition, some 50,000 inhabitants throughout Indonesia die each year from waterborne pathogens.[12] Across the planet, more than 2 million children die annually from water pollution, many of them in large cities in Africa and Asia.

New generations of smart sensors, including compact units that can be connected to mobile devices, can help cities monitor pollution levels and reduce the health and welfare costs associated with pollution. Many cities in China regularly exceed levels of 700 parts per million (ppm): a level of 0–50 ppm is considered "good" while a level above 201 ppm is considered "very unhealthy—subject to alerting the population". China's levels are regularly two to three times that of the levels already considered "unhealthy". The cost of this is borne by the city and its citizens over time with increased medical costs, emotional loss and through psychological impact.

Smart cities will monitor air pollution and take proactive action to bring it to safe levels. In cases where governments or utility companies intentionally falsify data, citizens should avail themselves of pollution sensors and take part in social media sites that publicise truthful reports. Air pollution sensors connected to smartphones can enable crowdsourced environmental maps that are freely available to the public. Such maps can record levels not only for cities overall, but within subsections of a large city, as pollution can have high variability within a geographic area and over time.

Some of the most promising technologies for this include localised carbon scrubbing or sequestration technologies that clean the air around cities. Boston is trialling the use of carbon-scrubbing artificial trees called "treepods" that use a technology called "humidity swing" to remove carbon dioxide and other particulates from the atmosphere. Start-ups like Carbon Engineering, based out of Alberta, Calgary, are looking at more

---

12 M. I. Duki, S. Sudarmadi, S. Suzuki, T. Kawada and A. Tugaswati, "The Effects of Air Pollution on Respiratory Health in Indonesia and Its Economic Cost," *Archives of Environmental Health* 58, no. 3 (2003): 135–143.

large-scale production of the direct capture of CO_2. Designer Daan Roosegaarde has recently deployed the largest air purifier ever built in Rotterdam, the Netherlands. The purifier is a tower that scrubs the pollution from more than 30,000 cubic metres of air per hour and then condenses the fine particles of smog into tiny "gem stones" that can be embedded in rings, cufflinks, etc. A research team at George Washington University has gone even further, developing a method to capture atmospheric CO_2 to produce high-yield carbon nanotubes, which could then be used in construction and manufacturing.

There are also new and low-cost options available to help with water pollution in the near term. New types of low-cost water purification units for individual households or communities can remove most types of dangerous chemicals, parasites and bacteria. Smart cities should have such equipment available in case of water pollution resulting from man-made or natural disasters, as well as from other causes. Inroads are already being made in this area. For instance, Dr Askwar Hilonga, a Tanzanian scientist, has created a water filter that utilises nanotechnology to filter 99.9 per cent of contaminants, bacteria, microorganisms and viruses.

> "In Tanzania, 70 per cent of households, of nine million households, are not using any kind of a filter. That is how big the market is. That is in Tanzania alone, nine million households. Now imagine in Kenya, Uganda, Ethiopia, sub-Saharan Africa, India and elsewhere. So the market is very big."[13]
>
> **Dr Askwar Hilonga via Reuters**

---

13 "Tanzanian engineer invents low-cost water filter," *Reuters*, 28 September 2015.

One of these filters, which costs around US$100 to manufacture, is capable of supplying the needs of a family with many litres of clean water per day.

Smart materials and nanotechnology will allow us to create very efficient filtering systems that make our air and water cleaner with much lower investments than we imagine today. Geoengineering the planet will be a popular career for Millennials and their descendants as the globe starts to feel the increased effects of climate shift, and as the old guard loses its influence on policymaking that protects incumbent industries.

Smart Emergency Response Systems

Keeping its citizens safe in times of emergencies or disasters is a major challenge for smart cities. Groups such as firefighters, paramedics, law enforcement and medical teams are collectively called "first responders". The ability to coordinate and deploy such first responders after a disaster occurs can save many thousands of lives during what are called the "incident response" (during and shortly after a disaster) and "recovery" (the weeks after the disaster) time periods.

Challenges for smart cities when it comes to disasters include:
- lack of integrated planning
- poor or non-existent communications during a disaster
- inability of different agencies (federal, state, local) to act together

The results of these challenges not being met have been amply demonstrated in the last decade during Hurricane Katrina, the Haiti earthquake, the Indonesian tsunami and hundreds of similar disasters. Fortunately, ICT solutions are available to help smart cities in this area.

Integrated planning requires that different agencies such as fire departments, local police, paramedics, hospitals, city and state governments as well as federal agencies must plan together, using common terminology and assumptions. The norm is for such agencies to each come up with a unique set of plans in what is termed a "silo" (i.e., remote and independent) environment. This consequently leads to chaotic responses when a crisis occurs.[14]

Integrated communications have also been a problem in the past, with each group of first responders having its own analog equipment. In past years, for instance, personnel from the Los Angeles County Sheriff's Department, Police Department, Highway Patrol and Fire Department could not talk with each other during crises because their equipment sets were incompatible, purchased through different contracts and procurement processes.

The inability of different agencies to act together has had dire consequences during disasters. During Hurricane Katrina, highway patrol deputies blocked access to New Orleans to technicians who had been called for and were desperately needed by the City Police Department to repair various infrastructures. After the 1999 Izmit earthquake near the city of Istanbul, Turkey, different response agencies were not only unable to operate together, but also had conflicts over which group actually had control over critical resources such as buses and helicopters. The resulting confusion slowed the response and contributed to the high death toll of more than 30,000. Similar chaotic conditions occurred in Australia during the "Black Saturday" bushfires of 2009, in which different agencies sometimes worked against each other, with one group closing highways that others had tagged as evacuation routes; 173 people died, and hundreds were injured.

---

14 Z. Baird et al. *Nation at Risk: Policy Makers Need Better Information to Protect the Country* (Washington, DC: Department of Defense, 2009).

Figure 11.5: The Rio Operations Center (Credit: IBM Smart Cities)

Smart cities will overcome this by insisting that all relevant agencies have smart devices that have resiliency features to help overcome occasional transmission losses, use common terms, plan together, and train and exercise together frequently, using daily the systems that they will need to use during a period of crisis. An example of a smart city disaster management system that is integrated and used every day, not just during disasters, is the Rio de Janeiro public information management centre, the Rio Operations Center, located in Cidade Nova.

This system for the city and county of Rio supports integrated planning for disasters, and links together police, military, medical services, electrical utilities, road construction and other organisations that can be involved in one of the many floods and mudslides the area is prone to during storms and hurricanes, or just even coordinating traffic, security and services during the annual Rio Carnival.

The Operations Center was built with the personal support and involvement of the mayor, in preparation for the 2014 FIFA World Cup and 2016 Summer Olympics. As the system is in everyday use, the operators across the city are familiar with each other and do not need the normal four to eight hours of "getting to know you" at the beginning of a crisis or natural disaster. This has a secondary benefit: since the groups are familiar with "who does what and in what sequence" for different contingencies, automated commands can be sent out upon warning (e.g., a report of an incoming hurricane) instead of consuming the many hours usually needed to generate, review, approve and issue orders to dozens of operators and emergency personnel.

Rio's integrated planning enables economies of scale and a reduction in repetitive actions. As the mayor of Rio said, "Why have the sewer department, the telephone company, the water company, the roads department and other agencies dug up the same street five times? Let them coordinate, and dig it up only once!" Woah, common sense!

Inputs to the Rio system include sensor networks that track rain and weather conditions. In addition, it incorporates predictive modelling to alert leaders as to what is going to happen rather than just react after an event has taken place. The system can be preprogrammed to send out alerts for incoming inclement weather or other emergencies to both government agencies and the populace (via phone messages, email and mobile phone texting). As aforementioned, it can also enable tasking, automatically sending out detailed orders or sets of tasks to relevant organisations, with follow-up for acceptance, processing and completion of such tasks. Not only that, the system will accept text messages and other inputs from citizens to report outages and crises. It thus provides an avenue for ordinary people to become actively involved in the safety and functioning of their neighbourhoods—and to feel that government leaders care about their inputs.

Augmented Cities

There are many possible ways to augment and enhance the quality of life of the citizens of smart cities with ICT, including smart unmanned aerial vehicles (UAVs), also called drones, enhanced computer generated displays such as AR, AI-supported decision aids for government and industry, and many more. Two examples with potential applications—AR and UAVs—are overviewed below.

The Potential for Augmented Reality in Cities

The advantage of AR for a smart city is that it can enhance real-world views at a physical spot with data and images to help the user to better understand the location, shopping or driving options and the historical context of real-world objects being looked at. It is thus ideal for applications including travel, tourism and the understanding of local cultural objects.

One common and useful application of AR overlays is in finding parking spots or locations of parked cars. For example,

Figure 11.6: Historical view overlaid on a real-world streetscape

an app that supports users in finding their cars allows a view of the real world (via the handheld's camera) but overlays graphics to guide them to and then identify their car.

AR can be especially useful to visitors and tourists in a smart city, as they are largely unfamiliar with the city's features and hate inefficient searching for where they want to go. Here are some sample AR apps:

- **Wikitude** is an AR aggregator of information from content sources such as Citysearch and Wikipedia as well as user-generated content. Users can choose categories to search (e.g., restaurants, sights) and explore other people's Flickr photos and comments.
- **Yelp Monocle** can be accessed via the "More" tab at the bottom of the screen of an Android phone. Holding the phone vertically in the desired direction pops up tabs of businesses and reviews while holding it horizontally generates a map view and route.
- **Metro AR Pro** is a "location-aware" app that automatically detects the city you're in and displays metro and other public transportation stops.
- **WhatWasThere** shows what the neighbourhood you're in looked like in the past.
- **Google Search** (or the Google Goggles app) enables the traveller to click on "Search" and snap a photo of an object the user wants more information on. The app then downloads prices, directions, history and other data. A photo of a sign in a foreign language can provide a quick translation.

Every large city usually has a wealth of cultural artefacts and locations, including monuments, museums, art displays and examples of local architecture. Unfortunately, relatively few of its citizens fully experience such marvels. Museums tend to have displays of many objects with little description—and an overwhelming number of objects (typically over 95 per cent) are locked away in basement vaults. Such objects can be brought to life with AR technology. The people in paintings can appear to "walk off the walls" and tell their story, statues can give their history and skeletons of dinosaurs and other animals can come alive to delight and educate young and old alike.

Smart cities can use AR to educate their citizens and keep alive cultural roots and traditions. City support of such efforts can include forming partnerships with educational centres teaching videogame, VR, AR, ICT and related technologies and city assets such as museums, outdoor art displays, monuments, cultural centres and high-traffic areas to not only help develop job skills and innovation but also bring the smart city to life. The emergence of PHUD units like Meta or Magic Leap will certainly enable smart cities to be creative with the use of AR.

Figure 11.7: NatGeo and Seef Mall in Dubai have incorporated AR into the shopping experience. (Credit: National Geographic)

Unmanned Aerial Vehicles in Smart Cities

The employment of UAVs for civilian tasks is increasing rapidly. Until 2014, UAV missions were almost exclusively military: for reconnaissance, weapons delivery and covert transport of special payloads. Only a dozen civilian companies had been granted permits by the FAA to use UAVs in the United States, and those were mostly for aerial filming on closed sets. This situation has changed radically. In the first half of 2015, over 500 permits to fly UAVs were issued by the FAA for missions including farm surveillance and servicing, security services and railway and pipeline inspections.

The number of suppliers is also increasing rapidly, with hundreds of start-up companies creating alternatives to the existing very expensive UAV systems manufactured by aerospace companies for government users. Other start-ups are creating electronics for UAV control and data analysis and display, including AI-supported software that is able to control multiple aircraft at the same time.

The Association for Unmanned Vehicle Systems International believes that drones will become ubiquitous in the United States, Europe and Asia, with priority missions including crop monitoring, atmospheric research, oil and mineral exploration, border and security fence monitoring, and law enforcement patrols. The recently published Drone/UAV Dictionary lists 300 major UAV applications.

Several types of UAVs may be of interest to a smart city. The UAVs listed below are not being recommended herein, they are only examples of size/function envelopes. Classes of UAVs for a city include:

- Lightweight, electric quadcopter UAVs such as the DJI Phantom 3 for patrols by guards and law enforcement, photography and inspection services.

- Lightweight, electric UAVs such as Aeronavics' SkyJib or Quadrocopter's CineStar, with enough lifting capability for professional camera rigs, short-range film and TV cinematography. These cost in the range of US$10,000 each.
- Medium UAV systems for extended field use, such as the Honeywell T-Hawk. The T-Hawk has seen limited service with the US Army and Navy, and has been used by ordnance disposal technicians to get overviews of deadly situations. For instance, a T-Hawk was used to provide close-up views of Fukushima Daiichi Nuclear Power Plant, which was damaged by the massive earthquake and tsunami that hit Japan in 2011.
- UAVs such as the Russian-made Chirok can assist with waterborne rescue in the event that the smart city is located near a lake or ocean. The Chirok can either fly at altitudes of 20,000 feet (6,100 m) or hover over water on its fan-generated air cushion. With a payload of 660 pounds (272 kg), it can rescue up to three people or carry significant equipment to any ground or sea location.

Figure 11.8: The Schiebel Camcopter S-100 (Credit: Schiebel Corp)

- Medium UAV systems capable of carrying 110 pounds (50 kg), such as the Austrian Schiebel Camcopter S-100. Designed to be used for law enforcement and surveillance, the system is compact, with a height of 3.6 feet (1.1 m), and can fly for 6 hours, with a range of 124 miles (200 km). It can carry urgent-delivery freight or packages across a city, such as dropping off emergency medical supplies. The system is capable of manual or fully automatic flight and carries a day/night sensor package. In chapter 4, we gave an example of an ambulance-style UAV that could drop a defibrillator or first aid kit in an emergency scenario.

A mix of two or three of these types of UAVs or drones could enable a smart city to:

- Carry high-value cargo across the city, unhindered by traffic.
- Perform search and rescue (SAR) operations on land or at sea.
- Perform inspections of critical infrastructure such as oil and gas lines.
- Conduct day/night patrols of the city for law enforcement.
- Quickly bring equipment that might not be accessible to normal vehicles to first responders, medical personnel or others.

The US Centers for Disease Control and Prevention (CDC) and Microsoft Research have started a project with drones to collect mosquitoes and conduct gene-sequencing and pathogen detection. The White House believes that "this technique has the potential to serve as an early warning system for vector-borne disease outbreaks and may assist health officials in planning for the impacts of climate change on public health." Another very recent UAV application is the prediction of global wildfires. Smart cities of the future will generate many pilot projects for new uses for UAVs, which could not only serve their citizens well but also create new business and entrepreneurial models and potential.

Will AIs Be the "Smart" behind Smart Cities?

Smart cities employ modern ICT to increase the health, safety, learning, job and recreational opportunities and sustainability of their citizens, and to engage more actively with them. New technologies such as smart sensor nets, easier-to-understand graphic displays, high-resolution smartphones, AR systems, smart UAVs and IoT offer new channels for collaborative problem solving and mutually beneficial collective action. Research centres such as MIT's Cities Lab are deep wells of innovation while cities such as Amsterdam, Copenhagen and Barcelona are pioneers in effective smart city development, and offer lessons learned and best practices.

Transforming our cities into the smart cities of the future will encompass incorporating technologies and key digital developments all linked by machine-to-machine solutions and real-time data analytics. Smart cities, however, must be underpinned by the appropriate infrastructure based on fibre-optic and high-speed wireless technologies. This infrastructure allows for the development of smart communities, supporting connected homes, intelligent transport systems, mHealth, eGovernment and massive open online courses/education (MOOC/E), smart grids and smart energy solutions, etc. Central to this will be infrastructure that starts to run itself, responding in real time. Automated UAVs, autonomous emergency vehicles and robots, and sensor nets giving feedback loops to the right algorithms or AIs to dispatch those resources.

Artificial intelligence will not only be an underpinning of smart cities, it will also be necessary simply to process all of the sensor data coming into smart city operations centres. Humans will only slow down the process too much. Strong AI involvement running smart cities is closer to two decades away. Within 20 to 30 years, we will see smart governance at the hands of AI—coded laws and enforcement, resource allocation, budgeting and optimal decision-making made by algorithms that run independent of human committees and voting. The manual counting of votes for elections will be a thing of the past, as citizens will BYOD (bring your own device) to the challenge of casting their votes. But that's only the start.

Within 50 years, it is entirely possible that partisan politics within local and state government will give way to delegating governance primarily or entirely to algorithms. The voting process is a largely inefficient mechanism for governance today. At the federal level in the United States, it involves the expenditure of billions of dollars in advertising, fund raising and hundreds of thousands of hours given to debate, analysis, posturing and so forth. Eventually, mankind will determine that such resource allocation in the process of electing leaders is as inefficient as using fossil fuels for energy or using a person to drive a bus or train. Government is one of the few industries left to disrupt and AI is going to be the key to that disruption.

Unfortunately, such smart cities are still the exception rather than the rule today. Millions of people die each year from the negative effects of living in large cities, including water and air pollution, large-scale corruption, traffic accidents, the depletion of natural resources, poor health care and ineffective responses to ever-increasing natural disasters. Smart cities offer a better, safer world; they are urgently needed, not only to increase the physical and intellectual capabilities of man, but for the sustainability of the planet.

12

The New Era of Engagement

Contributed by Andy Lark

Edited by Brett King

> "Great products are no longer good enough to win in business. Creative marketing and delightful customer service too are not enough to succeed. Success and the future of business is experiential and this is the time to learn how to create and cultivate meaningful experiences."
>
> From *X: The Experience When Business Meets Design*
> by Brian Solis

Depending on the day and our mood, shopping can be a necessity, a social event, a research project or an outlet for our emotions. Sometimes, we even call it "retail therapy". On some days, we attack it head-on with a list and a single-minded focus. On other days, we might join friends at the mall and shop with complete abandon, arriving home with goods we neither needed nor wanted. Then there are days we plan for extensively, seeking recommendations, reading reviews, researching online and comparing prices. The research might lead to an immediate online purchase or it might lead us to a store for our final part of the customer journey.

While the "why" of shopping has remained constant and survived as a central part of our lives, the "how" of shopping has been rapidly evolving, driven largely by technology change. Despite the birth of Amazon, Alibaba and others, the shopping experience is about to undergo its most radical transformation yet.

Technology is already augmenting our shopping experience. You can take a virtual tour of a house you are thinking of buying. You can hang a virtual representation of that new TV you're interested in in a virtual version of your living room created from an uploaded photo, you can take a virtual test drive in a new car or you can snap a selfie and use an app to "try on" some sunglasses. What we look at in the virtual world will soon be further enhanced by new sensory experiences spanning sound, smell and touch. Augmented shopping experiences will not only change how we buy, it will change what we buy as new experiences, products and services evolve to better meet our needs. This evolution won't stop at shopping either; it will span travel, tourism and more.

Augmented Moments

At the heart of the movement to augment how we shop and travel is a desire to address our **moments of desire, dissatisfaction and doubt** (MODs). These are the moments—sometimes measured in seconds—where we experience emotions in relation to a product, event or service.

- *Desire* must be fulfilled immediately, often in milliseconds. Left unsatisfied, we simply seek out other services and offerings.

- *Dissatisfaction* drives us to seek alternatives but also opens our minds to new products and services.
- *Doubt* is answered with information and data, allaying concerns or anxiety and providing reassurance as to the quality of the potential services.

For instance, think about the moments Uber has created as part of its experience. We *desired* taxis to be available with the same convenience as making a telephone call or checking an email. We were universally *dissatisfied* with taxis that didn't arrive or those that delivered poor service with impunity. The mere *doubt* of not knowing where our taxi was could create anxiety and stress, especially when we were in a hurry and the taxi hadn't shown up.

Uber managed to solve all three of these moments. When we open the app, immediately we know that there are cars available. We order with a click on the "Find an Uber" button and we can observe the journey of the taxi as it makes its way to us—the stress and doubt disappear with the certainty the app delivers. Most importantly, we are able to rate the quality of the experience, affording Uber the opportunity to improve the overall service and weed out substandard drivers or vehicles.

A recent *Quartz* article[1] identified that up to 30 per cent of Uber drivers in the United States have never had a bank **account**—many operated previously as taxi drivers in the cash economy. To be a driver on Uber, however, drivers need a minimum of a debit card to get paid. So Uber has had to solve this problem by allowing drivers to sign up for a bank account as part of the Uber driver application process, in real time. Unsurprisingly, this makes Uber the largest acquirer of small business bank accounts in the United States today, bigger than Wells Fargo, BofA and Chase combined.

---

1 Ian Kar, "Uber is trying to lure new drivers by offering bank accounts," *Qz.com*, 3 November 2015, http://qz.com/533492/exclusive-heres-how-uber-is-planning-using-banking-to-keep-drivers-from-leaving/.

You've probably never thought of Uber as an acquirer of small business bank accounts, but if you're an Uber driver and Uber can give you a debit card that enables you to get paid—then why would you go to a bank branch to open an account instead? It also means that as an entrepreneur bank account the next obvious move is to design day-to-day banking into Uber's app instead of standing alone as a typical bank account or mobile banking app.

For the millions of permalancers or gigging economy workers, it's highly likely that the first time a freelancer opens a bank account will be directly in response to a new gig or job offer—if that employer (like Uber or Airbnb) offers you a bank account as part of the sign-up process, why would you stop signing up for Uber, drive to a branch and sign a piece of paper?

Uber is also offering car leases to its drivers,[2] allowing drivers with no vehicle to sign up and get car financing backed by demand from Uber. This is what the new banking experience looks like for small business entrepreneurs. Uber is effectively doing all the sourcing for bank relationships, and has become an acquirer for bank accounts, leasing and insurance. An Uber driver has no reason to go to a bank branch for his needs today thanks to Uber's commitment to **experience design** enabling the needs of a new driver.

Uber is a brilliant example of how technology is being used to augment our everyday journeys, and the business of journeys. It doesn't rely on just one single technology but brings many together to transform a traditional service for its customers and drivers alike. Incumbents faced with the superior experiences offered by this new entrant often lobbied local regulators and lawmakers to outlaw Uber. When that failed, these same companies were forced to invest in similar technologies and experiences just so

---

2   Pavithra Mohan, "Uber to Lease Cars Directly to UberX Drivers," *Fast Company*, 30 July 2015.

they could remain relevant. Most could only approximate the new experiences Uber pioneered.

At the heart of Uber is the near-term benefit of augmentation. Take an existing service and make it simple and easy. Most new technologies are focusing on this near-term innovation opportunity. Many of the examples you will see across retail and travel today reflect this. Electronic bag tags, mirrors that show you how a shirt will look on you without trying it on and bracelets that track the journey of your child on a plane or in a theme park. All harness readily available technology to make the current experience better than before.

On the near horizon are promises of far greater innovation.

Augmented Service Delivery (2015–2020)

Over the next five years, most innovations will seek to transform current services and address our MODs. What we see today as major shifts like Uber and Airbnb will turn out to be small incremental improvements in hindsight.

The underlying theme of an augmented world is that technologies connect to create fundamentally new experiences that aren't possible in a manual or human process driver world. An example of what might be possible already today with a mash-up of a range of technologies is shopping for glasses. We snap a photo of ourselves on an iPhone, then select a pair of glasses from an online catalogue to see how they might look on our face (rendered via an app). Selecting the glasses we like, we then get a map of retailers with current stock of the frames we like. The closest retailer then serves an offer via text messaging to our phone but will take three days to deliver. A retailer in the same area can deliver in 24 hours but doesn't provide us with a discount offer to purchase. The decision is ours. This scenario is highly feasible due to the technology we already carry in our pockets, the capability of the computing cloud that is integrated into the world around us and specific application of data like geolocation or GPS and mapping technologies.

Already drones are taking to the air to test personal delivery of everything from books and smartphones to pizzas. Drones may initially be required to make deliveries to centralised locations like post offices, petrol/service and train stations for safety purposes. Five to ten years from now, those same drones and/or autonomous carts and pods (small robot vehicles) will come to wherever you and your smartphone are. Lily, a self-driving robot videographer drone that automatically follows you around capturing your life on video, pulled in a whopping US$34 million in pre-orders for more than 60,000 units when it went on sale over Christmas in 2015. We can be sure that drones will play a part in experiences in many ways.

Experiences Re-invented and Distributed (2020–2025)

Technology will reshape products and industries dramatically the further we get away from the 20th-century norms. As Brett discussed in his earlier chapters, when computers are everywhere and our environment is smart, always connected, the limitations of existing value chains, product life cycles and campaign marketing will be vaporised in favor of engagement that is real time and moulds itself to our needs, location and preferences. The businesses of the future will be in the business of experiences, not products and services.

Retailers that no longer sell goods but deliver experiences in which products feature will be a distinct element of the Augmented Age. Whether that is a gourmet food experience, a luxury lifestyle experience or an immersive entertainment experience, goods and services will be reframed as an experience you live. Goods or products may be embedded in the service, but individually branded products themselves will likely become less of a factor in a buying decision and more a "feature" of the experience itself. Will you buy an iPhone 11s or will you buy a personal AI and healthcare system supported by a smartwatch and what we'd call a smartphone today? Would you buy a VR headset or would you buy a subscription to an immersive storytelling and gaming platform that needs a VR headset to provide you with that experience?

Travel is going to be another one of these areas where the entire experience has the potential to be impacted by technology, from what you see out of your window through to the food you eat and media you consume will be a dynamic reflection of your personal preferences learnt through past interactions and behaviour. Some of these preferences you'll have told your personal AI (acting as a travel concierge) while others will be inferred from your data, behaviour or choices historically.

What will make a first-class experience for you? Will it be flying up front?[3] Will it be a shower on board before your long-haul flight lands? Will it be an à la carte dining service, high bandwidth data connectivity or a personal greeter who can rapidly get you through immigration and home faster once you land? In the past, marketers might have been tempted to call this a market-of-one segmentation, but this is more about behaviour-based adaptation of the market and service providers to the individual in real time through experience and interaction design. It's about technology that can learn about you, and services that can intelligently adapt to that knowledge.

The World of Instant Products (2025–2040)

In this 15- to 20-year timescale, our lives will be augmented by

---

3 There's a rumour that Brett King only knows how to turn left when boarding an aircraft. Can anyone confirm that?

products and services that are designed as and when we need them. Let's say you are planning that special night out and you'd like to give your significant other some jewellery to mark the occasion. We might no longer shop for a piece of jewellery but rather look simply for a cool design to fit the occasion. That design is downloaded and then printed on a 3D printer, but not before including some last-minute customisation that you've built in to personalise the piece. The Voxel8 is a 3D printer, retailing at US$9,000, that can print complex circuits using conductive ink, which hints at a future where we might even be able to print our own electronics at home.

A team of computer scientists from Germany's Saarland University has developed a technique that could allow anyone to literally print their own custom displays, including touchscreens. Using a regular inkjet printer equipped with special ink, a DIY thin-film electroluminescence (TFEL) display can be printed out from a digital template.

The team has developed two methods using either screen-printing techniques or off-the-shelf inkjet printers that can take anywhere from several minutes to four hours for a layman to create a custom display. The team claims that this results in "relatively high resolution displays" only one tenth of a millimetre thick. They say covering a standard A4 or letter-sized printer page with a display layer would cost about €20 (US$21.69), mostly due to the cost of the special ink involved.

Within ten years, it appears that we will be able to deliver circuitry and electronics into these downloadable designs and, by 2030 to 2040, your next iPhone might, in fact, be a file you download from Apple and not a physical device you buy from a store. The only physical product we'll absolutely have to buy in the future might be a 3D printer or fabrication unit.

Figure 12.1: A 3D-printed, TFEL high-resolution display

Reshaping How We Shop

To understand how we're going to get to the future, we have to understand how we got here. The dot-com boom of the 1990s gave birth to a new generation of retailers. E-tailers, as they became known, had no physical presence save a few warehouses from where their products were shipped. Armed with the global reach of the Internet, search engines and teams of programmers, they took traditional retailers head-on. Amazon unseated booksellers and quickly became the "everything store". Gilt, Rue La La, Alibaba and Zappos made the annual sale a daily event. Initially sceptical or even downright hostile, most incumbent retailers were dragged along kicking and screaming as these online players took market share. Some, like Blockbuster and Borders, just didn't make it.

This first phase of augmentation was basic but necessary. We could quickly experience products before heading to the store, maybe shopping online to compare goods or prices. We could choose pick up or delivery, a recipe quickly morphed into a shopping list with the click of a mouse and we could find out if the item we wanted was in stock and/or reserve it before we got to the store. The physical world was already being augmented by an online world that enabled us to time and place-shift our desires. We no longer had to wait to visit the store to see what we wanted. Instead we browsed, researched and ordered online.

Hampered with legacy cost structures and physical debt, it took decades for traditional retailers to make headway against new entrants. As Clay Shirky put it, "'You're gonna miss us when we're gone!' has never been much of a business model."[4]

Today, physical retailers compete toe to toe with online competitors, leveraging omnichannel marketing and merchandising and complimentary experiences to unify the digital and physical world. Recently, we have seen pure online stores opening physical storefronts such as Amazon and Microsoft.

The year 2015 marked another e-commerce boom after an already heady 2014, with US-based e-commerce reaching more than US$350 billion in sales. Global sales have expected to top out in excess of US$1.5 trillion. Online e-commerce over the Christmas holiday period showed an increase year-on-year of some 14 per cent,[5] with US$617 billion in sales globally, and US$80 billion in the United States alone (approximately 10 per cent of all retail sales).

Four Technology Forces Reshaping the Future of Retail and Travel

As Brett identified in chapter 2, the four most disruptive forces of the Augmented Age are artificial intelligence, distributed embedded experiences, smart infrastructure and gene editing and HealthTech. However, within those disruptive themes,

---

4   Clay Shirky is a well-respected writer, consultant and professor who has been a leading voice on the social and economic effects of the Internet. He lectures at Harvard's John F. Kennedy School of Government, New York University, the Interactive Telecommunications Program and the Arthur L. Carter Journalism Institute.

5   http://www.practicalecommerce.com/articles/92465-4-Predictions-for-2015-Holiday-Shopping-Season

> **"We always overestimate the change that will occur in the next two years and underestimate the change that will occur in the next ten."**
> Bill Gates, 1996

your shopping experience is also being transformed. There are four building blocks to Augmented Retail, around which thousands of other technologies and augmented experiences are starting to cluster.

First: Augmented by the Cloud

The cloud is perhaps the worst metaphor for computing power ever created. The name harks back to early network diagrams in which technology not on the physical site was represented with a diagram of a cloud. Today, the cloud is literally hundreds of hectares of computer and storage power operating as a massive, distributed system in service of everything from Facebook to email, photos and mapping software.

Brett discussed in chapter 3 that computers are becoming ubiquitous and essentially disappearing (by being embedded or diffused into the world around us). Today, entrepreneurs and individuals have access to computing power that was previously only available to the largest companies in the world. Any start-up with a credit or debit card can buy computing power for a few dollars to get started, and then, as the company grows, scale its spend and cloud-based platform as required.

Today, the cloud provides access to unprecedented computing power and storage, enabling any retailer to scale services. So just how big is the cloud? Unfortunately, cloud providers don't disclose too many details about their operations. However, we know that Amazon is the biggest since it recently reported US$7 billion in annual revenue for 2014.

First, let's look at the scale of Amazon's cloud operations. It's truly mind-blowing.

- Amazon Web Services (AWS) is carved up into **11 regions globally** where it has datacentres.
- Each region has at least two availability zones (AZs), for a total of **28 availability zones.**
- Most AZs have multiple datacentres. Amazon hasn't revealed how many datacentres it actually has but a recent EnterpriseTech article estimates that there are around **87 AWS datacentres.**
- Amazon has 50,000 to 80,000 servers in each datacentre, for a total of somewhere between **2 and 5 million servers.**[6]
- Power requirements for each datacentre are 25 to 30 megawatts, or **2+ gigawatts** for all of AWS.
- Amazon is building **solar farms** to make its datacentres 100 per cent renewable as well as working with Tesla to apply battery storage technology to address its power needs.
- As for network capacity, each datacentre has at least **102 Tb/sec of bandwidth** coming in, connected to each other through private lines. That is 100,000 times as much bandwidth as Google Fiber. In fact, Amazon has had to develop its own networking technology just to continue its growth.

We know that both Google and Amazon have over 1.5 million servers each. Facebook has at least half a million servers for its Facebook, WhatsApp and Instagram infrastructure. Each of these installations has more storage and computing power than the entire planet had in the mid-90s. If you add IBM, Oracle and then companies like Rackspace, as well as private clouds owned by banks, governments[7] and so on, we're talking tens of millions of servers spread around the globe, zettabytes of storage space and hundreds of gigawatts of energy

6 Some estimates are as high as 5 million. Amazon last confirmed that it had at least 1.4 million servers, but that was in December 2014.

7 The National Security Agency's Utah Data Center alone is said to hold more than 5,000 servers with 12 exabytes of storage space, throughout a building that spans 1.5 million square feet.

consumption. The size of the "cloud" is truly staggering. Maybe we should start calling it the "nebula" —cloud seems just too small.

We once worried about where our data was stored and bought physical floppy discs to do back-ups. Now our data lives in many places and flows to whatever device or application we link it to in real time. In many ways, we're still getting started on this journey. Between 2011 and 2013, the Internet population grew 14.3 per cent to 2.4 billion people. With 80 per cent of the world likely having a web-enabled smartphone by 2020, we can expect to add another 2 billion mobile consumers to this number within the next five years. Today, no device sends and receives more personal data than that of our smartphone.

Second: Augmented by Mobile and Wearables

The mobile device—smartphone, iPhone, whatever your flavour—has created a new connection point with the shopper and traveller. Part tracker, wallet, camera and interface to the physical world, it sits in our pocket, always on, always listening, dynamic in its ability to interact.

According to Deloitte research, smartphones used as part of a shopping experience could impact 17 to 21 per cent of retail sales by 2016—that's an incredible US$627–$752 billion. During the 2015 Christmas period in the United Kingdom, more than two thirds of shoppers were expected to use their mobile device to shop. Econsultancy's "Mobile Experience Trends Briefing" report in May 2015 also found that 92 per cent of shoppers utilise mobile to make buying decisions while completing their purchase in-store. Furthermore, eMarketer estimated an increase of 35 per cent increase in mobile commerce for the 2015 Christmas shopping period.

The data is clear. Today, there is no greater influence on our shopping behaviour than the mobile phone, and its influence is growing. To be fair, growth is happening across the board in retail and in commerce, but no channel or mechanism is growing anywhere as fast as mobile is. Mobile is growing at least three to five times faster than that of both online and conventional retail commerce and sales, and faster than online grew even at the height of dot-com.

The travel industry is being greatly impacted by mobile. Nowadays, 60 per cent of all travel is booked through digital, up from 0 per cent in the mid-90s. In 2007, that accounted for about US$94 billion in online sales but that will be closer to US$300 billion by 2020. In 2016, eMarketer estimates that 51.8 per cent of travel-related digital sales will be mobile or app-based. So the biggest single channel for travel booking will be a mobile phone. Obviously as apps get better, as hotels, airlines and travel agents streamline their mobile-based booking engines, this is likely to increase significantly. Of course, this doesn't even factor in Airbnb and the sharing economy.

Let's face it—the retail and travel industries may be growing, but the sweet spot is mobile engagement and revenue. Essential to our retail and travel experiences will be engagement and payments. Engagement is the new "marketing" when it comes to the retail space—how can we get you into our store (physical or virtual), and buying our product, then how do we make it as easy as possible to buy? The most efficient form of payment is one that isn't at a checkout but happens when you interact in the store, or even as you walk out of the store having picked out your goods.

In the future, your unique identity will be linked to preferential payment mechanisms coded into your smart device. As you have

Figure 12.2: Microsoft and Volvo are collaborating on AR "manuals" that show you how car features work. (Credit: Volvo/Microsoft)

your new shirt, automated personal drone or new foldable tablet scanned by an in-store representative for purchase, the in-store systems will have already negotiated with your phone and be ready to process the payment. As you walk out of the store, you'll see the receipt and transaction record (and warranty record) instantly on your device.

Augmented reality will be used for a variety of applications across the entire buying cycle from research through to purchasing and service interactions. Volvo cars and Microsoft HoloLens recently demonstrated a conceptual example of new service interactions with AR.

The rendered concept video shows how shoppers will be able to check out useful features that are often overlooked because drivers tend to no longer read car manuals. Detailed visualisations also help them understand how these features work in various scenarios. This will change support for technical products considerably. Imagine a help desk or customer support showing you a feature while you're wearing smart glasses.

If you use a pair of smart glasses, you might see options or deals in your personal head-up display. Augmented reality will be a stronger in-store trend looking at the middle of next decade. However, to accomplish that, we will need a new technology infrastructure underpinning store experiences.

Third: Augmented by Beacons

For smartphones, smart glasses, a personal AI or smart wearables to respond in the retail space, something must be listening.

Today, sensors and Bluetooth connected beacons surround us. iBeacons, NFC chips, radio frequency identification tags (RFID) and more sense our presence and communicate with our devices in real time. Most of the time, we're unaware that this is happening. Connecting to millions of phones in millions of pockets, with their connected location-based services, they signal the opportunity to deliver extremely tightly focused, personalised messages, offers and promotions in real time.

Beacons are the fastest-growing retail technology, growing 287 per cent to 5 million beacons[8] in the United States within the next four years, with most of them in use by retailers, according to BI Intelligence. By 2016, 85 per cent of the top 100 US retailers will have deployed beacons. Apple is deploying beacons in its own stores and in association with Disney for payments and in-store offers. Macy's recently rolled out beacons to 4,000 stores.[9] According to *Business Insider*, beacons directly influenced over US$4 billion in US retail sales in 2015 and will climb to more than ten times that in 2016.

Using a combination of virtual currency, apps and location-based services, the technology used by Macy's (and provided by Shopkick) has the potential to significantly change the way we shop.

---

8   http://www.businessinsider.com.au/beacons-impact-billions-in-reail-sales-2015-2
9   http://www.mediapost.com/publications/article/234217/4000-beacons-coming-to-all-macys-stores.
   html

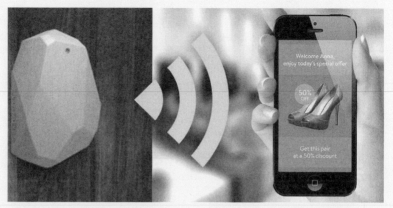

Figure 12.3: Beacons will dramatically change the ability to offer context digitally.

> "Shopkick has found a way to change consumer behaviour... We can influence behaviour in a measurable way. Shopkick users spend 50 to 100 per cent more than others."
>
> Cyriac Roeding, CEO of Shopkick

By augmenting your shopping experience with contextual, real-time rewards, Shopkick and Macy's can reward you for just visiting certain parts of the store. By scanning a barcode on a product, you get even more rewards. You not only get your shopping trip augmented with new experiences, you get an entirely customised experience.

> "If it's Chuck's Macy's, you experience a different Macy's store," said Roeding. "The whole experience becomes YOUR Macy's. Just like different stores carry different products. This takes 'My Macy's' to the next level. The store becomes an individual experience."
>
> Cyriac Roeding, CEO of Shopkick

To shoppers, the reality is that technology matters little. What matters is value delivered.

An interesting side effect of this technology will be a complete undermining of credit card reward programmes. As in-store offers emerge, rewards becomes easier and easier to redeem. As a direct result of this, there will be a decrease in the net number of customers who no longer claim rewards and, therefore, marginal profitability of current reward programmes will be hammered— quickly becoming unprofitable. If you get cashback today from your card, expect to have this disappear within the next five years. It's unsustainable in a real-time world with decreasing interchange models.

Gen Ys are much more attuned to the notional opportunity cost of rewards built into credit card schemes in particular, where they are not convinced of the trade-off between higher interest rates, frequency of spend and the tangible value of the reward. Even for cashback offers, it doesn't require much of a revolving balance over a couple of months for a consumer to wipe out any cashback benefits. In the era of the quantified self, the self-aware customer won't make spending decisions based on cashback, miles or trinkets offered, they'll make spending decisions based on whether they can afford to make a purchase, or whether this is a great deal in-store. Loyal customers will get great deals; that will be the new frequency model. Not miles or points you never spend.

Today, shoppers are surrounded by printed posters, displays and billboards illustrating these new retail experiences. We see smartphone ads encouraging the downloading of apps and connections to in-store WiFi networks. These posters and billboards are not about apps per se, but linking customers to coupons, discounts and offers in-store.

A great example is the Regent Street app promoted on double-decker buses across London.[10] Download the app and you will find yourself "beaconed" into any one of the hundreds of luxury stores and brands along Regent Street with messages correlated with your predefined interests. Westfield London shopping centre is working on similar technology.

Today, what happens on our handheld screen is fairly one-dimensional. The next level of retail augmentation is when auditory, visual and olfactory experiences are added to our reality.

Fourth: Augmented by Sensory Experiences

As Brett articulated in chapter 3, the current generation will be the last to use a physical keyboard and mouse. Soon, our so-called "phones"[11] will not only take instructions from us but also sense the tone and tenor of our voice, listening for choices, instructions or preferences, and making recommendations of experiences we might enjoy.

While the humble camera and speaker are how we most commonly experience visual and audio innovations today, what lies beneath them has far more revolutionary potential.

Next-generation retail experiences will evolve into something akin to neural and bio-synchronicity. The use of biometrics (fingerprint, facial, iris and voice identification), pattern recognition (emotional, stimulus response, location-based), behavioural psychology, sensory integration and augmented reality will change the retail experience into something that is a hybrid of technology and experiential design. We've talked about smart health care, smart banking, etc., in the other chapters of the book, so it's natural that retailers and hospitality will seek to merge retail, travel and tech as much as possible.

10 *See* Footmarks at http://www.footmarks.com/beacons-regent-street/.
11 Clearly, we're talking about devices that are no longer just smartphones but supercomputers that we carry on our person, linked not only to the cloud, but to smart glasses, beacons, sensors on and inside our bodies, the devices of others and a myriad of IoT devices and sensors.

The future of big retail will be undeniably smart and augmented, but just like in other industries, smaller retailers (read "mum and pop stores") will struggle to keep up with the changing conventions of experience and interactions.

The CEO of Whole Foods, Walter Robb, calls the future of their stores a "richer buying experience".

> "Imagine if you are picking up a head of cauliflower—and this platform allows you to actually have a video from the supplier saying 'here this is how this cauliflower was grown.' This is the ultimate endgame of matching up this platform with our product attributes [and] our product quality."
>
> Walter Robb, CEO of Whole Foods

The 2.4 million tickets sold for the 2015 Rugby World Cup featured augmented reality content to bring the experience alive for fans, both in the run-up to the competition and on the day of the games. Using an augmented reality app and a mobile phone or tablet, tickets could be scanned to reveal exclusive behind-the-scenes material hosted and delivered by Rugby World Cup 2003 winners Jonny Wilkinson, Lawrence Dallaglio and Will Greenwood.

Managing Director of England Rugby 2015 Stephen Brown hailed it as a sporting first: "using augmented reality technology as part of the ticket design enables fans to engage with the tournament through interactive content, which is a really exciting piece of activation."[12]

Of course, printed tickets are not long for this world as we're already seeing with airline boarding passes, bus tickets and so forth.

---

12 www.createtomorrow.co.uk/live-examples/rugby-world-cup.aspx

One of the world's leading high-street retailers, John Lewis Partnership (JLP), is now trialling AR tech in its flagship stores. JLP has created a virtual showroom in-store ahead of roll-outs in its Cambridge store. Basically, any physical space can be turned into a virtual showroom today. Rather than physical models, computer-generated models such as furniture and appliances can be added to the real in-store environment. Imagine technology like Magic Leap or HoloLens being made small enough to fit into smart contact lenses over the next two decades, and the possibilities for the in-store experience are almost limitless.

Matt Hully, head of brand innovation at JLP, said, "Technology will play a key role in the new Home Department at John Lewis Oxford Street, helping customers visualise new ways to personalise and design their home."

> "Central to this is our new partnership with Imagine. It allows customers to visualise products in life like 3D, rather than just on the pages of a catalogue; helping them to virtually 'try' an item before they buy it. We hope it will give our customers a taste of the future of shopping and enhance their overall experience. This is just the first step in using a very exciting technology."
>
> **Matt Hully, head of brand innovation at JLP[13]**

The use of technology like biometrics, pattern recognition and psychology is a win-win for retailers and consumers. Not only will these technologies dramatically improve our relationship with brands and stores, they will also revolutionise security, especially in the area of payments.

---

13 "John Lewis Adopts Augmented Reality," *Inside Retail Australia*, 9 September 2015.

Over the next five to ten years, nearly every transaction will be verified with some sort of biometric scan (facial recognition and fingerprint being the most common methods) combined with other data like heuristics and geolocation data. That same scanning technology that underpins payments security will be used to tailor offers and promotions and guide you through a retail experience. Looking ten to twenty years down the road, tourist attractions and in-store merchandising will take cues from your current "state", or your profile, and reshape the environment to appeal.

If you use your smartphone to pay today, we can use fingerprint for confirmation (this is very difficult to replicate), we can verify that your phone is in the same geolocation as the POS terminal where your phone is being presented (or tapped), we can use heuristics or behavioural data to verify that this is a typical transaction for you and we can tie the payment app to a specific mobile device (using Device ID). In mobile payments, we also use tokens. This is when the merchant receives a one-time code for a particular transaction so that even if the POS terminal is compromised, a thief can't reuse your card number for other transactions.

What this means in practical terms is that a phone-based payment in a store is 500 to 600 per cent safer than using your plastic card,[14] and this is just with current tech. In the future, we'll be able to use even your heart rate to uniquely identify you.

Biometrics Research Group predicted the global biometrics market to soar to US$15 billion by the end of 2015,[15] up from an estimated US$7 billion just three years ago. Technology consulting firm Frost & Sullivan forecasts that nearly half a billion people will be using a smartphone equipped with biometrics by 2017.

---

14 To think that some people are worried about the "security" around mobile payments!
15 "Your voice is your passport," *STORES* magazine, February 2015.

Figure 12.4: Smart changing rooms and mirrors allow a crossover between physical and digital. (Credit: Nordstroms-ebay fitting room)

Retailers and brands like Ugg Australia, Uniqlo and Burberry are already using "magic" or "memory" mirror technologies that utilise individual profiles. RFID tags identify the product while cameras capture your image and body shape, enabling you to try on virtual outfits in different colours and styles. Once you've had a shopping experience in-store, that profile can then be used at home for you to make sure online goods fit you properly and see how they'll look in a virtual fitting room experience. More sophisticated in-store displays can even change the context whereby you can try on an overcoat in the rain, a swimsuit in the Caribbean or sports gear on the track.

Bloomingdales has augmented fitting rooms with iPads to allow customers to ask for help, read reviews and see what sizes are in stock. C&A, a retailer in Brazil, has gone one step further, showing the number of Facebook Likes a particular product has, displaying this on the coat hanger in-store.

The smart dressing room is here to stay. In the future, alternatives will simply appear on the mirror in front of you if

Figure 12.5: C&A's digital coat hanger shows the number of "Likes" for a product in-store, in real time. (Credit: C&A)

your facial expression shows uncertainty with the choice you've made. Further out, the dressing room vanishes. Wherever we are, merchandise appears on mirrors and screens as if we were wearing it.

Online tailor InStitchu has teamed up with mPort to fuse the online and offline purchasing experience with 3D body scanning technology. 3D body scanners, similar to those used by the Transportation Security Administration (TSA) at US airports, have begun to be rolled out to shopping centres in Asia, enabling people to buy clothes tailored to their exact measurements.

> "The customer simply steps into a private enclosed area to scan themselves. Their precise body measurements are then instantly captured and stored on their InStitchu profile. Once they've designed a suit unique to their personal preference and style—right down to the stitch colour, buttons, materials and lapel—we send

Figure 12.6: This Lego AR display shows a virtual representation of the constructed Lego model. (Credit: Lego)

> their order to a team of Saville Row trained tailors who use their expertise to create the suit to the required measurements. The suit is then delivered direct to the customer, with the whole process taking just a matter of weeks."
>
> **Robin McGowan, co-founder of InStitchu**

Technologies like mPort with InStitchu address the MODs that I mentioned earlier. Imagine the following scenario. Perhaps I love the look of a suit but am disappointed that I can't find one that fits. What I'd really like is a tailored suit but I don't know where or how or if I can afford one—the smart dressing or changing room might be able to detect this just by watching my emotional response, and then send me an offer later online to have the clothes tailored to my individual body type.

Lego augmented reality kiosks (called the Lego Digital Box) enable you to see what the finished Lego construction will look like before you make a purchase. Similarly, the United States

Postal Service has a virtual box simulator that lets customers see if a package will fit into one of their flat-rate boxes, eliminating guesswork in choosing which packaging to use.

Brett referred to Amazon Echo in chapters 3 and 8. Amazon Echo looks like any ordinary speaker but it is listening. With technologies like this, you will never need a shopping list pinned to the fridge again. With a personal AI, wish list management will become a part of your life. Think of something you need, just get your PAI to tag it to your personal wish list, perhaps noting whether this is an immediate, medium-term or long-term purchase. Like many of the new generation of technologies that will augment our lives, they don't wait to be turned on, they don't require you to input anything on a keyboard, they are always on, waiting to adapt, learn or respond.

Human habit will be laid bare by technology shifts. Your loyalty to a particular retailer could be challenged. Augmented retail will make stickiness to brands both easier and much more difficult. What of our most emotional responses and senses?

Research by Nobel Peace Prize winners Richard Axel and Linda Buck[16] reveal that our sense of smell is perhaps the most emotional sense we have. With smells, we appear to "feel first" and analyse second. Studies have shown that we remember about 10,000 distinct odours, each of which can trigger an important memory, even taking us all the way back to our childhood.

Recently, I walked into the Crown Metropole in Melbourne, Australia, and was transfixed by a warm and inviting smell. Abercrombie & Fitch has its own line of men's fragrances called "Fierce". Fierce assaults the senses on entering a store to give off what A&F describes as a "lifestyle...packed with confidence and a bold, masculine attitude". When you smell like this, you inevitably start to feel and see yourself like the models depicted

16 Recipients of the 2004 Nobel Prize for Physiology or Medicine

in-store. Over the next five years, olfactory stimulus will become a powerful brand trigger and signifier.

Scent will augment our experience and create new brand experiences. Take Johnny Cupcakes, a retail T-shirt "bakery" that started out in Boston in 2001. When you walk into the store, your sense of smell is pleasantly assaulted by the smell of cupcakes, and when you buy a T-shirt, it's given to you in a box that looks like it came out of a bakery. The smell in a Johnny Cupcakes store is a big part of why people say they keep coming back. On 12th March 2011, the London store opened with hundreds of dedicated fans from around the world queuing up and camping out for more than 24 hours.

What does your brand smell like?

One additional area that was showcased in the science fiction film *Minority Report* is directed audio. In the film, protagonist Captain John Anderton is constantly identified by iris-scanning devices that direct advertising his way. This becomes problematic as these algorithms can also track him and enable the police to hone in on his location. Therefore, he gets a transplant—new eyes. After the transplant, Anderton walks into a retail environment and is identified by iris scan as a returning shopper of Japanese descent. Thus, the audio messages directed at Anderton before he boards a subway train and when he walks into a retail environment are for him specifically.

Such directed audio advertising technology is now coming of age and could be used in in-store or public space interactions in the near future. Prototypes of this technology, such as HyperSound directed audio solutions, convert audio into a highly directional, ultrasonic beam that only you would hear.

Other stores are already using subliminal audio messaging or hiding advertising prompts in high-frequency audio playing in the background of in-store muzak and soundtracks. You won't be able to hear this high-frequency audio, for example, but an app on your phone might hear this and use it to trigger an offer on your phone. Beacons and AR are more likely to replace this tech in the near term. Nevertheless, sound remains another area where the in-store experience can be augmented.

The Impact of Robots and AI on the Retail Industry

At the 2015 Gartner CIO Symposium, Gartner principal analyst Kelsie Marian challenged her audience to imagine what the retail store would look like without humans. Brett has explored the risk of being replaced by automation or robots in chapter 2, but while this is increasingly true of environments that we would likely rather not find ourselves in—say, a bank branch—it could be assumed that retail and travel environments are places we go to for reasons beyond the transactional.

> "Let's imagine that we in this room are the last generation of retailers to have humans working in our stores...Maybe this seems a little fantastic, but the truth is that we have a new class of smart machines that can get us closer to that reality. Probably the future is something between the store we know today full of associates and the idea of an associate-less store."
>
> **Kelsie Marian, Gartner principal analyst**

The potential for technology to not just augment the sales associate but become a sales associate in and of itself is profound. Take the OSHbot being tested by Orchard Supply Hardware store in San Jose, California. The OSHbot is multilingual,

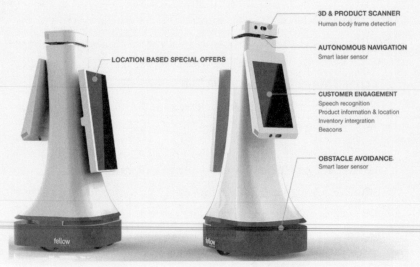

Figure 12.7: OSHbot in-store customer service bot (Credit: Fellow Robots)

capable of giving customers detailed information about a product in five different languages and can show customers on an onscreen map display where the item is located in the store, or you can just follow it physically to the shelf where the item is located.

> "We have amazing store associates, but very few speak five languages fluently, right? If there's somebody that can speak those five languages fluently, they probably don't know the real-time location of every single object in the store."
>
> Kyle Nel, OSH/Lowes Innovation Labs Director[17]

While workers are snug in their beds at night, the OSHbot roams the aisles. "The robot actually navigates by its own overnight," said Marco Mascorro, CEO of Fellow Robots. "So it learns when they move, for example, a shelf."

17 *ABC News* Oakland, CA, December 2014

OSHbot has an almost unassailable advantage over human store associates because it can communicate in multiple languages and knows where every product is in real time.

Technology like this doesn't have to replace the sales associate, but it could free them up to do work of more value. For instance, rather than being locked into a checkout counter, they could roam the store, advising, informing and guiding customers. Although robots like OSHbot are showing that humans may not be the best at that for much longer.

The Machines Are Watching and Listening

Scott McNealy, former CEO of Sun Microsystems, liked to say, "You have no privacy. Get over it!" Privacy is increasingly something we give up with the click of a button as we join WiFi networks, share photos and other particulars with all sorts of organisations. This crucial data drives how effectively our shopping experience will be augmented. Most people will agree that the trade-off is worth it; those who don't will suffer from a very traditional, non-augmented world. In fact, it will be increasingly impossible to not give this data to organisations like retailers.

As you enter a shopping centre or mall, the smart displays will notice who you are and match your face to a core database of previous shoppers who have visited. This data can then be shared with retailers who can start pinging you offers based on past shopping experiences or even matching a known wish list you have on Amazon, Pinterest or products you've talked about on your Facebook page.

These same cameras, and the machine algorithms tied to them, will notice what you did not buy. Say that you linger in front of a shop that stocks your favourite brand of jeans but you

Figure 12.8: Smart mannequins like the EyeSee from Italy use facial recognition to track you in-store.

don't enter—the camera notices. On returning to the shopping centre a few days later, you are then served offers for those jeans directly to your phone, and as you stroll past the store, a digital display changes to reinforce the offer or says, "Hey John Anderton, you'd look great in these new True Religion bootcut jeans!" Even that mannequin in-store might be tracking your movement with cameras that use facial recognition.

Worried about all this data eroding your privacy? You shouldn't be. Rather than removing freedom or privacy, the advance of technology is putting us more in control than ever before. Rather than being confined to opening hours, we now shop when we want, often having goods delivered when and where we want. Rather than have to grapple with a European clothing size when visiting London, our personal preferences could already be uploaded to the store as we walk in (via our phone talking to beacons, and the store talking to the cloud) and we could find that the sales assistant already has the information required to help us pick out the correct size.

Data and online collaboration also means that we are concentrating our buying power. In 2014, U.S. Cyber Monday sales were US$2.3 billion—up 29 per cent from the previous year. China's big buyer or "Singles' Day" (11th November) dwarfs it by comparison. In 2015, Alibaba only took two hours to reach US$2 billion in sales on Singles' Day and reported sales had surpassed US$9 billion by the end of the day.

Stores are getting smarter. They are starting to equip themselves with the technology not just to improve the in-store experience but to also learn about us like never before. The augmented world will know more about us than we even know about ourselves.

Smart retailers will learn that loyalty doesn't come from brand marketing, tear-jerking advertisements or airline miles. It comes from the ability to know what we need before we know it, and to personalise that in real time. Shopping in the future is all about the experience, and the experience is all about the data.

Conclusions: Life in the Smart Lane

Living in an Augmented World

Every aspect of our life will be augmented by technology. From devices that monitor our health, to the way we pay for goods and services, how we spend our spare time, how we move around, how we look for advice, how we interact and how we work—it's all fair game in the Augmented Age. Living "off the grid" will severely restrict your options, if not be impossible, and digital literacy will be a more important life skill than algebra, writing or geography. The most advanced technologies will become less visible and less intrusive, becoming smart, embedded and predictive in nature.

What is life going to be like in 2030 or 2040? It will be different on many different levels. Increasingly, immersion in a technology-based society won't be optional; it will be both preferred and inevitable for those of us in the developed world. For the developing world, the gap will rapidly close by the end of the next decade.

To illustrate how your life might change over the next couple of decades, I'm going to take you through a number of possible scenarios of what life might be like for different people in the near future. You might see yourself or your loved ones in these scenarios, you might disagree with the totality of these shifts—but try and recognise the potential for change, disruption and opportunity.

At the risk of offending friends and family, I'm going to use some people I know to illustrate their potential or possible futures in an augmented world. Am I sure that these predictions are going to be 100 per cent correct? Obviously that isn't the point—the point is to illustrate the dramatic changes our lives will take over the next 20 years.

I hope they don't mind. I'll try to be nice.

The Gigging Japanophile
Hannah King (Age 25)
Circa 2027—Tokyo, Japan

9 a.m.

Today's a busy day and coming off a late-night design assignment Hannah is a little slow to get started. She's already twice told Albert, her PAI, to dim the room lights and keep the curtains closed, as opposed to the normal wake-up setting that lets the morning sun into her Tokyo micro-studio. Her first alarm went off at 8 a.m. but she has already delayed the inevitable twice—it's time to get going.

Hannah lives in the Shibuya district in the heart of Tokyo, so smaller apartments are all the rage, and all most can afford. The 200-sq-foot apartment is barely three years old but is chock-full of home-tech and innovations that make the utility of the space greater than square footage. The primary, or largest, wall in the apartment is video-capable, but she generally uses it as a workspace or for various status updates and alerts. As she gets out of bed, the wall is showing the collective messages she's received, the time (with a red status alert because she's already running late), the weather forecast and a compressed run sheet of the day's activities.

She jumps in the shower and asks Albert to make it a little hotter than the usual temperature, before dialling it back 30 seconds later to the normal setting. While she's in the shower, she selects a K-pop playlist before deciding it's too pop for her this morning and instead asks Albert to play something new. Albert selects some Aerosmith from the 1980s; it seems to fit her mood.

As Hannah dries her hair, the mirror in the bathroom is displaying an increasingly worrisome alert status regarding her first appointment at Dentsu Digital at 9:30 a.m. She gets Albert to contact Hikado at Dentsu to let them know that she'll be 20 minutes late. It's not far, but she's running behind. Albert also provisionally moves her 11 a.m. call with her Hong Kong prospect so that her Dentsu appointment won't conflict if it runs over (it usually does), but then it looks like her lunchtime appointment is out—she tags it for rescheduling.

A small pastry and she is on her way to the train. It is a little cold but a small Under Armour smart sweater is enough to keep her warm, and keep her devices charged.

As she arrives at the transit station, she can see on her PHUD that the next train to Yokohama is in 2 minutes. As she walks through the scanner gate, she feels a vibration in her wrist as the station debits her account for access to the transit system. Calling the modern transit system a train is like calling the space shuttle a plane—these ultra-modern maglev units reduce the travelling time between Japanese cities by hours a day for commuters. It takes Hannah about 6 minutes to travel the 45 km (26 miles) to the main station where Dentsu's offices are located, and then another 5 minutes for the automated shuttle pod from the station.

The air is fresh today, but the weather has been erratic all month. She walks past the Meiji-Jingu gardens and can see the cherry blossoms are locked up in their special atrium, like some historical artefacts of the past. The increasingly unstable weather systems and higher temperature averages have played havoc on the delicate conditions required for cherry blossoms. She looks through the glass enclosure surrounding the cherry blossoms and can see data coming through on her PHUD about the blossoms and the ideal conditions created inside the atrium. Today, however, no visitors are allowed in the enclosure. She is saddened that these beautiful trees are relegated mostly to environments like this these days. When the cherry blossom season was cut short two years in a row in Tokyo by early heatwaves, the municipality stepped in with this preservation project.

At the Dentsu meeting, she's working with a team to promote a new VR series called *The Hab* produced by Electronic Arts and Amazon. The series is basically a fluff piece for NASA and the European Space Agency (ESA) on the colonisation of Mars, which is currently a subject of debate across the European Union and in the US Congress in respect to funding proposals. There are still those who argue that the problems of geoengineering the planet against the increasingly aggressive temperature changes should take priority. Nonetheless, the VR series is turning out to be extremely popular. Hannah is working on character pieces for electronic displays around Tokyo and Osaka to promote the series. She submitted a couple of concepts last week and the team is refining its pitch to EA before its presentation next week.

1:30 p.m.

After Dentsu and her Hong Kong call, Hannah catches the transit back to Akihabara to the small shopfront she's rented for the afternoon with her friend Tanaka. They run a trendy pop-up tattoo parlour and are making quite a name for themselves on SoMe. The variable location adds to the dynamics and mystery of their small start-up. Other artists and giggers are doing the same—moving their physical locations around, but having a central virtual presence where people do most of their shopping.

Hannah gets to work and takes off her smart sweater. After politely greeting Tanaka, she starts work on some of her new designs. All she really has to do is the sketch work; the experience of applying tattoos is not as thrilling or artistic as it used to be. These tattoos are applied through lasers for permanents or via activated e-Ink for dynamics. Hannah comes here to sketch every afternoon and works with her clients on application. Today, she has a client who has some degradation of her e-Ink, leaving some pixilation when she changes designs, so she's doing some maintenance.

One of her clients has an old traditional sleeve they want to update to e-Ink. Getting rid of tattoos is easier too, now. All you need is the same laser gear and a couple of weeks of derma-spray and your skin barely shows signs of the old ink. Sometimes, Hannah is still asked to do traditional designs with inks and needles for the purists, and she values this perhaps the most. She's heard chatter about someone trying to work on full body designs that include animated tattoos, but as far as her friends in the business are concerned, they're still a decade away from that sort of tech. For now, she's content to make some download fees for her designs on the tattoo cloud, and dream of the time she can either make her own VR anime series or do this full-time.

7 p.m.

Later she heads home, listening to a constructed playlist she made on the way featuring a new club band she heard some of her friends talking about online. As she hits the small laneway in Shibuya where she lives, automated lights illuminate her path and she can hear someone nearby talking a little too loud like they're talking through some old tech to someone far away. She asks Albert to heat up some rice and chicken for dinner, and then, as she jumps into the lift that's heading upstairs, she sends off a quick *vrm* to her mum in NYC to let her know that she's still alive. The cameras in the lift and in her apartment are stereoscopic and linked to the cloud.

The Biohacker
Alex Lightman (Chronological Age 68, Biological Age 35)
Circa 2030—Santa Monica, California, USA

Alex rode the solar wave as photovoltaics went from 1 per cent in 2014 to 50 per cent of electricity produced in the United States and cashed out in 2025 when the company he cofounded producing solar appliances with batteries was acquired. However, he had already begun to explore his real passion a few years earlier when he started to look for ways to maximise his personal fitness levels, optimising his day-to-day health and improving his longevity.

As a venture capitalist, Alex started to explore HealthTech and wanted to get technology and products to market faster than the FDA approval process allowed for processes to bioengineer better genes and health. He created a start-up with the team responsible for hypergravity clothing, along with some engineers who had been working on second-generation exoskeletons. He found a CEO and engineer to build two complementary business units, an aerospace division and a wearables health division. The core product—smart clothing and wearables that enabled progressively greater resistance training as you walked around—had also been adapted into prototype spacesuits to make working in microgravity environments easier.

The Mars power suit (MPS) that his team was working on used nanoengineered plating with the idea that it would both reduce radiation exposure and, through a combination of weighted resistance and exoskeleton support, simulate earth's normal gravity while on the Mars surface. Any crew on Mars would be able to use the suits outside not just to work safer, but also to keep their bones and muscles toned for when they returned back to earth. Many of the future colonists were going to be on a one-way trip but the early international crews set to first arrive on Mars were on sample return missions. By wearing an MPS, Mars visitors would have the experience of being much stronger relative to the planet's normal gravity, and also gain strength from their journey to Mars rather than potentially losing muscle mass and agility by the time they returned to earth.

The core technology advances of the MRS were twofold. The first was an elasticised graphene/rubber composite that generated a low power electrical charge as the user moved about. The charge could be stored or fed back into the second feature of the suit—a set of nanotech panels. These panels were inlaid to produce a magnetic field that worked like a miniature personal magnetosphere protecting the user from solar radiation. The panels also incorporated new flexible battery tech for storing charge.

The elasticised, smart fibres that formed the interior musculature of the suit could be activated by running a modulated charge through it that either substantially increased resistance (like weight training bands) or, via a pulsed charge, could provide a "muscle assist" to the user, enabling muscle-building or superheavy lifting mode. Of course these early suits had limitations, but they worked on the same principles as exoskeletons, which had been around for close to 30 years.

Elon Musk's SpaceX had already sent landers to Hellas Planitia and rovers that were beaming back pictures of Olympus Mons.

The race was on between whether Musk or NASA was going to get there first, with China being the outlier in the race. SpaceX had a contentious relationship with NASA. They played well together when it came to low-earth orbit (LEO), but when it came to Mars, Musk was just in too much of a hurry for the engineers at NASA, having staked his legacy on making Mars colonisation affordable for the average earthling. While SpaceX had succeeded thus far, NASA was betting that the commercial organisation was going to have some major setbacks due to the risks inherent in SpaceX adopting an accelerated programme.

Musk's approach was iterative and since the early days of the Dragon programme, he had been known to be willing to send up early prototypes and test them out with the expectation that they might fail the first few times, but that his team would learn faster through that approach. He didn't take that approach with manned flight, but he was more aggressive in testing. Whether it was commercial flights for NASA to the ageing International Space Station that had begun in 2017 or commercial tourist operations to the new space hotels being constructed in orbits, they had fortunately not lost a manned spacecraft so far.

Right now, Alex was sitting in a meeting with the SpaceX team, working out a testing schedule for the MPS over the next 18 months prior to sending the suits to Mars for testing. The cinematic visualisations were powerful, especially considering that SpaceX owned some of the best Mars VR content from its light-field cameras deployed on the surface of the red planet. However, the suit models were giving them some anomalous readings on the effectiveness of the panels in the simulation that was meant to be showing a worst-case scenario of a person caught outside the radiation-hardened domes, in solar flare conditions. Alex finished up the meeting as he got a video call on his PHUD. His agent working with Under Armour had set up a meeting to enable him to pitch his latest hypergravity sportswear. He handed all the details to Alexa, his PAI.

By the time Alex got home, he was ready to eat and do some light exercise. He set his Natural Machines 3D food printer (he was the first outside investor in NM, and felt nostalgic making meals with an old model) to make a turkey burger, hummus and falafels while checking his vrmail for a few minutes. But first he had his robo-chef whip up a Bulletproof coffee, using a recipe from the first man to become a billionaire via biohacking, Dave Asprey. Alex still regarded Asprey as he had done since 2012, as both friend and rival. Alex jumped on his treadmill desk and set it to a walking pace of 4.5 mph at an incline of 15 per cent while he generated the MPS iterations on to his holoprojector workstation. The new simulation showed an effectiveness of 75 per cent with the new magnetosphere panel updates, but there was a slight degradation in the panel lifetime based on the revised graphene structure so he flagged it for follow-up.

Seven minutes later, he sat down to his fresh turkey burger courtesy of his robo-chef equipped with a 3D printer. Vatmeat™ was very common today, and it was having a dramatic effect on the farming sector as commercial cattle farms were being decimated by the uptake in artificially engineered meats. Amazon now just sold the constituent components in pods for the 3D "foodie" printers that were all the rage on the West Coast. Restaurants still used "original" meat but the low-fat, lean, organic make-up of Vatmeat™ was hard to beat. The gene editing of lean cattle couldn't even keep pace with the 3D-printed stuff.

After the meal, he slipped on his bio suit and asked Alexa, his PAI, to run a full body scan. It looked like Alex was going to have to replace his arterial flow cardio-sensors next week as the readings were starting to fluctuate; these ingestibles didn't last forever. He saw that most of the statuses were in the green, but his triglycerides had spiked last Monday for some reason. He pinged his health service, asking if he should make a modification to his diet or supplement intake for the next couple of weeks.

He brought up the AR site for a new start-up he had heard of that was spinning off out of Johns Hopkins Tech called GenomixRe. GenomixRe was promising a new gene splicing technology that had a higher resolution than the previous generation of editing tools. The collection of human genomic data collected globally now was on the verge of reaching a yottabtye[1] of aggregate, personalised biodata and the correlation mapping was producing new systemic understanding of DNA, particularly in relation to what scientists used to understand as "junk" DNA. He ran a profiling algorithm over its social and media presence and mentions and tried a correlation with its hiring and patent releases to see if its momentum was backed up by a growing team. The results were promising so he asked Alexa to monitor chatter from the venture community and search traffic in respect to the company, and report back in a week.

He then settled back and put his glasses into VR mode, dimming the house lights so that he could try out his new

---

1 A yottabyte is one septillion bytes. In 2015 terms, the storage cost would be approximately US$100 trillion but, by 2030, it would equate to less than US$100 billion of today's dollars. Given the role in health care that such data will play, this sort of storage space will be affordable and necessary.

Apollo 11 simulator. Later, his PAI gently pinged him. His readings: 6,000 calories burned for the day, including 42 splat points (minutes in which his heart rate was above 83 per cent of his maximum heart rate). In a few days, he had a Master's track meet with Santa Monica Track Club and was on track to run a sub-six minute mile for the 44th year in a row. It was going to be another year of getting younger.

The Hackathon Apprentice
Matt King (Age 23)
Circa 2026—New York (Lower East Side), USA

By 2025, the United States had seen record decline in college admissions for three years straight accompanied by the failures of more than 100 colleges and business schools. The year 2026 was on track to see college admissions fall to below those of the 1970s. For US graduate schools, it was largely a problem of return on investment (ROI). It had been demonstrated that the average student outlays of US$45,000 to US$100,000 in tuition and fees were not converting to better employment prospects, and the incidence of bankruptcy from student loans was at its highest ratio in history. Universities were responding by offering free online and VR courses that transitioned to degrees, but the response so far had been lukewarm.

Matt, like a growing number of his generation, wasn't really fussed about attending college full-time, given that environment. He was hacking his way through vocational education and picking up work in a manner that baby boomers might have called an apprenticeship. He was increasingly taking on gigs at start-ups and incubators on the East Coast of the United States, working for whomever would take him on as an intern, or just hanging out with other like-minded giggers experimenting and collaborating. He referred to himself as an experimental AR-tist using AR/VR story forms, but mostly he was getting bits and pieces of work worldbuilding.

Companies like Ubisoft, Square Enix, Electronic Arts, Activision/Treyarch, Valve, Microsoft and others had been building virtual worlds for games since the 1990s, but the requirement was now for rich, cinematic reality, so those worlds were getting rebuilt and recoded onto much richer pallets, with great levels of detail. For worlds like 18th-century London or 22nd-century New York and Los Angeles, there were already very comprehensive public libraries of street-level stock VR footage available that was constantly being updated, but environments inside buildings, shopfronts and in warehouses were deeply customisable.

Today, Matt was hacking some footage that had been taken last week in an abandoned subway station and mapping it onto an immersive (as the playable VR movies seem to be collectively named) story grid. It was an amateur piece by some group that was trying to create an interactive adaption of a James Bond movie from a couple of decades ago. They didn't yet have the rights to the Bond name or character, so the working title was just *Double-O*. The game/movie/immersive wasn't so much crowdsourced as crowdbuilt. AR-tists and coders from around the world would bid or auction their time on various projects and would get units in the film, sort of like equity. One project that Matt had worked on earlier in the year had already gone to market and he was getting a small amount of cash trickling in.

Matt was a decent digital artist, but the tools they used these days were part animation tools, part worldbuilding and part video editing software. Matt was doing a MOOC programme in Los Angeles part-time, learning lighting and shader techniques, but most of what he was doing these days was self-taught. Matt and his contemporaries were starting to redefine working patterns and habits pretty significantly. No one in the working space he was hanging out at today worked regular hours, some got paid, some were studying, some were here every day, others might just be there for a few hours and then go off to find some new space. Work was a much more fluid concept to Matt and his friends.

A good analogy for Matt's generation was environments like Minecraft, which had become hugely popular in the early 2010s. Minecraft was part game, part puzzle, part coding problem; Matt had learned some basic Java when he was ten just so he could code up a mod for some of his friends who were in a Minecraft mob. Hacking together cloud-based servers, setting up local instances of dev platforms and pushing code and AR models out to other teams working around the world was a pretty basic skill set to these guys.

Matt was using a next-gen Magic Leap visor and he was right now dealing with some pretty significant latency with the environment the UK team had set up for the immersive. He quickly dumped the 10 terrabyte model onto a local server located somewhere in Philadelphia so that he could do some localised testing, and then he merged his packet back onto the dev server in the United Kingdom once he was done. The 3D scaffold he had been sent had some design errors in it, like solid walls where utility access panels needed to be modelled, etc., so he was going to have to either fix it himself later or ping the dev group for some help.

As he was working, he got a call from his pal Nick. Nick had joined his dad's architectural design firm when he graduated from Columbia but was working on some 3D-printed hab designs for India in his spare time. Matt was still using the AR rig so he accepted the call and selected conference room mode.

"Hey Nick, what's up?" said Matt.

"Hey Matt. I just did this new mock-up for a hab, but they don't like me using the work printers here for my personal stuff. Do you guys have a fabber there in your workspace?" Nick asked. As he was talking, Nick had sent Matt the new design file and it was rendered on the worktable in their shared virtual space.

"Sure, I can print it, but you'll have to ping me some credit. The public fabber units here are really expensive, dude!"

"Ok, will $100 cover it?" Nick asked.

"Should do... I'll send you the job record once it's done," Matt offered. "Are you going to come by and pick up the print?" He could see Nick had sent $100 to his public wallet and he felt his personal device vibrate in his pocket to give him an added confirmation of the ping.

"Sure, let me come by around 6 and I can buy you dinner. You're at spARce, right?"

"Yes, yes and you can read my geoloc just like the rest of humanity, so you already know the answer to that redundant question. Ok, gotta run, one of my PMs is hassling me on another screen."

Later that day, Matt got a message from Nick asking him to bring the model to a restaurant a couple of blocks away around 6:30 p.m. The message was tinged with embarrassment and a big favour emotive. Matt messaged back an AR image of Nick's hab model getting crushed by a Metro EBus and the message "Sure... but no guarantees."

He had better get going. He had classes starting at 8:30 p.m. and he wanted to be home before they started. He thought of using UberAI to get home but his PHUD was telling him that he couldn't afford to Uber it and eat out tonight. It was time to make a choice. Instead, he fired up his Apple Car app with the car he part-owned in Connecticut where his parents lived, and traded some time for Uber. The autonomous iCar he owned had banked about 30 hours this month on UberAI and he took his share of miles and credited them to his own Uber account. Problem solved. Time was on his side tonight ... just.

The Social Producer
Rachel Morrissey (Age 37)
Circa 2023—Bay Area, California, USA

10:30 a.m. PST

Rachel is working on some news stories on cities adapting to self-driving cars and proposals to ban human drivers. Autonomous vehicles are now regularly featured on many European roads, in the United States and in much of the developed world. New York and London have both had proposals to ban human drivers from their city centres, but so far the numbers aren't carrying, so Rachel asks her permanent show hosts if they think the story has legs, and they are keen to pursue it.

Rachel does a curated news search and gets a nice summary of headlines and key points based on her initial show abstract. She then starts the process of content acquisition. She posts on some reporter and podcaster auction sites for submission of news content related to the show, giving a brief, sample questions and the required interview lengths. Within a few minutes, she has reporters from Shanghai, Sydney, London and New York ready to participate. She contracts all of the relevant players and asks them for submissions in 72 hours' time. Only one of them opts out due to timing.

72 hours later

Rachel now has 20 hours of interview footage from five cities on the topic. She's also pinged the Apple and Tesla teams and got some written responses to her questions. She runs the video and audio raw material through her curation algorithms and her smart editor software identifies 17 candidates for inclusion in the piece, sorted by significance and alignment with her original story premise. She gets through 14 of the candidate pieces before guessing she has enough content.

She throws the pieces up on to the studio digital wall and reviews them for placement. She has seven vid pieces, four audio only pieces and two written pieces. She extracts a couple of quotes from the written pieces and has one of her hosts record an independent entry and summary pieces, along with some segues and commentary on the written quotes.

She wraps up the editing in about an hour and then publishes the video, radio and podcast versions and the written stories simultaneously from the edited content. The written stories carry more of the written pieces, plus transcripted and curated content from the audio and video. As some of the audio stuff is great, the algorithm throws up some storyboard images so that it can be combined into the video footage for the TV and video streaming outlets.

She sends an extract of the story to NPR and NetflixNews and gets a bite. She then auctions the ad slots and product mentions to be embedded in the pieces, throwing it off to Volvo, Tesla and Google for sponsorship. She fills her sponsorship quota in about 15 minutes—looks like this positive story is about to go live and is oversubscribed! She sells some additional ad time for reruns of the piece over the coming six weeks before she's happy enough to wrap it up.

3 p.m.

By mid-afternoon, Rachel does a revised and most likely final push of the content to the outlets and on the subscription channels for her shows. She asks her network to put it out on social media, too. She can see it trending in real time with her audience so she decides to take a couple of hours off and get that lunch she missed out on earlier.

I would like to do a few more of these stories, but let's get to the BIG predictions behind the Augmented Age.

The Big Predictions

At the end of the day, we know that the way people work and the way they live will radically change. Here are a few key projections for the next 20 to 30 years:

Jobs like loan officers, bank tellers, financial advisers, tax advisers, financial planners, etc., will mostly be replaced by algorithms that are less prone to mistakes, human biases and restricted by limited data or information. Advice will be delivered in real time via your personal Life Stream.

The **most powerful energy conglomerate** in the world will not be invested in coal, gas or oil and the largest net new employment will likely be in retooling economies for solar energy, moving away from the wooden poles and wires that currently distribute centralised generation. More broadly speaking, energy systems will become highly distributed, both to reduce grid-based reliance and failures, and as we build energy efficiency into the world around us. Supporting service industries will explode from the retooling of our grids and energy systems across to renewables, replacing large property developments with windows that generate energy, the installation of battery and energy storage systems, wireless/microwave transmission systems, vehicle charging stations, etc.

Amazon will be the first (but not last) to deploy **drones and robots for delivery** of products, but **self-driving transport and 3D printing** will further disrupt the value chain, making intellectual property ownership (design) and access to these new distribution networks essential. Stores will become inefficient distribution models for a vast swathe of products, especially where advice is currently part of the experience. By 2030 to 2035, we'll regularly download products for printing at home, inclusive of electrical circuits, displays and other tech.

Our kids won't own the stuff we own today as revised notions of ownership come to reshape asset management. Airbnb, SocialFlight, Lyft, Sailo and others are only the first wave of shared asset systems. In the future, you'll be able to take a different car to work every day (autonomous, self-driving vehicles) at a much cheaper rate than you could ever do owning a car of your own, live month by month or week by week in a different room and work in a different workspace every day. Because these experiences are personalised, it will still feel like our own personal style is shining through. Generations Y and Z will trade assets for experiences—the American Dream of the white picket fence will likely give way to a dream of a lifestyle.

The **biggest entrenched economies today will be those most disrupted** by the Augmented Age, largely because of their hesitancy to change from reliance on long held investments in existing technologies. It is why China, which is investing heavily in new technologies and infrastructure, will likely eclipse the United States and Eurozone rapidly as the most valuable economy in the world, why unemployment is likely to grow in the United States as the economy resists infrastructure improvement[2] and climate change,[3] but why the US stock market will thrive. Legacy infrastructure will curtail future economic growth severely. Silicon Valley and venture capital (VC) investment will be seen historically as one of the primary reasons why the US economy remained globally viable in the face of crumbling incumbent industries, government mismanagement and infrastructure.

---

2   Steve Kroft, "Falling Apart: America's Neglected Infrastructure," *CBS News*, November 2014.
3   "France warns climate change threatens global security," *Associated Press*, 30 May 2015; http://www.salon.com/2015/05/30/ap_interview_france_warns_climate_change_threatens_security/.

The **biggest companies in the world** will all be technology companies, and commodities and service companies that aren't technology-based will find themselves losing market share rapidly over the next decade. The biggest banks in the world will likely be technology companies emerging out of developing economies serving the 2.5 billion people who today are without a bank account, but most of whom will have a smartphone by the end of the decade. In 30 years, the biggest companies will be based around personalised AIs, new energy and infrastructure, and even possibly Asteroid mining for rare metals powering technology. Mobile and digital money will be significant players, too.

The moniker **citizen of the world** will become a more viable proposition. On a longer-term horizon as immigration and border control is given over to algorithms, travel will likely resemble the world prior to World War I when travel was more informal, and you could cross a border in Europe without papers. Why? Because it will be automated. From the moment you enter the airport to depart to the moment you hit your hotel in a distant foreign land, the various immigration departments, the departing and arriving airport operators, the airlines and the hotel will already know who you are. Additionally, countries like Estonia and Singapore and associations like Asia-Pacific Economic Cooperation (APEC) are developing e-Citizen programmes that could give you a form of citizenship that allows freedom of travel and employment in a broad range of geographical locations.

Virtual and augmented reality will be your reality. Magic Leap calls its conceptual technology "cinematic reality", but the journey that started with Google Glass in 2013 is only just beginning. We've started a 50- to 75-year journey towards neural integrated biocircuitry that will be able to display information in our visual field in the form of a personal head-up display. Augmenting our vision will be a major feature of bioaugmentation whether it is through wearing tech or engineering and upgrading our eyes. Some say the eyes are the windows to the soul but, in the future, they'll be the windows to a whole range of feedback loops, enhanced context and overlays.

New art forms will continue to emerge as we start experimenting with storytelling and experience design in many ways. The world of gaming, movies, VR and AR will all be rich landscapes where stories will be told, lived and experienced. Some users will become addicted to virtual worlds that let them escape to a better place than their real world, and for a time the world will become immersed in VR in a way that raises the shackles of conservatives and traditionalists. But like the world of social media and smartphones, this will normalise to an extent where it will be integrated into our lives much like TVs and computers are today. The *Star Trek* holodeck will become a possibility as people establish rooms with whole-room projection or spaces optimally designed for VR encounters. Augmented reality and augmented virtuality will constantly blur the lines between what is real and what is not.

Your health will be a known quantity and **health care will be a dynamic, technology-based industry**, and we'll start to **live longer, healthier lives**. The world of sensors, shared data, genomics, 3D printing, bioengineering, biorobotics and mimicry, underpinned by artificial intelligence, will radically change the way we manage our health.

History credits the Egyptian official Imhotep (c. 2650 BC– 2600 BC) and the Indian physician Sushruta (sometime between

1200 BC and 600 BC) as being amongst the founding fathers of surgery, but since then we've been trying to repair damage, excise disease and transplant organs to restore health. We've gone from using herbs, extracts and crushed minerals to pharma companies that charge thousands of dollars for a formula developed in a lab. In the future, doctors won't be practising medicine; it will be a precise, measured, exact science. We still need to understand more about internal medicine, how the brain works and what various protein chains do on a long-term basis, but decoding and editing our DNA, designing personalised medicines in near real time, and synthesising replacement organs and components will become increasingly viable.

You will be friends with an AI. Within 10 to 15 years, one of the most frequent relationships you will have, based on daily contact, will be with a synthetic intelligence. While these machine intelligences will be highly interactive, they won't be sentient or self-aware in the sci-fi sense of the word, but that won't stop them from becoming a proxy for a companion, butler or digital personal assistant. As depicted in movies like *Her* and *2001: A Space Odyssey*, games like Halo and science fiction stories of the last 50 years, an AI will have profoundly personal implications, the least of those being that as the algorithms associated with our personal AI get to know us, they will know us better than our own mother and father.

Will people fall in love with their AI? Yes, but thankfully that will be an outlier. Will we be debating AI rights to vote, own property, etc.? It's unlikely until AGIs become sentient 20 to 30 years from now, and by then machine intelligence will already be integrated into society in such a way that they have effective control (not ownership necessarily) over a myriad of resources, purely because they are much more efficient than human operators and processes. To the disdain of capitalists the world over, considerable resources required to run urban centres like data, utilities, emergency services, transportation and the like will become shared resources managed by centralised algorithms.

Education will be revolutionised. When writing this, I kept coming back to the apprenticeship and guild models of old, rather than the modernised knowledge-based systems around universities and colleges. As we augment our intelligence through AI and always on access to data, knowledge will tend towards ubiquitous access, and knowledge as a scarcity mechanism or barrier to entry will become indefensible—but skills will remain sought after. The Augmented Age will be dominated by the need for creative thinking and the ability to design new experiences embedded in the world around us based on new capabilities, smart everything and predictive behavioural modelling.

Students will still go to university, but the economic models of universities will be challenged as the ROI of a degree becomes increasingly questioned and the burden of student loans reduces an economy's ability to compete. In practical terms, every course at a progressive, modern university will be a STEM-based programme because if your profession is not using technology, students won't be able to apply their skills vocationally.

Finance competencies like risk, trading, asset allocation and market analysis will increasingly be about coding or codifying the systems that execute these black-box functions. Medical students will learn to use a broad range of technologies, understand smart diagnostics, learn about sensor networks and learn to operate robotic surgery equipment. New medical fields will be increasingly common.

The augmented generation will have "life" as their career. We've discussed the strong entrepreneurial sentiment of Gen Y and Gen Z, but there's another overarching objective emerging in a generation that grew up with a perceived social connection with thousands of casual Internet friends from across the globe. In a generation that has faced the rise of the Islamic State, the global financial crisis, the Arab Spring, diseases like Ebola, the emergence of AI and self-driving cars, ballooning student debt and record rates of unemployment, you can't blame them if they are more interested in waking up every day and doing things that they love, things that they are passionate about, rather than a dead-end job to pay the rent.

The augmented generation will be able to travel more than their predecessors. They'll change jobs more frequently, and stock options and a promotions path won't be able to retain them unless they love what they're doing. They'll team and join forces with others who share their same passion to create crazy new things, even if those collaborators are on the other side of the planet. They'll be artists, lovers, dreamers, thinkers and doers.

They'll be resolute about unwinding the damage that their parents did to the environment. They'll be increasingly sceptical about religion and its place in the world. They'll be much more accepting towards technology, and look to science to increasingly solve the world's problems. They'll want to do things bigger and better. They'll want to invest in making the world a better place, not making as much money as they can at the expense of others. Yes, they'll be idealists—I hope we don't destroy that passion in them.

Employment and Business in the Augmented Age—
Winners and Losers

Large human-dominant or process-based industries will be decimated by the AI, experience design and smart infrastructure disruptions that underpin the Augmented Age.

The losers will be:

1. **Big Energy**. Four key forces will challenge any fossil fuel producer or incumbent energy system:
    -   ultra-cheap renewables
    -   smart grids
    -   electric vehicles
    -   energy storage systems (batteries like the Tesla Powerwall, fuel cells, etc.)

    Droves of gas (or service) stations will go out of business, wired electricity poles will fall into disrepair as whole cities and regions become net energy producers and mining will shift away from extracting fuels to extracting resources to power the new smart world.

2. **Big Health Care and Pharma**. The competency for the new healthcare businesses will be data, engineering and models, not chemistry, patented medicine and surgery time. We'll still need hospitals and doctors' surgeries, but if you are a medical professional, you'll diagnose from sensors. Medical emergencies will peak in the late 2020s as events like heart attacks become predictable and as treatment becomes prescribed by self-learning, healthcare-dedicated AIs that are better at diagnosing and offering treatment suggestions than any human.

3. **Small- to Mid-sized Colleges and Universities**. Student debt, unemployment and the perceived decreasing effectiveness of graduate studies, particularly at business

schools, will lead to a significant consolidation in tertiary education. Markets like Australia, United States and the United Kingdom, which have departed from government-sponsored systems, will be hit the hardest as the augmented generation travels to countries open to foreign students and offer reduced tuition fees, signs up to online MOOCs and/or chooses gigging apprenticeships.

4. **Big Government**. Government is perhaps the last industry to be disrupted by technology and the Internet. AI will demonstrate its ability to greatly reduce processes both around laws and resource allocation that is currently dominated by humans, hard-coded processes and trademark government inefficiency. Governments will tend towards more socialist policies as AI-managed government becomes radically cheaper and more efficient than human-led administration.

5. **Banking, Insurance, Regulators and Finance in general**. Whether it is a teller in a bank branch, a financial adviser, an accountant, a loan officer or anyone else who has made their business around "advising" you on bank products or financial rules, all of these professionals will be at threat. Any financial institution that cannot shift away from paper application forms and signatures will be in rapid decline by the early 2020s, and will probably no longer exist by 2025. In 100 years' time when we look back at the Augmented Age, we'll recognise that bank tellers were the biggest and fastest impacted profession as a result of experience design changes around mobile distribution. Risk models will dramatically shift, as will product design and compliance approaches. The 2 billion newly banked consumers using smartphones won't use branches, plastic

cards or chequebooks. They'll create new lean, low-margin superbanks based on technology, real-time financial advice and superior utility (payments, credit and value stores).

The winners of the Augmented Age will be:

1. **Tech Majors**. These will continue to invest in new tech because it is their power alley. We'll see an ebb and flow like we have with Microsoft over the last couple of decades, but players like Apple, Google and Facebook still have plenty of growth left in them.

2. **Artificial Intelligence Start-ups**. These are the players building the architecture of the world moving forward. Google DeepMind, Facebook's Wit.ai, MetaMind, Sentient Technologies, The Grid, Enlitic, x.ai, to name just a few. Don't forget the machine intelligence players either though—self-driving car companies, healthcare diagnosis and sensor networks, IBM's Watson and others. We haven't even seen the start of this industry but, without doubt, it is going to be like the dot-com, the social media boom or the PC boom all over again, just bigger.

3. **Smart Infrastructure**. Autonomous, electric vehicle manufacturers, smart grid operators, consumer renewables and household battery deployment, nanotech-based water treatment and desalination, robot and drone delivery networks and general smart city infrastructure will all be booming businesses within the next two decades. Around 30 million people will be deployed in retooling the world with solar and renewables by 2030 alone.

4. **Internet of Things**. Everything will start to get smart around you. This will start with smart appliances, smart cars, smart homes, smart glasses and then extend to sensors,

screens and algorithms that are embedded in the world around us. When we go fully machine-to-machine for all sorts of day-to-day applications early in the next decade, sensor nets will explode and small ubiquitous computing devices will be everywhere: everything that can be turned on or off, or needs to be monitored in some way, will be an IoT device linked to the cloud. A huge subset of this will be wearables, ingestibles and sensors that monitor our health in real time and well-being in real time.

5. **Networking the Developing World.** Led by the likes of the Bill and Melinda Gates Foundation, Facebook, Google and Internet.org, we'll move to give 2 to 2.5 billion people access to the web via mobile devices predominantly. Cheap, ubiquitous smartphone access will emerge, and slowly but surely so will Internet access, followed by commerce.

6. **Developers, Human Computer Interaction and Experience Design Practitioners**. The whole world will need to be coded into new experiences and new processes built into technology all around us.

7. **HealthTech and FinTech Providers**. These two industries, in particular, will be dominated by new technology expertise. They will displace incumbents, they will partner with them to bring the core capabilities they lack and they will be acquired and grow to become the unicorns of tomorrow.

8. **Personal AI Providers**. Whether Facebook's M or next-gen Siri, Cortana, Alexa/Echo, Jibo and others, the emergence of smart digital companions and personal assistants will be big business. Especially as devices get smart enough to listen and respond to our needs dynamically, and passively.

9. **AR, VR, AV and PHUD.** The arena of augmented visual experiences and the incorporation of digital reality into our visual field will be a huge area of investment and consumer adoption. Movies will morph into interactive storyscapes, games will look more and more like movies and we'll escape to virtual worlds regularly. Social interactions will become increasingly AR or VR enabled, especially in the workplace where interactions are required.

10. **Exotic Metamaterials and 3D Printing.** It sort of does an injustice to put these two areas together, but it's essentially smart manufacturing and construction, along with the advanced application of materials using techniques like nanotechnology, etc. We will build transparent aluminium, carbon-fibre nanotubes, smart clothing, reactive and responsive materials that morph or alter their properties, smart polymers, piezoelectric, thermoelectric and photomechanical materials, and many more. Materials that are engineered at the atomic level. 3D printers that can build machines, homes, appliances and those that sit on your desktop at home.

The Roadmap for the Augmented Age

So what is in store for humans, the planet and our AI robot overlords? The basic principle here is that change is speeding up and we are approaching the most dynamic period of technology disruption in human history. In this future, you will either be seen as pro-tech, pro-AI, pro-robot, pro-advancement or you will be relegated to a minority who push back at an ever-increasing technology-based culture.

Overleaf are the major milestones of the Augmented Age that we can expect over the next 20 to 30 years.

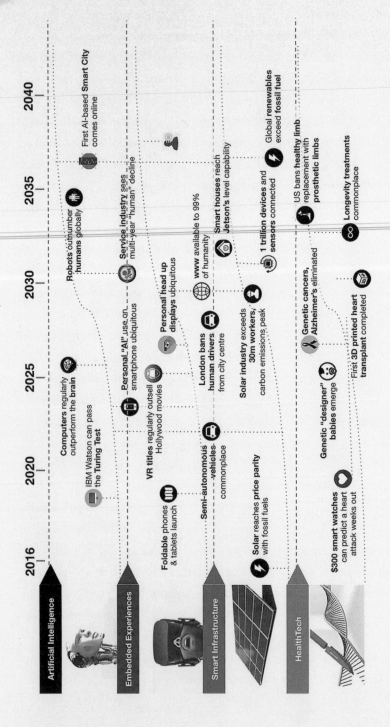

Artificial Intelligence

Computers regularly outperform the brain
IBM Watson can pass the Turing Test
Robots outnumber humans globally
First AI-based Smart City comes online

Embedded Experiences

Foldable phones & tablets launch
VR titles regularly outsell Hollywood movies
Personal "AI" use on smartphone ubiquitous
Personal head up displays ubiquitous
Service industry sees multi-year "human" decline

Smart Infrastructure

Semi-autonomous vehicles commonplace
London bans human drivers from city centre
www available to 99% of humanity
Smart houses reach Jetson's level capability
1 trillion devices and sensors connected

HealthTech

Solar reaches price parity with fossil fuels
Solar industry exceeds 30m workers, carbon emissions peak
Global renewables exceed fossil fuel
US bans healthy limb replacement with prosthetic limbs

$300 smart watches can predict a heart attack weeks out
Genetic "designer" babies emerge
First 3D printed heart transplant completed
Genetic cancers, Alzheimer's eliminated
Longevity treatments commonplace

2016   2020   2025   2030   2035   2040

Since the invention of the wheel, the steam engine and the computer, each consecutive generation has been fearful of the impact of technology, and each new generation has embraced that new technology in order to change the world. It's only now that technology is moving at a speed that is outpacing generational change, so that everyone today has to deal with these incredible changes. The coming generation is one that will embrace change as they have known nothing else since the day they were born, so this won't be a challenge for them, but for those with conservative values and belief in simpler times, or those who hark back to the "good ole days", the Augmented Age will represent constant threats to the status quo. As the great Marty McFly said in *Back to the Future*, **"Your kids are going to love it!"**

We have within our grasp the technology not just to make the world a better place, but to usher in a world where diseases that have existed for millennia are eliminated, and where we have a chance to live much longer, more productive lives. Lives that aren't dominated by working for 40 years, just to eek out a retirement. To take advantage of this, we will need to abandon the economic and political concepts of the 18th and 19th centuries. We will need to embrace technology like solar energy—not because of climate change alone—but because it is radically cheaper, cleaner and smarter. We will need to embrace new concepts of value because commodities like oil will plummet in value and banks won't be in buildings anymore. We will need to think about health care in radically different ways: we'll no longer take a pill to hide a symptom, instead we will reengineer our own biology to eradicate maladies. We will work very differently. We'll have to adjust to mass-scale automation and the deconstruction of multiple distribution methods and value chains. Our children will work multiple jobs simultaneously, and their careers will be focused on the things they are passionate about, in place of a career they trained for at college or university.

Within 250 years, we've learned that no industry, no business, no product has survived the impact of technology unscathed. This is a fight that history tells us will be emphatically won by the inevitable march of technology. However, like Peter Diamandis, Ray Kurzweil, sci-fi writers like William Gibson, David Brin and Ramez Naam, and techno-industrialists like Elon Musk, Larry Page, Bill Gates and Steve Jobs, I am essentially an optimist when thinking about this future. An Augmented Age infused with technology advancements is better than the alternative by a wide margin.

The Augmented Age will give us the greatest advantages and potential of any generation in the entire history of humanity, but only if we embrace change, transformation and innovation.

Get ready for *Life in the Smart Lane!*

About the Author

Brett King is a four-time Amazon bestselling author, a renowned commentator and globally respected speaker on the future of business. He has spoken in over 40 countries, to half a million people, on how technology is disrupting business, changing behaviour and influencing society. He has spoken at TED conferences, given opening keynotes for *Wired*, Singularity University's Exponential Finance, the *Economist* and many more. He has visited the White House to advise the National Economic Council on the Future of Banking and been invited to meet with regulators from the United States, China, the European Union and the World Bank.

King hosts the world's leading dedicated radio show on technology impact in banking and financial services "Breaking Banks" (72 countries, 1 million listeners). He is also the founder of Moven, a successful mobile start-up, which has raised over US$24 million to date, with the world's first mobile, downloadable bank account, available in the United States, Canada and New Zealand.

Named "King of the Disruptors" by *Banking Exchange* magazine, King was voted *American Banker*'s Innovator of the Year in 2012, voted the world's #1 Financial Services Influencer by The Financial Brand and was nominated by Bank Innovation as one of the top 10 "coolest brands in banking". He was shortlisted for the 2015 Advance Global Australian of the Year Award for being one of the most influential Australians living offshore. His books have been released in more than a dozen languages and he has achieved bestseller status in 20 countries, with many of his books still appearing in bestseller lists more than 18 months after their initial release. His fifth book is *Augmented: Life in the Smart Lane.*

King has been featured on Fast Company, TechCrunch, *Wired, Fortune* magazine, Fox News, ABC, CNBC, Bloomberg, BBC, *Financial Times,* the *Economist, ABA Journal, Bank Technology News* and many more. He contributes regularly as a blogger in *Huffington Post.*

In his spare time, he is an IFR-rated private pilot, scuba diver and gamer.

About the Contributors

Andy Lark

Andy Lark is a globally awarded marketer and business leader. Today, he is the chief marketing and business officer of Xero, the cloud accounting software leader and one of the world's fastest-growing software as a service (SAAS) companies. Xero was named the world's most innovative growth company in 2015 by *Forbes*. For the past two decades, Lark has worked alongside CEOs and their leadership teams to define—and then attain—digital and brand greatness for their institutions. These include Air New Zealand, Brocade, Commonwealth Bank, Coles, Dell, Emirates Team New Zealand, IBM, Simplot, Southwest Airlines, Sun, the New Zealand government, Visa and Xero. As an entrepreneur and marketer, Lark has built some of the world's most successful e-commerce sites, online communities and applications for smartphones.

Alex Lightman

Alex Lightman is an award-winning inventor, artist, entrepreneur and government advisor. He is the author of the first book on 4G wireless, *Brave New Unwired World*, as well as *Reconciliation: 78 Reasons to End the US Embargo of Cuba*. His awards include the first Economist magazine Reader's Award for the Innovation That Will Most Radically Change the World, SGI's Internet VR contest grand prize (out of 800 entries), and Avatars '97. He is the chairman of Witkit, Everblaze, and GINET, and director of a venture fund. He is a graduate of MIT and attended graduate school at Harvard's Kennedy School of Government.

JP Rangaswami

Born in Calcutta, JP Rangaswami (@jobsworth) read economics and worked as a financial journalist before changing careers over three decades ago to enter that strange space where society, technology and banking converge. Now 58, Rangaswami works as chief data officer at a major financial institution, having previously been chief scientist and chief information officer at a number of global institutions. He is Adjunct Professor at the School of Electronics and Computer Science at the University of Southampton. In addition, he is a Fellow of the British Computer Society, a Fellow of the Royal Society of the Arts and Venture Partner at Anthemis. Rangaswami is a popular keynote speaker, having given a popular TED Talk—Information Is Food, and can be found blogging at ConfusedofCalcutta.com.